Social Security in Religious Networks

Social Security in Religious Networks

Anthropological Perspectives on New Risks and Ambivalences

Edited by

Carolin Leutloff-Grandits,
Anja Peleikis
and
Tatjana Thelen

Berghahn Books
NEW YORK • OXFORD

Published in 2009 by
Berghahn Books

www.berghahnbooks.com

Library of Congress Cataloging-in-Publication Data

Social security in religious networks : anthropological perspectives on new risks and
ambivalences / edited by Carolin Leutloff-Grandits, Anja Peleikis and
Tatjana Thelen.
    p. cm.
Includes bibliographical references and index.
ISBN 978-1-84545-576-7 (alk. paper)
    1. Social service—Religious aspects. 2. Religion and social problems.
3. Religion—Economic aspects. 4. Social networks. I. Leutloff-Grandits, Carolin.
II. Peleikis, Anja. III. Thelen, Tatjana.
HV530.S56 2009
361.7'5—dc22
                                                        2008054016

British Library Cataloguing in Publication Data

A catalogue record for this book is available from
the British Library.

Printed in the United States on acid-free paper

Contents

Acknowledgements

This volume developed from the conference 'Social Security in Religious Networks' held at the Max Planck Institute for Social Anthropology, 10–11 November 2005 in Halle/Saale, Germany.

We thank the Max Planck Institute for providing us with the facilities and its financial support. Franz and Keebet von Benda-Beckmann have supported the project from the beginning. We thank them for their constructive criticism and intellectual support. We are also thankful to the two reviewers from Berghahn Books for their thoughtful comments that facilitated the reworking process.

Many thanks go to the contributors for their essays, for their spirited discussions and for their patience through the rewriting and publishing phase of the project.

We are deeply indebted to Sunniva Greve, who worked with patience on the manuscripts written by non-native speakers, and to Gesine Koch, Annett Mögel and Cornelia Richter for their work when organising the conference and preparing the manuscript.

Chapter 1

Social Security in Religious Networks

An Introduction

Tatjana Thelen, Carolin Leutloff-Grandits and Anja Peleikis

Human being always have to deal with insecurity and risk.[1] Rather then jumping into the emptiness as Yves Klein on our cover photograph they usually seek security in different kinds of safety nets such as kinship or friendship networks or formal insurances. In recent decades intensified globalisation, new epidemics such as HIV/AIDS, natural disasters and radical political change have posed new challenges for such social security arrangements worldwide. Simultaneously, the role of religion in society, once thought to have diminished in the process of modernisation, has regained public and scholarly attention. This volume sets out to explore the roles and relations of various religiously motivated actors in the creation of social security.

The potential of faith-based communities to contribute to social security has evoked contradicting appraisals. When globally distributed faith-based organisations, such as Caritas or Buddhist and Islamic Relief, provide aid to those who suffer most in times of crisis, global religious networks are frequently judged in a positive light as delivering the social good, strengthening worldwide solidarity and securing stability in the process. On the other hand, religious networks are simultaneously seen as ideologically driven to support their own members only, at the expense of excluding or even harming others. Their provision of spiritual and material security in this context is considered damaging to society, especially against the background of September 11. Likewise, on a smaller scale, local religious groups receive praise for their capacity for community development and the provision of social integration, but are accused at the same time of alienating their members from other social networks, such as their families

---

Notes for this chapter are located on page 15.

or society in general. These conflicting assessments of religious activities in the field of social security are often based on a conflation of different layers of actors, practices and ideologies. In this volume, we move away from one-dimensional images of the kind contained in ideological visions and policies. We aim instead at developing well-defined analytical concepts and a profound ethnographic knowledge of local circumstances in an attempt to grasp the ambiguous role of religious networks in creating social security. In order to approach this field of inquiry, we propose to combine network and social security concepts as developed in anthropology. Bringing these perspectives together will allow us to generate innovative insights, with particular regard to situations of accelerated social change, increasing global connectedness, and the interrelatedness of religiously informed relations and other social networks.

The Dynamics of Social Security Arrangements

Anthropological research on social security emerged in the 1970s and 1980s in the context of scholarly debates on development in the Third World. In these countries, state-organised provisions reached only a small section of the population and social security relied on complex arrangements between family, kinship and community (Partsch 1983; Midgley 1984; von Benda-Beckmann et al. 1988, 1994; Ahmad et al. 1991; Lachenmann 1996, 1998). Consequently, the concept of social security that focused on provisions distributed or organised by the state in industrialised countries hitherto taken for granted was criticised as inapplicable to developing countries. At the same time scholars began to recognise the pluri-agent nature of social security provision in Western welfare states as well (Johnson 1987; Zacher 1988). As evident in the concept of welfare pluralism, most people in Western countries also receive resources from state agencies, NGOs or insurances, and simultaneously from their personal network of kin, friends, neighbours or co-believers. Thus scholars dealing with social security in both contexts began to criticise the singular dichotomies of public/private, formal/informal or even modern/traditional types of provision. Care provided by parents for their children, for example, is rarely seen as formal social security, although in many cases it is to a certain extent legally prescribed (von Benda-Beckmann and von Benda-Beckmann 2000). Following these considerations, we rely on the wide concept of social security as developed by Franz and Keebet von Benda-Beckmann (2000). They define social security as 'the dimension of social organisation dealing with the provision of security not considered to be an exclusive matter of individual responsibility' (2000: 14). This broad definition leaves room for the notion of social security as provided by a variety of sources, agents, institutions and networks. It also indicates that risks and responsibilities are not given but socially constructed. Furthermore, analysing social security entails taking actors' expectations of the future and of the actions of others into account. Comparing elderly care in the US and Japan, Hashimoto (1996), for example, has convincingly shown that differences in the provision of kinship care are informed by life scripts and expectations concerning anticipated needs in old age.

This and other studies have likewise shown that social security is not merely a matter of providing tangible material resources, such as food, shelter, or health care to people in need, but also contains important social as well as emotional and spiritual aspects. Very often it is not the material outcome that makes people feel secure, but rather a network of social relations to which they can relate and refer in times of crisis and need (Risseeuw 2001; see also Caldwell 2007 and the various articles in Pina-Cabral and Pine 2007). However, the embeddedness of security in social networks incorporates an inherent ambiguity. A social network to which an individual (or a group) belongs or can refer makes the future more predictable. At the same time, inclusion in one network frequently means exclusion from others.

While earlier studies on social security were influenced by a somewhat 'positive mood' or modernist discourse based on the notion of potentially enhancing worldwide welfare, recent studies tend to underline its 'fragmentation' (Carter 1998) and the production of insecurity and exclusion in specific settings of welfare arrangements (Nettleton and Burrows 1998; Risseeuw 2001; van Euwijk 2004; de Jong and Roth 2005; Rohregger 2006). This ambivalence is also evident in social security arrangements created by religious networks presented in various chapters of this volume.

In an effort to understand the ambivalent character of social security in religious networks, we consider the five layers of social security as proposed by Franz and Keebet von Benda-Beckmann (2000: 14) valuable. They conceptualise the first layer as the above-mentioned *ideological notions*, and their cultural and religious ideals with regard to risk, vulnerability and caring responsibilities. These can differ from one society to another, between the various agents of social security such as the state, the family or religious networks, and also between the individual members (see also K. von Benda-Beckmann 1994; Zelizer 1997; Hashimoto 2000; Haney 2002; Bartkowski and Regis 2003; Marcus 2006; Murphy 2007). Secondly, they describe the layer of *institutional provision*, which is often based on legal prescriptions and clearly defined rights and obligations and is usually more restrictive than the ideological background. The *social relationships between recipients and providers* constitute the third layer, which again can differ from the normative and institutional level, focusing as it does on the interactions between people. The authors refer to social security *practices* as the fourth layer, where concrete social security provisions take place. Finally, there is the layer that deals with the *social and economic consequences* of social security practices for the providers and recipients, as well as for the wider social field.

Applying this approach to social security also allows us to cross the nation-state boundaries so prevalent in the numerous comparative studies on welfare state typologies (cf. Esping-Anderson 2003). Globalisation and increasing migration flows lead to the travelling of ideas about need and obligation, and produce transnational social security practices. The effects again are ambivalent (von Benda-Beckmann and von Benda-Beckmann 2000: 10). Migrants, for example, provide, on the one hand, for their families back home by sending money and material goods. As a result of their absence at home, on the other hand, they may fail to provide social and emotional support to their families. When young people leave home and migrate to look for work, those who stay behind bear the brunt – especially if they are unable to fulfil work obligations (in agriculture, for example) or caring activities that were primarily carried out by those who had left (Leliveld 1994, 2000). Although there may not be a distinct lack of labour, those who stay behind could feel left alone. Many who migrate perform care work in richer countries, leading to the development of new forms and mixtures of social support/dependencies in global care chains (Hochschild 2000; see also Ehrenreich and Hochschild 2003; Constable 1997; Parrenas 2003). Applying a broad concept of social security allows for an assessment of the ambivalent contribution of religious networks in a globalised world. At the same time, using the term *network* in the anthropological tradition enables us to emphasise an actor-centred and relational perspective.

The Making of Religious Networks

Speaking of 'religious networks' rather than 'religion' helps to avoid an ethnocentric definition of religion in the institutional sense of the church, for instance. In addition, the term facilitates highlighting the diversity of religious social formations (*Vergemeinschaftung*) in several social and geographical settings. Unlike a group, which is assumed to be constructed by relationships of one type, social networks are created by overlapping relations such as kinship, friendship and religion (Mitchell 1969: 15). Although we concentrate on a specific content of the relation in employing the term *religious network*, we do not rule out that actors may attach additional or overlapping meanings to their relationships.

Originally developed in the context of African inner migration, anthropologists introduced the term *network* to grasp the seemingly new fluidity of social relations in urban conditions. In these early studies, researchers of the later so-called Manchester School focused on certain social relations rather than norms, and analysed their influence on behaviour, above all with regard to conflict resolution (Epstein 1969; Kapferer 1969; Mitchell 1969). With her study on married couples in London, Elisabeth Bott (1971 [1954]) introduced the specific notion of personal networks (Wellman 1993: 432; see also Jansen 2006: 42–44). Despite the fact that social network theory lost its attractiveness in anthropology from the 1970s on, it continued to be applied in sociology in the context of sophisticated computer-based methods. Nevertheless we use the term in its anthropological tradition to underline the fluidity of social relations and the interconnectedness of networks, and their extension to non-members and the outer world in general. Rather than aiming at formal descriptions of religious networks in terms such as density or reachability, we seek to stress the multiplexity of relations and interactional criteria, as well as the ways in which norms and values are communicated. In our understanding, religious networks include organisations with formal membership regulations as well as informal links between individuals. We therefore propose to define a religious network as composed of social actors linked to each other through religious practices, ideologies or institutions.

Employing a flexible religious network concept does not mean that boundaries have no meaning for the actors concerned or the forms of social security these boundaries create. Religious networks are constructed by means of constant boundary work, where the most salient distinctions lie between religious specialists and lay people, long-time believers and newcomer adherents, and insider congregants and outsider non-members (Bartkowski and Regis 2003: 17). The essays collected in this volume concentrate on lay people who regularly attend religious services as well as on religious experts such as Christian pastors, Voudou priestesses or Islamic teachers. The network concept allows for a description of diverse relational patterns, thereby making it possible to comprehend various types of hierarchies within the religious network, such as clientelist or egalitarian relations, and individual positions. Single actors in the network, for example, could occupy a central role or act as so-called bridge persons that link the religious network to other networks and groups. The papers in this volume represent this diversity and include loosely knit religious migrant networks, locally and translocally based individuals and institutions, as well as highly formalised Catholic congregations. Several organisational principles and religious ideas influence how social security is created within the framework of these networks. Using the concept of network, we can also grasp also less-institutionalised patterns of behaviour (Schweizer 1996: 37) and analyse a variety of religious activities in the context of creating social security.

Social Security in Religious Networks

Combining the theoretical concepts outlined above allows for a better understanding of how religious networks create notions of social security and develop specific forms of provision. In exploring these processes we will take the different layers as described above as points of departure. Hence we focus on the ideas, relations and practices that surface in religious networks, analysing them in their interrelatedness to other providers.

Firstly, as mentioned above, social security is always bound to future expectations, and religious belief contributes to these expectations. Instead of taking need as obvious, the authors in this book explore the social construction of specific perceptions of risk and security in religious networks. One of the principal forms of social security provided by religious networks is undoubtedly spiritual or ontological security. However, we should not overlook that the spiritual security religious faith provides can simultaneously enhance material vulnerability.

Ideas on what constitutes legitimate need and assistance contribute to the second layer of analysis – the different relationships through which care is or should be provided in religious networks (Zelizer 1997; Bartkowski and Regis 2003; Read 2005). 'Visions of charity', as Allahyari calls them in her comparative ethnography of a Catholic and a Protestant-based food programme for the urban poor, provide 'blueprints for how food is served, for understandings of the poor as guest or clients, and for organizational relations to the state' (2000: 13; see also Murphy 2007). Charity ideologies differ and authorise religious actors to direct their services and provisions to a certain strata of the religious network only, and sometimes to all of the co-believers, occasionally also to strangers. Consequently members and non-members are provided with different forms of social security that pursue different sets of rules, logic, ideas and strategies with regard to the solidarity of its members, and result to varying degrees in institutionalisation. Adherents of a specific community may in some cases even be unaware of social security provision, a side effect of network membership, since believers might not see this as constitutive of their network activity and instead stress the idea of a common faith. Other religious networks give more prominence to mutual assistance. Support given or received on the basis of moral attributes could allow members to consider themselves more or less as insiders, essentially defined as in need of, or eligible for care. With regard to accusations of sorcery in Burkina Faso, Badini-Kinda argues that religious belief can even legitimise nonassistance, that is, to family members, friends, and co-believers, as well as to strangers (2005: 155). In their comparative work on poverty relief programmes of various congregations in the south of the US, Bartkowski and Regis (2003: 19) phrase this ambivalence by distinguishing between two forms of faith-based social capital. Bonding faith-based social capital refers to 'strategies of congregational inreach such as communal worship and mutual aid', while 'congregational outreach to disadvantaged non-members and the formation of interdenominational relief agencies' constitute examples of bridging faith-based capital. These practices highlight the ambiguity of social security provided by religious networks and demonstrate that religious ideology can also mean social exclusion.

The question of eligibility hints at the practices of inclusion and exclusion implied in the concept of need and charity developed by religious networks. Material resources such as food and shelter or access to medical care are frequently limited and hard to come by. Once social networks provide access to these resources, it can be assumed that the latter will be cut off to those who are not members of the network. To belong or not to belong to a social security network can therefore turn out to be a question of access to resources, and in a wider sense one of social inclusion or exclusion. In addition, it can be taken as given that members in hierarchical positions pursue disparate aims. Franz and Keebet von Benda-Beckmann (1998) argue with regard to state officials that their respective social security arrangements should be part of the analysis, because their personal needs and obligations greatly influence the distribution of state resources and community networks. In the same vein, the inclusion of church officials or other key figures in the analysis allows for challenging insights into the nature of the relation between religious networks and social security. Religious experts, much the same way as state officials, pursue their own social security strategies, for example, by making pleas for donations to enhance their own well-being, or distributing resources differentially for their own purpose. In line with this thought, the chapters in this book look at the various social security ideologies and concepts that circulate in religious networks, and the resultant relations that exist between recipients and donors, as well as the respective practices and consequences. Several contributions highlight the ambivalent nature of these ideologies and practices, since they are in most cases embedded in hierarchies and entail exclusionary practices, or even the denial of assistance. The authors describe various forms of security ranging from spiritual to material provision, religious ideologies of solidarity, and concepts and practices of charity aimed at non-members.

The different layers of creating social security in religious networks can only be satisfactorily analysed when seen in their embeddedness in society as a whole. Prevailing ideas on need and social security practices are either in accordance with or in opposition to other normative systems in the respective society, such as state legal prescriptions or kinship norms and values. The manner in which charity is practised in religious networks is often closely linked to state and kinship frameworks of provision. The state is not only a key provider of social security but also in a position to legally define who is needy and what type of social security should be provided. As Marcus (2000) has shown for the homeless in New York, broader political tendencies can contribute to the definition of new groups in need. Also, most states define, enable or restrict the scope of other actors in the provision of social security. In many Western countries, for example, legislation takes the charitable nature of churches for granted (Dal Pont 2005). Still, current social security arrangements differ greatly. Whereas in some countries of continental Europe, such as Germany and Austria, relations between the state and Christian churches with respect to the distribution of welfare are close, in liberal states such as the UK or the US they are less pronounced. Nevertheless, even here policymakers show increasing interest in involving religious communities in welfare delivery (Lowndes and Smith 2006). In the US, for example, the introduction of a new welfare law in 2001 presented churches in the realm of charity organisations and the provision of welfare with more resources and more space to manoeuvre (Bartkowski and Regis 2003; Adloff 2006: 20). As witnessed in socialist countries, however, the state also has the potential to suppress faith-based welfare activities.

Not unlike the state, family and kinship networks are key providers of social security. They represent systems of mutual assistance and obligation along gender and generation, on which most people can rely for at least a certain period in their lifetime. How balanced and unbalanced reciprocity and solidarity actually work depends on norms and values inherent in the respective society. The significance of religious-based charity varies according to change in the wider social framework and in the course of people's lives. Kinship caring obligations can be enforced in religious networks or, on the contrary, the withdrawal of the individual believer from his or her family demanded, as evidenced in the call by many African Pentecostal churches for a break with the past (Meyer 1998).

In order to systematise the different forms of social security created through religious networks and to demonstrate the interrelations between religious networks and other providers of social security, we have grouped the chapters of this volume around the themes of (I) the response of religious networks to new risks, (II) the ambivalence of 'religious gifting' and (III) transnational networking.

Part I: Responding to New Risks and Crisis

Due to their embeddedness in the wider social context, social security arrangements are not stable, but react flexibly to changes in society. Hence, the role and meaning of religious networks is also subject to change. The material resources distributed via religious networks, for example, are highly dependent on the wider social context and vary with the changing risks in society. New diseases, political reforms and war are challenges that induce transformations in the provision of social security by religious networks, as well as in their underlying ideas and ideologies, and can put them under immense pressure or even threaten their existence and/or content (Risseeuw 2001; K. von Benda-Beckmann 2005: 7).

In crisis situations and periods of rapid social change, concepts of inclusion and exclusion transported in the ideologies of religious networks seem of particular relevance to the receipt of the social good offered by these networks or

– on the contrary – to establishing the ineligibility for such provisions. In fact, all four chapters in this section highlight the ambivalent nature of the charity extended by religious networks and its often-ambiguous consequences. The way in which faith-based charity is linked to political transformation and crisis will be dealt with in the first section of this volume.

The occurrence of new diseases, for example, AIDS, introduces new notions of risk in society and can thus alter social security arrangements. If significant sections of the population are affected, as in the case of several African countries, existing systems of kinship support can become overburdened. When families are no longer able to support their relatives, the latter may find additional assistance in religious networks. Multilateral and governmental agencies have recently shown appreciable interest in increasing the role of faith-based organisations in mitigating the impact of the pandemic (Christensen and Janeway 2005: 9). In her chapter, Catrine Christiansen explores the ambivalence of Christian church assistance in the form of social development programmes and pastoral care to families affected by HIV/AIDS. The HIV/AIDS epidemic has taken a heavy toll on young and middle-aged carers, altering the demographic structure to a disproportionate number of (orphaned) children in need of care, hence stretching the meagre resources of surviving relatives. Based on examples from Pentecostal and Catholic Church programmes in Busia District, Uganda, Christiansen argues that church responses to this situation did help individual members of HIV/AIDS-affected families, but failed to a great extent to strengthen family networks. The focus of both programmes and pastoral care on the individual is a contributing factor to this development. She describes how social programmes for orphans tend to facilitate the creation of networks among the young as distinct from strengthening commitment to their families. Furthermore, there is evidence that churches have banned traditional rituals with the potential to restore family relationships among kinsfolk, or even performed rituals to empower individuals to break kinship ties, as seen in the case of the Pentecostalists.

Perhaps the most blatant instance of changing social security arrangements in face of crisis is war or the breakdown of state structures as experienced in former Yugoslavia. The contribution by Leutloff-Grandits discusses the different types of support provided by a charity campaign in the ethnically mixed town of Knin in Croatia in the aftermath of the Croat-Serb war, and their exclusionary consequences. The author illustrates that while the campaign successfully mobilised material and spiritual aid all over Croatia, this support had an ambivalent impact on the various population groups in the region – Serbs, native Croats and new Croatian settlers. For many of the new settlers from Bosnia, spiritual support was key. It gave them emotional security to belong to the Croatian national community, albeit at the expense of the Serbs, for whom this campaign meant exclusion and insecurity. The native Croats, who had weaker links with the Catholic Church than the new Croatian settlers, also felt disempowered by the campaign. The chapter raises the vital question of the nature of charity in the wake of civil war. Whereas this example highlights the overestimation of the material transfer, it does reveal that the real transfer is that of emotional security based on national group membership. The effect of the latter on the society of the region as a whole, however, was of separation rather than integration.

Other postsocialist states present more peaceful examples of political reform that create new risks and simultaneously define new roles for the faith-based provision of social security. During the socialist era, the role of religious organisations in providing material forms of security and their public role in morally defining need was in most cases radically reduced or even oppressed by the state. Notwithstanding the existing differences that religious actors in socialist states still had, the political and economic reforms in the 1990s generally granted more religious freedom and more room for faith-based charity. In Hungary, for example, citizens can decide to delegate part of their tax to religious welfare institutions (Mahieu 2006), and in Russia non-Orthodox religious organisations are only allowed to enter the country on condition that they act as NGOs assisting the needy (Caldwell 2004). These examples also demonstrate that, contrary to the widespread image of state withdrawal from social security provision, the postsocialist state continues to play a decisive role in the regulation and allocation of specific tasks to religious groups (see also Read and Thelen 2007).

Despite regaining its status as a state partner in welfare provision and in contrast to many other postsocialist countries, the Protestant Church in eastern Germany has failed to increase its membership. Focusing on the network of Protestant women engaged in a nonprofit association in eastern Germany, Thelen argues in her chapter that the efforts of individuals to reassure meaningful biographies not only impact on their social security arrangements, but shape this specific outcome of political transformation. Thelen's analysis is based on a comparative description of the provisions and risks faced by this religious network during the socialist era and after unification. Under socialist rule, these women were religiously active and practised an 'alternative' lifestyle in opposition to socialist doctrine. She explores the interrelation between their seemingly private decisions on religious faith and mothering in relation to changing state policies. As social security is deeply interwoven with the individual life course, the ambivalent contribution of the religious network and wider consequences can only be understood against the background of these personal biographies embedded in changing state policies.

Similar to the German example, Kupfer's chapter shows how religious networks can be interpreted as simultaneous producers of risk and security for their members in periods of political reform. She compares social security provision by Qigong and Christian religious networks in relation to the dismantling of state social security arrangements after the Cultural Revolution and the subsequent period of economic growth in China. Although the public images, organisational structures and religious teachings of these religious groups differ, they have developed similar features, reflecting their position in the Chinese political and socio-economic system. Both types of spiritual groups establish networks of mutual assistance, particularly in the case of illness, and enable members to climb the hierarchies, gaining social prestige and security in the process. For the members themselves, however, the most important aspect is that of spiritual healing, which alleviates psychological suffering and creates a utopian vision of society in terms of social justice and moral values. In addition to demonstrating the complex reactions of religious networks to changes in state policy, Kupfer shows that strong ties within religious networks simultaneously imply a reduction of complexity in the individual social security mix.

In fact, the various religious networks discussed in this first section all react to current forms of crisis and need, but reduce at the same time access to other social security providers and/or exclude certain strata of the population from benefiting from them.

Part II: Ambivalences of Religious Gifting

The second section of the volume focuses on the resources available to and distributed within religious networks, as well as the values attached to them by the various social actors. In the eyes of the policymakers, religious networks have the specific capacity to provide social security in the form of staff and volunteers, and networks of trust and reciprocity (Lowndes and Smith 2006: 6). The distribution of these resources and their attached meanings vary in different religious groups, organisations and institutions. The chapters in this section allow for a comparative view of religious networks and the different meanings they attach to their practices in the more affluent setting of the Czech Republic (Read) as well as in high-poverty environments in Africa (de Bruijn and van Dijk; Rohregger).

As mentioned earlier, ideas on reciprocal solidarity and charity frequently circulate in religious networks, one example of which is the free gift. Analysing these networks and their ideologies therefore ties up with the rich anthropological literature on the nature of the gift as a form of reciprocal exchange (e.g. Sahlins 1965; Gouldner 1973; Parry 1986; Mauss 1990; van Dijk 1999).[2] For Mauss, gift exchange consists of three obligations: to give, to receive and to reciprocate. He denied the possibility of a free gift and instead stressed exchange as an important means of demonstrating status. However, religious charity is often based on the concept of a free gift where reciprocity is not expected. Furthermore, there is obviously no unilinear translation from norms into practices. In order to highlight the specific character of religious charity, the analysis of notions and practices of gifting in religious networks must be carried out empirically. The chapters by de Bruijn and van Dijk, and Read disclose how different the effect of such ideologies can be. In their contribution, de Bruijn and van Dijk take a critical look at the impact of religious charity on the material well-being of the inhabitants of two African communities. Comparing Sufi Islamic and Pentecostal Christian networks, the authors examine local notions of need and emphasise that charity and gift giving neither aims at nor results in reducing the vulnerability of the population. The examples of Islamic charity towards children in Chad and the Pentecostal involvement of gift giving in Ghana both describe the logics of charity as pursuing the goal of individual salvation. Rather than delivering a general social good, social inequality is enacted in charity. Notwithstanding the unlikelihood that charity programmes are ever beneficial to all, the chapter allows us to rethink the application of an abstract notion of social security in different cultural contexts. The chapter hints at the ambiguity of goods and services delivered by and within vertically structured religious networks. It furthermore provides us with a comparative viewpoint on different ideologies of social security and the critical question of how to evaluate its various dimensions. In regions of extreme poverty, inclusion in a religious network that provides members with emotional security may not be enough to ensure survival.

In contrast to de Bruijn and van Dijk, Read's analysis shows how the idea of the free gift can be used to formulate a critique of prevailing social conditions. Faith-based charity is habitually constructed as being rooted in altruism and community service, and in opposition to the state and to market sectors of provision that are seen as characterised by self-interest, instrumentalism and impersonality (Baggett 2001; see also Bartkowski and Regis 2003: 18–19). This is also the case in Read's study on the religious network of volunteers and nuns from the Borromean order in a day-care centre in Prague. In the specific case study, Catholic nuns provide a service demanded and financed by the Czech state. Read pursues the question of how nuns and volunteers articulate the character of the social security they provide as distinct from that of the state. She explores the volunteers' identification with the nuns, arguing that the former are motivated not merely by a shared religious faith but by admiration and affinity for the particular kind of caring environment the nuns are perceived to create for the patients. The care is seen as emotionally warm and highly personalised: a gift of the self, which becomes a model for the volunteers. These assertions and new forms of fundraising downplay the role of the state as the chief source of funding for the nursing home. The emphasis on the personalised gifting of care among contemporary volunteers draws on and reworks cultures of volunteering associated with the socialist past, critiquing the perceived individualism of the capitalist present. Focusing as they do on care as an essentially free gift, actors at the same time, however, defend another brand of individual agency.

Taking up the debate on the materialistic orientation of Pentecostal churches in Africa, Rohregger argues that this discussion has been overstated, since materialist aspects are also pertinent in other denominations. The author examines social security in relation to religious networks in a former squatter settlement of Lilongwe City, Malawi. Concentrating on new migrants to the city, Rohregger argues that the religious affiliation migrants bring with them facilitates their integration into urban communities. Engagement with religious networks does not constitute a replacement for kin or country left behind, nor is it the result of a break with the past. Instead, Rohregger finds that religious networks have a range of functions that are not necessarily related to the town as a locality, but contain translocal dimensions and appeal. In this context her case illustrates once again that while the vertical level of support in religious associations may have a low profile in material and instrumental terms, on the horizontal level networks can create a sense of identity and belonging that is pivotal in the migrant situation.

Part III: Transnational Networking

The third section takes up the issue of migration with a specific focus on transnational relations in religious networks. Religious actors such as Sufi orders, Catholic missionaries or Buddhist monks have carried religious thinking and practice across vast spaces and hence been involved in creating transnational networks for a long time. They can therefore be described as 'the oldest of the transnationals' (Hoeber Rudolph 1997: 1). However, the relationship between religion and transnationalism has not attracted much attention in the social sciences, contrary to the manifold discussions on transnational migration that have developed since the beginning of the 1990s.[3] Attempts have recently been made, nonetheless, to analyse the emergence of religious networks in a transnational world (Hoeber Rudolph and Piscatori 1997; van Dijk 2002; Allievi and Nielsen 2003; Vertovec 2003; van der Veer 2004). Religious networks are an integral part of the dense and highly active networks that span vast spaces, transforming diverse social, political and economic relationships in the process. Against this background, the contributions in this section go on to analyse how transnational religious networks were established and how they parallel, intersect or substitute kinship and locality networks with regard to social security provision at distinct points in time.

Hüwelmeier's contribution on a female Catholic order that spread transnationally illuminates, for example, that the order was initially the principal institution in securing the nuns' emotional, spiritual and financial needs, thereby substituting family and kinship obligations. The order became the family and provided social security for the constructed kin, 'the sisters'. However, Hüwelmeier shows that with changing political and social circumstances both in and outside the order in the mid-twentieth century, nuns were able to mobilise both their native kin as well as the state for the provision of social security. Similarly, taking the example of a local parish in the Curonian Spit in present-day Lithuania, Peleikis demonstrates how religious, kinship and locality networks partly coincided over time. Rather than focusing exclusively on transnational kin and locality connections, she demonstrates that the connectedness based on Lutheran beliefs and local religious practices greatly contributed to people's spiritual, emotional and ontological security, particularly in the course of forced displacement and the postwar era. Concentrating on religious experts in the transnational social field between Haiti and Canada, Drotbohm shows that religious, kin and locality networks repeatedly overlap. At other times, however, religious networks provide a distinct form of social security that kinship networks are unable to offer. Thus, all three contributions give space to the religious dimension in transnational connections, and analyse from a historical perspective how these networks contribute to the social security mixes of the actors involved.

Not unlike the religious aspect in transnational networking, social security has played only a marginal role in transnational studies.[4] The three chapters, however, pinpoint the significance of social security needs and provisions in the making of transnational and translocal networks. Peleikis, for example, describes how in post-Soviet times very different social actors were drawn together in a heterogeneous Lutheran network based on specific needs. She argues that the act of exchanging social security practices virtually became a catalyst in establishing these transnational and translocal connections.

In the same vein, Drotbohm argues that the Haitian Vodou priests have become vital agents in the maintenance of transnational connections. While on the one hand they look after the specific religious, emotional and material needs of transmigrants living in Montreal, they have, on the other hand, become authoritative reminders of the migrant duty to support kin back in Haiti. While establishing and reproducing a transnational religious network via their social security practices, Vodou priests contribute at the same time to the reproduction of transnational family relations by advocating transnational needs and responsibilities. With the sending of remittances to their native localities, migrants contribute to local social security systems. Thus, migration has the effect of coupling local and wider regional, national or transnational support systems and in this sense is both a source of and a response to insecurity (von Benda-Beckmann 2000: 10).

Looking after less-prosperous family or parish members back home and sending money and other items demonstrates that transnational religious and family networks take on caring activities for weaker members. In this context, Hüwelmeier reveals that the sisters in Germany and the US received social security in the form of health insurance and pension schemes from their respective countries of residence, while nuns in the so-called Third World are dependent on aid from their co-sisters in the industrialised world. Hence, religious networks establish new social security relations to meet different needs. Similarly, Peleikis sheds light on how members of a religious and a family network took care of less-fortunate members. The Second World War refugees who arrived in the western part of Germany received support from the state and the church. They redistributed these resources by sending parcels to destitute family relatives and parish co-members who had been deported to Siberia. When the latter were finally permitted to leave the Soviet Union, the transnational social support networks changed as a matter of course. This section of the book attempts to gain a greater understanding of and to analyse the ongoing dynamics and continuity of these transnational religious networks, and how they changed over time.

In sum, the diversity of religious networks described in the various chapters of this volume allows for a deeper understanding of the dynamics of religious works as an ambivalent blessing with regard to social security.

Notes

1. This introduction began as the background paper for an international conference on 'Social Security in Religious Networks' held at the Max Planck Institute for Social Anthropology, Halle/Salle, 10–11 November 2005. We thank Franz and Keebet von Benda-Beckmann, Thomas Zitelmann, Michael Schnegg and the two reviewers from Berghahn for their thoughtful comments.
2. A newer compilation on the topic with a good introduction to the discussion is Osteen (2002).
3. The most prominent author on transnational migration is Nina Glick Schiller, who defined transnational migration as the process by which immigrants forge and sustain simultaneous multi-stranded social relations that link their societies of origin and settlement together. See Glick Schiller et al. (1995: 48); see also Glick Schiller et al. (1992) and Glick Schiller and Fouron (2001).
4. For an exception to the rule see, for example, K. von Benda-Beckmann (1991); Moore (2000); Leliveld (2000); and Brouwer (2000), all of whom focus on migration and social security.

References

Adloff, F. 2006. 'Religion and Social-Political Action: The Catholic Church, Catholic Charities, and the American Welfare State'. *International Review of Sociology* 16(1): 1–30.

Ahmad, E., et al., eds. 1991. *Social Security in Developing Countries*. Oxford: Clarendon Press.

Allahyari, R. A. 2000. *Visions of Charity: Volunteer Workers and Moral Community*. Berkeley, Los Angeles, London: University of California Press.

Allievi, S. 2003. 'Islam in the Public Space: Social Networks, Media and Neo-Communities', in *Muslim Networks and Transnational Communities in and across Europe*, ed. S. Allievi and J. S. Nielsen. Leiden, Boston: Brill, 1–27.

Allievi, S. and J. S. Nielsen, eds. 2003. *Muslim Networks and Transnational Communities in and across Europe*. Leiden, Boston: Brill.

Badini-Kinda, F. 2005. 'The Gap Between Ideas and Practices: Elderly Social Insecurity in Rural Burkina Faso', in *Ageing in Insecurity: Case Studies on Social Security and Gender in India and Burkina Faso*, ed. W. de Jong and C. Roth. Münster: Lit, 139–66.

Baggett, J. P. 2001. *Habitat for Humanity: Building Private Homes, Building Public Religion*. Philadelphia: Temple University Press.

Bartkowski, J. P. and H. A. Regis. 2003. *Charitable Choices: Religion, Race, and Poverty in the Post-welfare Era*. New York and London: New York University Press.

Benda-Beckmann, K. von. 1991. 'Developing Families: Moluccan Women and Changing Patterns of Social Security in the Netherlands', in *Het kweekblad ontkiemd: opstellen aangeboden aan Els Postel ter gelegenheid van haar afscheid als Hoogeleraar*, ed. H. Claessen, M. von den Engel and D. Plantenga. Leiden: Faculty of Cultural Anthropology and Research Centre for Women and Autonomy of the University of Leiden, 35–60.

———. 1994. 'Social Security in Developing Countries: A Mixed Blessing', in *Social (In)Security and Poverty as Global Issues*, The Hague:, Development Information Department of the Ministry of Foreign Affairs, 10–24.

———. 2005. 'Soziale Sicherung und ihre vielen Gesichter', Antrittsvorlesung an der Martin-Luther-Universität Halle-Wittenberg, http://www.eth.mpg.de/people/kbenda/pdf/Antrittsvorlesung-Halle-Soziale-Sicherung-und-ihre-vielen-Gesichter.pdf.

Benda-Beckmann, F. von, et al., eds. 1988. *Between Kinship and the State: Social Security and Law in Developing Countries*. Dordrecht, Berlin: Foris, Walter de Gruyter.

Benda-Beckmann, F. von and K. von Benda-Beckmann. 2000 [1994]. 'Introduction', in *Coping with Insecurity: An 'Underall' Perspective on Social Security in the Third World*, ed. F. von Benda-Beckmann, K. von Benda-Beckmann and H. Marks. The Netherlands: Focaal Foundation, 7–34.

———. 1998. 'Where Structures Merge: State and Off-State Involvement in Rural Social Security on Ambon, Indonesia', in *Old World Places, New World Problems: Exploring Issues of Resource Management in Eastern Indonesia*, ed. S. Pannell and F. v. Benda-Beckmann. Australian National University: CRES, 143–80.

Bott, E. 1971 [1957]. *Family and Social Networks*. London: Tavistock Publications.

Brouwer, R. 2000 [1994]. 'Insecure at Home: Emigration and Social Security in Northern Portugal', in *Coping with Insecurity. An 'Underall' Perspective on Social Security in the Third World*, ed. F. von Benda-Beckmann, K. von Benda-Beckmann and H. Marks. The Netherlands: Focaal Foundation, 153–75.

Caldwell, M. 2004. *Not by Bread Alone: Social Support in the New Russia*. Berkeley: University of California Press.

———. 2007. 'Elder Care in the New Russia: The Changing Face of Compassionate Social Security', in *Social Security and Care After Socialism: Changing Notions of Need, Support and Provision*, ed. T. Thelen and R. Read. *Focaal* 50(2): 66–80.

Carter, J. 1998. *Postmodernity and the Fragmentation of Welfare.* London and New York: Routledge.

Christensen, A. and P. Janeway, eds. 2005. *Faith in Action: Examining the Role of Faith-Based Organizations in Addressing HIV/AIDS.* Washington, DC: Global Health Council.

Constable, N. 1997. *Maid to Order in Hong Kong: Stories of Filipina Workers.* London: Cornell University Press.

Dal Pont, G. E. 2005. 'Charity Law and Religion', in *Law and Religion*, ed. P. Radan, D. Meyerson and R. F. Croucher. London and New York: Routledge, 220–43.

Dijk, R. van. 1999. 'The Pentecostal Gift: Ghanaian Charismatic Churches and the Moral Innocence of the Global Economy', in *Modernity on a Shoestring: Dimensions of Globalization, Consumption and Development in Africa.* Leiden: EIDOS, 71–89.

_____. 2002. 'Religion, Reciprocity and Restructuring Family Responsibility in the Ghanaian Pentecostal Diaspora', in *The Transnational Family: New European Frontiers and Global Networks*, ed. D. Bryceson and U. Vuorela. Oxford, New York: Berg Publishers, 173–96.

Ehrenreich, B. and A. R. Hochschild, eds. 2003. *Global Woman: Nannies, Maids and Sex Workers in the New Economy.* New York: Metropolitan Books.

Epstein, A. L. 1969. 'The Network and Urban Social Organizations', in *Social Networks in Urban Situations*, ed. J. C. Mitchell. Manchester: Manchester University Press.

Esping-Andersen, G. 2003. *The Three Worlds of Welfare Capitalism.* Cambridge: Polity Press.

Euwijk, P. van. 2004. 'When Social Security Reaches its Limits: Long-term Care of Elderly People in Urban Indonesia', in *Exploring Social (In)Securities in Asia*, ed. R. Büchel. Bern: Institut für Sozialanthropologie, 74–90.

Glick Schiller, N. 1995. 'From Immigrant to Transmigrant: Theorizing Transnational Migration'. *Anthropological Quarterly* 68: 48–63.

Glick Schiller, N., L. Basch and C. Blanc-Szanton, eds. 1992. *Towards a Transnational Perspective on Migration: Race, Class, Ethnicity and Nationalism Reconsidered.* New York: New York Academy of Sciences.

Haney, L. 2002. *Inventing the Needy. Gender and the Politics of Welfare in Hungary.* Berkeley, Los Angeles and London: University of California Press.

Hashimoto, A. 1996. *The Gift of Generations: Japanese and American Perspectives on Aging and the Social Contract.* Cambridge: Cambridge University Press.

Hochschild, A. R. 2000. 'Global Care Chains and Emotional Surplus Value', in *On the Edge: Living with Global Capitalism*, ed. W. Hutton and A. Giddens. London: Jonathan Cape, 130–46.

Hoeber, Rudolph, S. 1997. 'Introduction: Religion, States, and Transnational Civil Society', in *Transnational Religion and Fading States*, ed. S. Hoeber Rudolph and J. Piscatori. Boulder, CO: Westview Press, 1–24.

Hoeber, Rudolph S. and J. Piscatori, eds. 1997. *Transnational Religion and Fading States.* Boulder, CO: Westview Press.

Jansen, D. 2006. *Einführung in die Netzwerkanalyse. Grundlagen, Methoden, Forschungsbeispiel.* Wiesbaden: Verlag für Sozialwissenschaften.

Johnson, N. 1987. *The Welfare State in Transition: The Theory and Practice of Welfare Pluralism.* London: Wheatsheaf Books.

de Jong, W. and C. Roth. 2005. *Ageing in Insecurity: Case Studies on Social Security and Gender in India and Burkina Faso.* Münster: Lit.

Kapferer, B. 1969. 'Norms and the Manipulation of Relationships in a Work Context', in *Social Networks in Urban Situations*, ed. J. C. Mitchell. Manchester, University Press.

Lachenmann, G. 1996. 'Informal Social Security in Africa from a Gender Perspective', in *Searching for Security: Women's Responses to Economic Transformation*, ed. Isa Baud and Ines Smyth. London and New York: Routledge, 45–66.

_____. 1998. 'Constructs of Social Security: Modernity and Tradition in West Africa', *Working Paper No. 304.* Bielefeld: University of Bielefeld.

Leliveld, A. 1994. *Social Security in Developing Countries: Operation and Dynamics of Social Security Mechanisms in Rural Swaziland*, Tinbergen Institute Research Series. Amsterdam: Thesis Publishers.

———. 2000 [1994]. 'The Impact of Labour Migration on the Swazi Rural Homestead as Solidarity Group', in *Coping with Insecurity: An 'Underall' Perspective on Social Security in the Third World*, ed. F. von Benda-Beckmann, K. von Benda-Beckmann and H. Marks. The Netherlands: Focaal Foundation, 177–97.

Lowndes, V. and G. Smith. 2006. *Faith Based Voluntary Action*. Swindon: ESRC.

Mahieu, S. 2006. 'Charity in the Hungarian Greek Catholic Church: An Alternative Model of Civility?' in *The Postsocialist Religious Question: Faith and Power in Central Asia and East-Central Europe*, ed. Chris Hann and the 'Civil Religion' Group. Berlin: Lit, 315–32.

Marcus, A. 2006. *Where Have All The Homeless Gone? The Making and Unmaking of a Crisis.* New York and Oxford: Berghahn.

Mauss, M. 1990. *The Gift: The Form and Reason for Exchange in Archaic Societies.* New York: Norton.

Meyer, B. 1998. '"Make a Complete Break with the Past": Time and Modernity in Ghanaian Pentecostalist Discourse', in *Memory and the Postcolony*, ed. R. P. Werbner, Postcolonial Identities Series. London: Zed Books, 182–208.

Midgley, J. 1984. *Social Security, Inequality and the Third World*. Chichester: John Wiley & Sons.

Mitchell, J. C. 1969. 'The Concept and the Use of Social Networks', in *Social Networks in Urban Situations*, ed. J. C. Mitchell. Manchester, University Press.

Moore, S. F. 2000. 'Law In Unstable Settings: The Dilemma of Migration', in *Coping with Insecurity: An 'Underall' Perspective on Social Security in the Third World*, ed. F. von Benda-Beckmann, K. von Benda-Beckmann and H. Marks. The Netherlands: Focaal Foundation, 141–52.

Murphy, J. 2007. 'Suffering, Vice, And Justice: Religious Imagineries and Welfare Agencies in Post-War Melbourne', *Journal of Religious History* 41(3): 287–304.

Nettleton S. and R. Burrows. 1998. 'Insecurity, Reflexivity and Risk in the Restructuring of Contemporary British Health and Housing Policies', in *Postmodernity and the Fragmentation of Welfare*, ed. J. Carter. London and New York: Routledge, 153–67.

Parrenas, R. S. 2003. 'The Care Crisis in the Philippines: Children and Transnational Families in the New Global Economy', in *Global Woman: Nannies, Maids and Sex Workers in the New Economy*, ed. B. Ehrenreich and A. R. Hochschild. New York: Metropolitan Books, 39–54.

Parry, J. 1986. 'The Gift, the Indian Gift and the "Indian Gift"', *Man* 21(3): 453–73.

Partsch, M. 1983. *Prinzipien und Formen Sozialer Sicherung in Nicht-Industriellen Gesellschaften*, Sozialpolitische Schriften, Heft 48, Berlin: Duncker & Humblot.

Pina-Cabral, J. and F. Pine. 2007. 'On the Margins: An Introduction', in *On the Margins of Religion*, ed. J. Pina-Cabral and F. Pine. Oxford: Berghahn, 1–12.

Read, R. 2005. 'Altering Care: Gifts and Emotion in Nursing Practice within a Czech Nursing Home' in *Generations, Kinship and Care: Gendered Provisions of Social Security in Central Eastern Europe*, ed. H. Haukanes and F. Pine. University of Bergen, Centre for Women's and Gender Research 17: 137–62.

Read, R. and T. Thelen. 2007. 'Introduction: Social Security and Care after Socialism: Reconfigurations of public and private'. *Focaal* 50(2): 3–18.

Risseeuw, C. 2001. 'Policy Issues of Inclusion and Exclusion in Relation to Gender and Ageing in the South'. *European Journal of Development Research* 13(2): 26–48.

Rohregger, B. 2006. *Shifting Boundaries: Social Security in the Urban Fringe of Lingowe City, Malawi.* Aachen: Shaker.

Roth, C. 2005. 'Threatening Dependency: Limits of Social Security, Old Age and Gender in Burkina Faso', in *Ageing in Insecurity: Case Studies on Social Security and Gender in India and Burkina Faso*, ed. W. de Jong and C. Roth. Münster: Lit, 107–38.

Schweizer, T. 1996. *Muster Sozialer Ordnung: Netzwerkanalyse als Fundament der Sozialethnologie*. Berlin: Reimer.

Standing, G. 1996. 'Social Protection in Central and Eastern Europe: A Tale of Slipping Anchors and Torn Safety Nets', in *Welfare States in Transition: National Adaptations in Global Economies*, ed. G. Esping-Andersen. London, Thousand Oaks, New Delhi: Sage Publications.

Veer, P. van der. 2004. 'Transnational Religion: Hindu and Muslim Movements', *Journal for Studies of Religious Ideologies* 7: 4–18.

Vertovec, S. 2003. 'Diaspora, Transnationalism and Islam: Sites of Change and Modes of Research', in *Muslim Networks and Transnational Communities in and across Europe*, ed. S. Allievi and J. S. Nielsen. Leiden and Boston: Brill, 312–26.

Zacher, H. F. 1988. 'Traditional Solidarity and Modern Social Security: Harmony or Conflict?' in *Between Kinship and the State: Social Security and Law in Developing Countries*, ed. F. von Benda-Beckmann et al. Dordrecht: Foris Publications.

Zelizer, V. A. 1997. *The Social Meaning of Money: Pin Money, Paychecks, Poor Relief and Other Currencies*. Princeton, NJ: Princeton University Press.

PART I

Responding to New Risks and Crisis

Chapter 2

When AIDS Becomes Part of the (Christian) Family

Dynamics between Kinship and Religious Networks in Uganda

Catrine Christiansen

Introduction

The AIDS pandemic has posed profound challenges to the Christian churches in sub-Saharan Africa. Despite the diversity of these churches, it seems fair to state that church responses have changed noticeably since the first diagnosis in the 1980s (Clifford 2004; Tiendrebego and Buykx 2004; Christensen and Janeway 2005). The attitude marked by silence and a denial that the disease could affect church leaders and members of the congregation has evolved into a common recognition that even the faithful can be infected with the AIDS virus. Early fear and resentment towards people living with HIV/AIDS has likewise turned into active caretaking and efforts to combat stigmatisation. Churches in many African countries have thus become sites of comfort for the infected and, in addition to the notion of HIV infection as divine punishment, churches commonly recognize the link between poverty, inequalities and HIV infection (Bate 2003; Lwaminda and Czerny 2004; Czerny 2005).

Based on an interpretation of the biblical notion of marriage as the relationship between one man and one woman who remain together for life, the family as the site of well-being, solidarity, discipline and caretaking tends to take centre stage in church responses to mitigating the impact of AIDS on society (PAC-ANet 2005; Bate 2003). This centrality of the family resonates with both local and scholarly notions of extended family networks as the relations through which people in Africa find both moral and financial support. Since the AIDS epidemic has taken a heavy toll on both young and middle-aged care-givers, thereby altering the demographic structure to a disproportionate number of children in need of care and surviving relatives expected to stretch their meagre resources, the increasing 'poverty of people' has worsened the long-standing 'poverty of economics', and led to severe strain on family support systems.[1]

In the Ugandan context, in addition to the pastoral care of prayers, compassion and giving hope, the churches have become increasingly involved in the implementation of external aid (cf. Christiansen forthcoming). The mission-based Roman Catholic Church and the Anglican Church of Uganda have a history as key actors in providing social welfare in terms of education, health facilities and income-generating projects, whereas Pentecostal-Charismatic churches are a more recent phenomenon in Uganda. However, the latter have also become engaged in social welfare in terms of establishing schools and distributing external aid. The reasons for Pentecostal involvement in 'the social gospel' can probably be traced to the local need level and the increased availability of international funding to these churches. The Catholic and Pentecostal-Charismatic churches are, at least in eastern Uganda, currently the main source of externally funded social welfare (Christiansen 2005b). Most church-based projects are framed in the discourse that the economic deprivation of extended families is jeopardizing the basic social unit in Uganda and that this breakdown could lead to untold consequences for society. Following a logic within social policy, substantial resources are allocated to the people assumed to form the heaviest burden on family networks: children, youth, widows and people living with AIDS.

It is important to note the concurrent emergence of Pentecostal-Charismatic Christianity and HIV/AIDS during the 1980s in Uganda. This line of Christianity emphasizes the individual, who makes a personal commitment to God, and through strong faith and tight fellowship lives according to the divine tenets, experiencing the fruits of the faith (van Dijk 1992; Christiansen 2003; Meyer 2004). This prescribed living in faith would appear to correspond to the moral responsibility of the individual to avoid HIV infection. The focus on the salvation of the individual and the pressure to break the bonds with nonsaved kin, at least in a spiritual sense, differs notably from the Catholic and Anglican encouraging of members to maintain family networks, a point to which I will return later. It is furthermore notable that the emergence of HIV/AIDS has equipped churches with a powerful argument against a range of so-called traditional practices, which the various churches agree are *not* compatible with Christianity. One such practice is the custom of widow inheritance (Kirwen 1979; Christiansen 2004); another is the sacrificial rites to restore relations between kinsfolk, as will be discussed later on in the chapter.

This chapter seeks to discuss the consequences of Christian church assistance to families affected by HIV/AIDS. It will combine the two perspectives of churches as agents of social development implementing externally funded aid projects and churches as moral communities that support members afflicted by illness through pastoral care (Christiansen forthcoming). Based on ethnographic data from eastern Uganda, I will argue that the response of the churches to HIV/AIDS reinforces family networks to a limited extent only. First of all, this is because social welfare programmes commit participants, particularly the young, to religious fellowships rather than to family networks. Secondly, the churches have banned traditional rituals of restoring relations between kinsfolk without providing an alternative. In pastoral practice, mission-based churches address family disunity in the common language of forgiveness in sermons and in individual prayers with people living with AIDS, whereas Pentecostal-Charismatic churches perform rituals where healing is brought about by empowering the individual to break their kinship ties (cf. Meyer 1998; Christiansen 2003). Thus the approach of the pastoral care is to deal with the situation of the individual rather than to restore social relations, although the latter is generally considered fundamental to preventing further disintegration of family networks. When disputes among relatives in the parent generation are not resolved, the tensions are often continued between relatives in the younger generation. Social welfare activities facilitate young people to establish relations through education and religious networks, which they include in their social security nexus with expectations that these relations will somehow replace the kinship relations that have been disrupted. Since social welfare activities can also strengthen family relations, the linkages between church social security practices and family relations are ambiguous. The analysis draws on historical and contemporary literature on the Christian integration of proselytizing and the provisioning of social development in Africa (e.g. Gifford 1994; Smythe 1999; Hearn 2002), as well as on anthropological literature on kinship, rituals and HIV/AIDS (e.g. Whyte 1997; Yamba 1997; Meyer 1999). I argue that the approaches of the various churches are only to a limited extent able to strengthen kinship-based care and that this limitation is grounded in theological positions and ritual practices. It is important to note that the distinction between churches as agents of social development (in the form of aid programmes) and as fellowship communities (in the form of pastoral care) is an analytical distinction whilst in practice these dimensions overlap (e.g. see Bornstein 2002).

After a brief introduction to the research site, a Catholic-run education programme for children affected by AIDS will form the basis for discussion on the churches as agents of social development and as resourceful social networks.[2] Drawing on data gathered through participating in regular church services and accompanying clerics in their pastoral work, the following section will shift to a perspective on churches as moral communities in the social fabric that give social and spiritual support. Finally, Christian-based material, social and spiritual provisioning is considered from the perspective of local 'social security mixing' and its implications for kin-based networks (von Benda-Beckmann and von Benda-Beckmann 2000).

Setting the Scene

Christian churches in Uganda have been influential in the public policy process through representation in HIV/AIDS policy bodies and national committees (Christensen and Janeway 2005). This active engagement was encouraged by the presidential approach to involve all social sectors in combating the spread of HIV and mitigating the effects of AIDS (Christensen and Janeway 2005; Parkhurst and Lush 2004). When the prevention campaigns began in the 1980s with the slogan 'Love Carefully', the Christian churches joined hands with the secular campaign under the motto 'Love Faithfully' (Seidel 1990). This intersectoral approach led to the rare accomplishment in Africa of reducing HIV prevalence, a success that has made Uganda popular among international donors and a recipient of extensive development aid, of which a considerable part is allocated via Christian organisations (Richey and Haakonsson 2004). At the local level, campaigns to prevent infection, to treat the infected and to look after both the infected and the affected have become integrated into the general work of the churches (Tiendrebego and Buykx 2004; Christensen and Janeway 2005).

A mapping of religious organisations in Busia District, which serves as a case study in this chapter, indicates a widespread practice of embracing infected people in church fellowships and attending to their health both in the church and at their homes.[3] The Christian landscape in Busia District consists of the mission-based Roman Catholic Church and the (Anglican) Church of Uganda, and numerous Pentecostal-Charismatic denominations.[4] In addition to pastoral care in the form of prayers, compassion and giving hope, churches allocate a substantial amount of the external aid in the district.[5]

The district is situated in the corner of south-eastern Uganda, bordering Kenya on the eastern side and the shores of Lake Victoria on the southern side. While the national HIV prevalence of HIV/AIDS has dropped to approximately 7 per cent, local prevalence is approximately 10 per cent (District Director of Health Services, May 2007). This could be explained by the constant flow of money and people in the border town and the fishing villages, which are fertile grounds for transactional sex (Obbo 1993; Talle 1995). Most people rely on small-scale farming and fishing; however, they face severe economic difficulties, as population pressure has led to land scarcity and the cost of living exceeds well beyond the income from these activities. Jobs are few and far between, although a fish factory and several new schools have brought employment to the area in recent years. The area itself is also known as Samia-Bugwe, referring to the two *Abaluya* groups that make up the majority of the approximately 230,000 inhabitants (Katahoire 1998; Rwabwoogo 2002). The Samia people form the majority, yet peaceful coexistence, a common language and long traditions of intermarriage have led to the local practice of referring to the people as Samia rather than Basamia-Bagwe, a practice I will continue in the following.

Kinship among the Samia is patrilineal and virilocal, meaning that children are born into their father's clan and often grow up in close proximity to paternal relatives. While clan membership is still a vital marker of identity and engages bonds of affection, the former stronghold of clans as access to resources is declining. Elderly men reason this weakening as due to more frequent land disputes, legal empowerment of women to have a say in their husband's clan land, reduced respect for elders in general and for issues of uniting clan members and keeping peace between clans in particular, interference from other influential social networks (religious and work-related) and the transfer of authority to settle unresolved clan disputes to local government and the police. Symptoms of this decline can be seen in increased selling of clan land to (rich) people from other clans, thus altering the social geography, and in reduced support between clan members. Additional factors such as land shortage, the rising cost of living, unemployment, frequent instability in relations of procreation and, as will be described later, HIV/AIDS all add to changes in the networks of social support among close kinsmen (Weisner 1995; Nyambedha et al. 2003; Christiansen 2005a). These alterations can be encapsulated as growing uncertainty or instability in kin-based relations of assistance. This uncertainty has led particularly the younger generation to complain that family life today is not what it should be. Instead it is fraught with quarrels and dissension, with mothers the only ones interested in the well-being of their children. The next section will illuminate inferences of these uncertain patterns of assistance between kin in the context of AIDS and the actions taken by individuals to benefit from economic and social resources in Christian-based networks.

Church Provisioning of Education and Social Mobility

In Uganda, as in most other African countries, Christian missionaries introduced formal education (and biomedical health care) as part and parcel of Christianising, or civilising, local societies (see, e.g., Gifford 1998; Spear 1999). While this type of education was also perceived as a means of attracting local interest in Christianity, education became a key asset for social mobility, as this competence paved the way for employment within the colonial and Christian administrations (Spear 1999; Smythe 1999). Although the correspondence between education and employment is now of a historical nature, Ugandans still consider education as *the* access to social mobility (Meinert 2003). This notion of education as the key to individual and societal development and awareness of the negative consequences of HIV/AIDS on poor children's access to education is not restricted to the Ugandan setting. It is reflected in the Millennium Development Goals, and international aid agencies have increased funding to educational components as part of programmes aimed at mitigating the consequences of HIV/AIDS (see, e.g., Danida 2005). Considering the historical intertwining of education and Christianity, and the widespread perception of churches as locally rooted organisations in a position to reach deprived children and families (Hansen and Twaddle 2002; Gifford 1994, 1998), Christian denominations seem particularly suited to implement aid-funded educational programmes.

For the past five years the Catholic Church in Busia District has been running two large programmes for youngsters who dropped out of school. An international NGO has funded polytechnic education for 340 orphans,[6] and twenty-five young people have been given accommodation at a hostel run by Catholics. An American-based ecumenical organisation has furthermore enabled a local parish priest to build a fully equipped secondary boarding school for approximately 700 students, of whom approximately 360 are enrolled in a sponsorship programme for orphans and deprived children. In both cases the process of selecting students involved local public structures (Parish Development Committees), and the principal selection criteria referred to the economic resources in the household and the position of individual children in the home rather than to religious affiliation (Christiansen and Whyte 2008).

The section below seeks to illustrate how churches assist families affected by HIV/AIDS through aid programmes by presenting two adolescents enrolled in sponsorship programmes. The focus is on the family situation, the enrolment process and the young people's ideas about being schooled and away from the family setting. Sarah and Anthony[7] are in their late teens and have lived as boarders for more than three years, apart from holidays. Sarah is enrolled in the polytechnic programme and accommodated at the hostel next door to a Catholic mission, whereas Anthony is enrolled in the 'orphan' programme and is a secondary-school boarder.

Enrolment: Family Dissonance and Motherly Efforts

The families of these young people, as is common in Busia District, are heavily affected by poverty and AIDS. Sarah[8] and Anthony lost their fathers to the disease, and in both cases the paternal relatives drove their widows and children off the land and sold the fathers' belongings. Both fathers were polygamous and the HIV infections caused immense problems among the co-wives, and between certain wives and the respective husband's relatives. The crux of the matter seems to have been discovering which woman had had extramarital relations and infected the husband. Sarah's mother was the first wife (of three) and a rather successful businesswoman. For a long time she had been frustrated with her husband, who spent her income on alcohol. When he 'purchased' a third wife, she left the household. She returned with her children to her natal family home 4 kilometres away, a decision that caused outrage between her own family and her in-laws. When her husband developed signs of AIDS, she returned to the household to perform the caretaking obligations of a first wife. During the last months of his life, the children remained at the home of their maternal relatives because their mother was afraid one of her co-wives might perform witchcraft or poison them. Sarah's mother is a nominal Anglican whereas her parents are 'saved' (or 'born again') Anglicans, and she believed the stronger Christian commitment of the grandparents would prove a better position to protect the children from witchcraft. Shortly after the burial rites, the children's paternal relatives seized her belongings and drove her not only out of her house (each wife has their own residence within the larger homestead) but also off the land she had been farming, and which her sons were entitled to inherit.

Anthony's mother was the youngest wife in a polygamous household of four co-wives and lived in a homestead where the wives collaborated with each other, for example, shared the task of rearing a large number of children. This spirit of cooperation changed when the husband developed signs of AIDS. As in the case of Sarah's mother, the identification of AIDS led to allegations among the co-wives as to who had 'gone outside', but also gave rise to suspicions of witchcraft. According to Anthony's mother, and a common understanding beyond this area (see, e.g., Yamba 1997), the inscrutability of how women who sexually share the same man avoid infection when the husband is infected leads reasoning to the idiom of witchcraft. Yet, since the wives and close paternal relatives were committed Catholics (several had positions on parish committees), no one dared to go against the Catholic proscription of consulting a diviner to investigate the suspicion. According to Anthony's mother, the first wife convinced the husband's relatives of her own innocence and formed an alliance that after the burial led to the paternal relatives seizing the property of the three younger wives and driving them from the homestead and the land. Due to the internal conflicts and 'bad death' of the husband, Anthony's mother still feels threatened by the 'evil heart' of the first wife.

Fortunately both Sarah and Anthony's mothers are of Samia origin and could count on maternal relatives nearby for a small piece of land they could till and on which they could build a new household. Life is difficult, however, since the maternal relatives have enough problems and expenses of their own. Sarah, Anthony and their siblings therefore depend exclusively on their mothers to provide for their daily bread and education. The seizure by the paternal relatives of their land and belongings – which in the case of Anthony's father included a herd of thirty cattle – caused such anger among the maternal relatives that contact with the paternal sides of the families has almost ceased. When Sarah's mother began to develop signs of AIDS in 2001 (loss of weight and facial skin complaints), an adolescent son was forced to take over the business. Sarah and her older sister found employment in a small restaurant and the oldest brother went to work for a maternal uncle in Kampala. Anthony's mother is an illiterate farmer unable to generate money for more than basic domestic needs. Anthony became involved in smuggling petrol from Kenya to Uganda, his two younger brothers helped their mother with farming and his older sister got married. Only the youngest sister was able to continue primary education.

As widows with almost no contact to paternal relatives and originating from poor families themselves, these mothers were obliged to involve other people in the duty of educating their children. It is a common element of maternal care to engage other adults in the responsibility for the well-being of the offspring (Mogensen 1999). Children can be considered as symbols of links between adults, hence caring for other people's children indicates caring about their parent(s) and, conversely, mistreating other people's children refers to a discrepancy in the adult ties between a parent and a caretaker (Bledsoe 1995). As a result of their impoverished situation, none of the neighbours was able to give educational support. Anthony's mother approached the Catholic priest, pleading with him to educate or employ her bright teenage son, who was currently undertaking great risks to provide for the home. Fortunately the parish priest was aware of her family situation and was prepared to provide secondary education for Anthony, whom he knew well from the youth club and from the overall commitment of Anthony's relatives. Sarah's mother, on the other hand, did not turn to the Anglican parish priest because she knew he had no resources to offer. When rumours of a polytechnic programme circulated, Sarah's mother approached her neighbour and close friend, who was on the Parish Development Committee, and begged her to nominate Sarah for the programme. The neighbour was familiar with her ill-fated marital history and current situation, and she knew of Sarah's positive performance at primary school. Following Mogensen and Bledsoe, the adult relations between Anthony's mother and the parish priest, and between Sarah's mother and the committee member next door facilitated the youngsters' access to sponsorship. Hence it was the mothers' relations with adults beyond the extended family that enabled one of their children to obtain the desired education. While the role of the religious (Catholic) network was pivotal in Anthony's enrolment, religion also became vital for Sarah, since she is enrolled in a Catholic-run programme and lives in a hostel next door to a Catholic mission. The following section will centre on the young people's experiences of schooling in these settings and living away from the family.

Schools as Asylums: Skills, Relations, and Religion

The boarders (at the secondary school and the hostel) praise the Catholic Church for providing them with a highly desired combination of education and institutional living. The close association of boarding schools with prosperity gained ground because most of today's leaders spent many years of their youth at various educational institutions, where they obtained the formal education, social skills and relations that paved the way for such advancement. When asked to describe living in an institutional setting, several students commented along the same lines as Anthony:

> If you're at home you *just sit*, you just dig the land, have no job or anything where you could earn something and solve your problems. Then if you go to school but live at home, the minute you finish class your mother or someone else will be waiting for you to fetch water, dig the garden, help the young ones. They never give you a minute off. That's why it's good here at boarding school. We do preparations two hours before we begin class and then again after dinner. We even read during the weekends.

Accordingly, living at school means 'becoming someone', that is, an educated person who can provide for themselves (and for others), can gain a professional title and who knows how to interact. The contrary of what they call 'becoming someone' is, as Anthony says, 'just to sit'. At first I thought this phrase referred to laziness, but in reality the person digs the land and does household chores. Yet that person is not developing the skills or resources that will make the future more promising than the present. Considering that formal education is indispensable to social, political and economic advancement, the notion that a young person who is not enrolled for any kind of formal education is at a standstill, 'just sitting', is understandable (cf. Meinert 2003).

Young people at school form friendships, share ideas and experiences and with time engage in each other's problems, such as passing exams or overcoming illness. They also enjoy light-hearted moments. It takes time to become good friends and most young people manage to have only a few close friends, while others are 'just friends'. Yet most students underline the importance of at least being on good terms with their fellow students, since one of them might eventually be their future employer. According to male students it is not their family but their friends, and especially their workmates, who in the future will contribute to their bride wealth, a notion they share with most adult males, who see education as the key to starting their own families. Young males in circumstances similar to Anthony's are aware that they are second in line for assistance from maternal relatives, and that the likelihood of receiving assistance from paternal relatives is minimal. In addition to this link with aspirations for the future – for work and for marriage – it is conspicuous that young people frequently draw attention to the fact that friends do not carry evil spirits against them. This appears to be common among youth exposed to serious family problems.

Apart from friendships with peers, living as a boarder in a religious environment can strengthen commitment or motivate conversion to a particular religious fellowship. This was the case with Sarah and several other Protestant boarders enrolled in the polytechnic programme, as she explained:

> Staying here at [the adjoining hostel to] the [Catholic] mission, I really like the Catholics and their way of praising the Lord. Father [the parish priest] welcomed me just like he welcomed the Catholic girls…. They [employees] have taken good care of me, given me food every day and sometimes meat on Sundays…. I learnt Catholic prayers and hymns, and one of the teachers taught me the Holy Mary…. After about one and a half years I told Father that I wanted to become a Catholic. He said I should ask my mother and possibly my [maternal] uncle … and they agreed.

The construction of a hostel for students next to a Catholic mission and the provision of formal education, proper care and instruction in Catholic interpretations of Christianity is a well-known recruitment strategy (Smythe 1999). According to the parish priest, it was the donor and the local environment that requested that the students' composition within the boarding facilities should reflect the religious division of the area. The employees at the mission agreed with the priest that converting non-Catholic students was not the original objective, but that their faith motivated their concern for the well-being of individual students in terms of educational skills, anxiety about the home situation, and physical and spiritual health. This 'lifestyle evangelism' (Bornstein 2002) practised as caring for the students and empowering them with skills to prosper contributed to a common notion among the students of boarding facilities as a refuge from family suffering. That boarding school was preferable to home was evident, for instance, in Anthony's reason for asking to remain there during the holidays: 'When I get to my mother's home I'm faced with so many problems. No food, no clothes, no water, just a grass-thatched hut, illness, quarrels, oh … and she expects me to solve all that! How can I manage? I am only young and still studying. Me, I'd prefer to stay at school and read.' Living in the enclosure of a well-equipped school with food, water, electricity and permanent buildings, and the undertaking of being educated and socialised in a modern way of life, may thus make school holidays unwanted because it means facing the reality of home. Although having a schooled identity gives young people some competence to participate in decisions affecting the family's situation (Meinert 2001), as Anthony expresses, it is beyond his power to change the wretched situation at home. This attitude should not be understood as indifference to the well-being of his mother and his home, but rather as recognition of an inability to improve the standard of living or to settle family disputes.

The educational support for the younger generation in families affected by AIDS is considered the chance of a lifetime, which the youngsters would not otherwise have had. Samia children belong to their father's clan and paternal relatives are expected to take responsibility for the welfare of the children and their mothers (Christiansen 2005a). As in the cases of Sarah and Anthony, when the symptoms of AIDS become part of family life, kinfolk (related by descent or affinity) speculate about who brought the disease into the home, and latent conflicts between kin may find a new outlet. The subsequent dissension (and poverty) in the homestead may compel a mother to take her children to her natal home, where poverty and her position as a married daughter will frequently force her to look for resources outside kin relations. Neighbours and friends typically are usually just as strained, hence churches with aid funding become attractive resourceful organisations. Whether a mother can avail of a particular programme or not depends to a great extent on her personal network. Although both youngsters enrolled in programmes in this case maintain strong emotional bonds with their mothers and close family members who are 'on their side', they attempt to establish relations with peers and often consider a new religious fellowship. They have great hopes that their new friends will with time become a substitute for the kinsmen they considered 'not to be on their side'. These young people and their relatives at home both tend to evaluate friendships formed through education or religious fellowship channels as a resource in the process of growing up. The fact that the inclusion of friends rarely leads to the exclusion or lessening of relations with supportive kinsmen may be the reason for this positive assessment. The church provisioning of material resources may thus alter the 'social security mix' of young people, as they strengthen kin-based relations with some relatives while simultaneously seeking to enhance independence from other kin. The following section sheds light on why churches seem reluctant to engage in restoring relations among kinfolk.

Church Provisioning of Spiritual and Social Support

The association of HIV/AIDS with sexual misdemeanour and death means that when a sexually active person develops signs of AIDS, relatives are not merely concerned with taking care of the patient; they also endeavour to make someone responsible for the deadly infection of a beloved one. As the cases above illustrate, attempts to place blame may cause strife within collaborating families (Anthony's case) or may escalate existing conflict between family members

(Sarah's case). The person infected may also be accused of immoral behaviour, as in the case of Sarah's mother when she developed AIDS symptoms as a widow. According to leaders across the Christian landscape, churches attend to the social disruptions caused by AIDS by seeking to alleviate the stigma of the person infected and to mitigate the negative impact on the affected family. I will argue below that the approaches of the various churches are inadequate to restore family relations and that this is due to theological positions and ritual practices. This section thus shifts to the perspective of churches as key actors in providing social and spiritual support in the social fabric. It will pay attention to local ideas of aetiology through which HIV/AIDS is ascribed meaning, and as such inform the understanding of actions people take to deal with affliction (Whyte 1997; Clifford 2004), and to ritual practices of prayers and restoration of relations.

Preaching and Prayers with Patients

The Catholic parish priests were the first to repeatedly include the danger of HIV infection in their sermons, a practice that dates back to the launching of the national prevention campaigns in the late 1980s. In burial sermons, the most outspoken of the three parish priests in the district also pointed to AIDS as the cause of death, thereby giving rise to local rumours that the priest himself was infected with the AIDS virus. Priests, however, broke the silence and encouraged catechists to approach the issue openly, although many catechists were ill informed and chose to remain silent. The Anglican priests and lay readers, on the other hand, seem to have kept a comparatively low profile with regard to including HIV/AIDS in their sermons. Even today the local Anglican church leaders show little engagement in this domain. The abundant Pentecostal-Charismatic churches that entered Uganda around the same time that the national prevention campaigns were launched integrated HIV/AIDS into their preaching – a practice that relates to the correspondence between fear of AIDS and the assertion to 'convert to salvation'.

Most preachers across the Christian landscape base their sermons on notions of AIDS as the divine punishment of sin. Yet this perception rarely leads to resentment towards or fear of infected people. Instead this view is embedded in theologies that all human beings are sinners and, as a Pentecostal pastor formulated, 'God is the one to judge, not we, the sinners'. Situating the 'sin of HIV infection' in the context of the common sinfulness of Christians (or human beings), the sermons are often linked to the Christian obligation to forgive and to care for those who are in need. Many preachers, especially the well-educated Catholic parish priests, also seek to encourage caretaking and reduce stigma by informing the congregation that the AIDS virus is not transmitted through touching or sharing food and utensils with those who are HIV positive.

All priests and catechists pray for the sick and many of them stress that visiting AIDS patients at home bears witness to others that talking to and praying with those who are infected does not pose a threat. The long-established Christian practice of praying for the sick takes different forms and illuminates different theological positions that have implications for the relationship between patients and relatives. Below are some extracts from notes I made after visiting sick members of the congregation with the Catholic catechist Henry and a Pentecostal-Charismatic pastor:

> When we arrived at the first home, a woman greeted us warmly and showed us into a very dark hut where her husband, somewhat older, was sitting comfortably in a large chair.... The man gave us a long account of his life in English.... Henry said the standard prayer for forgiveness and health improvement. When we said goodbye he assured the man that he would be back the following week. On our way to the next home, he told me that the man was suffering from AIDS, two of his wives had died and he himself would die soon.

Henry recounted that his principal task was to comfort the sick by visiting the patients at home and praying for their recovery or, at their deathbed, exhorting them not to fear death. When Henry talked to the patients about pain and access to medicine, food and safe water, he rarely enquired about the care provided by relatives, even when it was obvious that the basic care of water or cheap painkillers had not been provided. As evident from my notes below, the situation was quite different with the Pentecostal-Charismatic pastor, Emmanuel:

> Before arriving at the next home he told me about the patient: a second wife, suffering from AIDS, claims to have been infected by her husband who is 'getting slim'; her children take care of her; she was 'saved' before she developed symptoms; the home is otherwise Anglican. A young girl greeted us and showed us to the hut. A very thin woman was lying on a mattress, covered with a blanket. The hut was dirty. Emmanuel sat next to the woman and began to enquire what I could follow was about the pain she was in, her hatred of the husband who had 'killed' her, the first wife who does not care, fear of death, and concerns for her children. He questioned her as to how she became infected, pressuring her to confess.... He prayed for a long time, raising his voice when he cast out spirits.... After we left the home he explained, 'the patient has to confess before the relationship with God can be restored, that is why I was obliged to counsel her in-depth before giving her the medicine. Our home-based care is to counsel and to pray.

In Emmanuel's view, confession of sins, such as hatred and the possible source of the HIV infection, was part of 'counselling', after which prayers to cast out evil spirits would restore her relationship with God. It is common in Pentecostal-Charismatic practice that confession is the first step in ritual healing processes and the casting out of evil spirits (Meyer 1999). These spirits are assumed to be present when relations with other people in the social world are strained, and deliverance from spirits is believed to empower the person to remain at a distance from the people concerned (Christiansen 2003). In this context, the power of God liberates the woman from being influenced by hatred towards the husband who infected her and towards the co-wife who is not infected despite having sexually shared the same husband, and who does not care about her suffering. The Pentecostal-Charismatic prayers thus approach the individual as a socially embedded person with strained family relations, whereas the Catholic 'prayers for the sick' approach the individual as a person in need of material and spiritual support, without explicitly enquiring about the social relations through which such support is provided or not provided. In the language of prayers, the Pentecostal-Charismatic pastor addresses the strained relations between the patient and his or her relatives, yet these relatives are not present and hence not confronted with her complaints about their lack of care. Similar to the Catholic prayers, the focus is on the well-being of the individual rather than the social persona. In the context of reuniting two parties, these prayers seem one-sided.

Traditional Restoration and Christian Rupture

The current strife between family members is a concern people share across generations, although young people are the most vocal about the lack of solidarity and cooperation between family members. While they acknowledge the ambiguous relations between co-wives, for example, many bemoan the inability to reduce the tension between the offspring of co-wives. Traditionally this restoration required mobilisation of the clans of those involved (the patient and the offender) and the performance of rituals where the people concerned were confronted and where animal sacrifices symbolised their reconciliation (Whyte 1997). The rituals of restoration formed part of an aetiology that an agent (living person or ancestral spirit) deliberately caused the patient suffering and the only remedy was to resolve the troubled relationship. Among the living, the 'usual suspects' are people with whom the offended contends over resources (especially co-wives, step-siblings or a neighbour competing over land) and those with ill feelings towards the offended (such as a barren sister-in-law, an aggrieved mother-in-law or a neighbour). Among the deceased are spirits of genealogical ancestors and spirits of people who may have been harmed by an ancestor (a common example is the spirit of a person killed by an ancestor). In order to identify the agent 'behind' the visible suffering, a person related to the patient must consult a diviner (Whyte 1997). In addition to divinations, daily interaction discloses other people's feelings, sincerity and intentions towards the patient. Thus the cause of the illness is established through enquiries as to who might have something at stake in his or her relationship with the patient. It is conspicuous that while kinsmen are perceived to make up the principal network of assistance, they are also typically the prime suspects when misfortune occurs.

Today these rituals are rare phenomena, as all churches have banned Christians from performing or partaking in sacrificial practice. 'The Lord Jesus Christ gave His blood to revitalize the connection between God and human kind, and therefore', as most Pentecostal-Charismatic pastors claim, 'sacrificial blood must be for the Devil'. Apart from animal sacrifices, it is the interrelated communication with ancestral spirits (through diviners) that makes these rituals part of cultural practices, which in the eyes of the priests are incompatible with Christianity. As one Anglican pastor explained: 'If we [a church] allow Christians to conduct rituals, they will think it correct to consult diviners, to drink their mixtures, to dance all night and to fornicate. No, Christians need clear guidance and we should not allow them to bring our culture into this.... They must learn to forgive in a Christian manner.' Regardless of the prohibition by the church, people frequently consider it too complicated to mobilise the necessary people and resources for the ritual to achieve its purpose. As Sarah's mother said:

> These days there is no way [of reconciliation].... We fight too much among ourselves. There is so much hatred. How am I to get mine [natal family] to mobilize all those people and all that food and *amalwa* [local beer]? Everyone has their own reasons for not coming, they all have their own problems. No, these days we no longer care about each other.... I am ill, but whenever I can, I work hard to make my children strong. I concentrate on them and pray that the hatred remains in that home. It has no place here.

Sarah's mother was expelled from her husband's homestead and has tried to establish a life with her natal family. She has been unable to mobilize sufficient interest or resources even among her own kinsmen to attempt reconciliation with her in-laws. From her perspective the best option is to focus on her own offspring, to pray for protection against the ill will of her in-laws and to keep her hatred towards them under control.

Relentless poverty aggravated by AIDS and weakening family solidarity means that many widows find themselves in a similar position to that of Sarah's and Anthony's mothers. While the churches are not distressed about the inability to perform the traditional rituals reconciling kinsmen, many pastors are indeed concerned about the growing dissension in family relations. The Catholic Church has attempted to prevent the complete breakdown of kin relations, as expressed in widows being driven from the husbands' property, by encouraging men to write wills. These are kept with the parish priest, who claims authority to ensure the will is respected. Yet this practice has only been implemented sporadically and can likewise trigger conflicts, since the priest then seeks to overrule the authority of the paternal owners of the land, women and children according to customary law. Moreover, the will itself does nothing to reconcile the dissent between the widow and the in-laws, and may leave the former in a vulnerable position in the home, since in-laws entrust her to the priest if she is in need (Christiansen and Whyte 2008). The Church of Uganda also seems unable to provide Christians with an approach to the breakdown in kinship relations and merely seeks to reconcile relatives through sermons and individual prayers for forgiveness.

The Pentecostal-Charismatic churches, on the other hand, incorporate witchcraft suspicions and allegations into ritual practices, where the divine power enables them to identify the agent behind the suffering, and alleviate the latter by exorcising the demons. It is also integrated practice to protect believers from the ill will of relatives by empowering people to keep their nonconverted kinsmen at a spiritual distance. While these churches approach vital issues for people who associate HIV infection with witchcraft, the ritual practices encourage the individual believer to break away from troubled relationships (at least spiritually) rather than attempt reconciliation with relatives. While the theology of salvation is focused on the individual and the fellowship of Christians as distinct from nonsaved kin, the mission-based Catholic and Anglican churches tend to encourage cooperation with family members who belong to other religious fellowships. Without disregarding that the discourse and practice of forgiveness and protection enables Christians to interact with family members whom they resent or fear, the mission-based churches do not provide a practice to restore relations within the families affected by HIV/AIDS.

Family, Friends and Fellowship

'When AIDS enters the family, it eats the people and the property', a young male student claimed. 'You even see strong homes collapse.' Homes collapse in both a physical and a metaphorical sense, since the virus 'eats' up the people and the resources in the home. In a context of rampant poverty and lack of access to public social services, civil society organisations seem to have gradually gained significance for young people as a means of improving their present situation and their personal development.

The space between family and state in Uganda is dominated by formal and informal networks, which are linked to a variety of religious and nongovernmental organisations as well as to schools, ethnicity and places of origin. Social relations, especially with influential friends and religious networks, are well known to be key for the attainment of desired positions in both private enterprises and public institutions, and to a certain extent could be the reason for the younger generation's expectation that relations with friends and religious fellows will provide prosperity. The severe discord between many family members in the adult generation, including the paternal relatives whose role it is to provide the sons with land, bride wealth and a burial site, and to protect the daughters from ill treatment in marriage, also reduces the variety of kinsmen young people perceive as relevant for their social well-being.

The quantity versus quality of people in personal networks may be irrelevant, if relations of friendship, kinship and between fellow believers overlap, but they can also tear apart. In the local Ugandan context there are several examples of young people who shift religious fellowships in order to obtain social welfare at the same time as enrolment in such a project might well motivate conversion. When young people shift between religious networks these movements spur discussions between kinsmen but do not necessarily influence kin-based assistance to the young. Knowledge of the consequences church-based social welfare has on the long-term well-being of young people and their social networks and orientations is scant. Mission-based and Pentecostal-Charismatic churches implement similar social welfare programmes for young people, yet differ markedly in pastoral care based on the integration of family and fellowship, focusing on forgiveness (mission-based) and, on the other hand, distance between fellowship and nonsaved relatives and the identification of harmful relatives from whom they must be released (Pentecostal-Charismatic). Thus young people's 'social security mixing' reveals further insights into the dynamics between kinship and religious networks in the context of HIV/AIDS and poverty.

Notes

1. The distinction between 'poverty of people' and 'poverty of economics' seeks to emphasise the particular kinds of loss that families affected by AIDS experience. It is inspired by a common notion in Africa about 'wealth in people', that is, a wealthy family has many people and many of them are financially well off. While it is possible to have a wealth in people and poor economic resources, families affected by AIDS become particularly deprived of both human and financial resources.

2. The data underpinning this chapter was produced in the course of two research projects carried out in the location of Busia District, Uganda, between 1998 and 2005. Initial research (1998–2001) attended to Christian church practices in relation to health and healing, especially links between religiosity, sociality and health-seeking behaviour. The later study (2002–2005) focused on patterns of raising young people in household and institutional settings, and implications of aid directed towards youth living in a poor rural context inflicted with HIV/AIDS. In the fourteen months of ethnographic fieldwork, the main methods used were participant observation, mapping exercises and a variety of interview techniques.

3. In the course of 2006, research assistants mapped out the religious organisations in Busia District, focusing on organisation, integration of issues related to HIV/AIDS, youth and development projects. The mapping was carried out in five (of ten) subcounties in Busia District and involved 366 churches and 19 mosques.

4. The Christian churches engage about 75 per cent of the population and are, similar to the national level, divided into a resourceful Catholic Church (approximately 35 per cent), a poor Anglican Church of Uganda (approximately 30 per cent) and a multiplicity of both rich and poor Pentecostal-Charismatic churches (approximately 10 per cent).

5. Based on a mapping of all ongoing projects in Busia District in 2004, which I renumerated in cooperation with the Community Development Office of the Social Department at the district level (Christiansen 2005b).

6. The programme is directed towards providing 'domestic child workers' with skills training in order to improve their employment opportunities. In the local setting, however, these are interpreted as 'orphans' as a result of the regularity with which orphans work both within and outside their homes.

7. This selection criterion is based on the recognition that resources in the household are not distributed equally among the members (see also Bledsoe 1995). Children without a father often lack the material resources ascribed to the role of the father and the paternal relatives, whereas children without a mother often suffer from lack of care because the father remarries and leaves the children in the care of a stepmother or the grandparents (Christiansen 2005a).

8. All names are pseudonyms and their backgrounds slightly altered to ensure anonymity.

References

Bate, S. 2003. *Responsibility in a Time of AIDS: A Pastoral Response by Catholic Theologians and AIDS Activists in Southern Africa*. Pietermaritzburg: Cluster Publications, South Africa.

Benda-Beckmann, F. von and K. von Benda-Beckmann. 2000. 'Coping with Insecurity', in *Coping with Insecurity: An "Underall" Perspective on Social Security in the Third World*, ed. F. von Benda-Beckmann, K. von Benda-Beckmann and H. Marks. The Netherlands: Focaal Foundation, 7–34.

Bledsoe, C. 1995. 'Marginal Members: Children of Previous Unions in Mende Households in Sierra Leone', in *Situating Fertility: Anthropology and Demographic Inquiry*, ed. S. Greenhalgh. Cambridge: Cambridge University Press, 130–53.

Bornstein, E. 2002. 'Developing Faith: Theologies of Economic Development in Zimbabwe'. *Journal of Religion in Africa* 32(1): 4–31.

Christensen, A.-M. and P. Janeway. 2005. *Faith in Action: Examining the Role of Faith-Based Organizations in Addressing HIV/AIDS*. Washington, DC: Global Health Council.

Christiansen, C. 2003. 'Conditional Certainty: Ugandan Charismatic Christians Striving for Health and Harmony', in *Uncertain in Contemporary African Lives*, ed. L. Haram. Uppsala: Nordic Africa Institute.

_____. 2004. 'Living in A Christian No Mans Land: Ugandan Widows Facing Dilemmas of Salvation, Social Support, and Sexuality', in *African Christianity in the 21st Century*, ed. P. Hasu. Uppsala: Nordic Africa Institute.

_____. 2005a. 'Positioning Children and Institutions of Childcare in Contemporary Uganda'. *African Journal of AIDS Research* 4(3): 173–82.

_____. 2005b. *Developing Busia District 2004*, unpublished report.

_____. forthcoming. 'Church-based Aid to Youth Affected by AIDS in Uganda: On Connections between Church and Development', in *Religious NGOs and the Politics of Development*, ed. T. Tvedt and P. Opoku-Mensah. London: James Currey.

Christiansen, C. and S. R. Whyte. 2008. 'Arenas of Child Support: Interfaces of Family, State and NGO Provisions of Social Security', in *From Subject to Citizen: Institutions for Inclusive States*, ed. A. Dani and A. de Haan. Washington, DC: World Bank Publications.

Clifford, P. 2004. *Theology and the HIV/AIDS Epidemic*. London: Christian Aid.

Czerny, M. S. J. 2005. *AIDS and the African Church: To Shepherd the Church, Family of God in Africa, in the Age of AIDS*. Nairobi: Paulines Publications Africa.

Danida. 2005. *Children and Young People in Danish Development Cooperation. Guidelines*. Copenhagen: Danida.

Djik R. van. 1992. 'Young Puritan Preachers in Post-Independence Malawi'. *Africa* 62: 159–81.

Gifford, P. 1994. 'Some Recent Developments in African Christianity'. *African Affairs* 93: 513–34.

_____. 1998. *African Christianity: Its Public Role*. London: Hurst and Company.

Hansen, H. B. and M. Twaddle. 2002. *Christian Missionaries and the State in the Third World*, ed. H. B. Hansen and M. Twaddle. Oxford: James Curry.

Hearn, J. 2002. 'The "Invisible" NGO: US Evangelical Missions in Kenya'. *Journal of Religion in Africa* 32(1): 32–60.

Katahoire, A. R. 1998. *Education for Life – Mothers' Schooling and Children's Survival in East Uganda*. PhD thesis no. 10, Institute of Anthropology, University of Copenhagen, Denmark.

Kirwen, M. C. 1979. *African Widows: An Empirical Study of the Problems of Adapting Western Christian Teachings on Marriage to the Leviratic Custom for the Care of Widows in Four Rural African Societies*. New York: Orbis.

Lwaminda, P. and M. S. J. Czerny. 2004. *Speak out on HIV and AIDS: Our Prayer is Always Full of Hope*. Catholic Bishops of Africa and Madagascar. Nairobi: Paulines Publications Africa.

Meinert, L. 2001. *The Quest for a Good Life: Health and Education among Children in Eastern Uganda*. PhD thesis, Institute of Anthropology, University of Copenhagen, Denmark.

_____. 2003. 'Sweet and Bitter Places: The Politics of Schoolchildren's Orientation in Rural Uganda', in *Children's Places: Cross-Cultural Perspectives*, ed. K. F. Olwig and E. Gullov. London: Routledge, 179–96.

Meyer, B. 1998. 'If You are a Devil, You are a Witch, and If You are a Witch, You are a Devil: The Integration of 'Pagan' Ideas into the Conceptual Universe of Ewe Christians in Southeastern Ghana'. *Journal of Religion in Africa* 28(3): 316–49.

_____. 1999. *Translating the Devil: Religion and Modernity among the Ewe in Ghana*. Edinburgh: Edinburgh University Press.

_____. 2004. 'Christianity in Africa: From African Independent to Pentecostal-Charismatic Churches'. *Annual Review of Anthropology* 33: 447–74.

Mogensen, H. O. 1999. *Mothers' Agency – Others' Responsibility: Striving for Children's Health in Eastern Uganda*, PhD thesis no. 13, Institute of Anthropology, University of Copenhagen.

Nyambedha, E. O., S. Wandibba and J. Aagaard-Hansen. 2003. 'Changing Patterns of Orphan Care Due to the HIV Epidemic in Western Kenya'. *Social Science & Medicine* 57(2): 301–11.

Obbo, C. 1993. 'HIV Transmission through Social and Geographical Networks in Uganda'. *Social Science and Medicine* 36(7): 949–55.

PACANet. 2005. *The Church's Role in Strengthening the Family in an Era of HIV/AIDS*. Position Paper. Abuja, Nigeria: Pan-African Christian AIDS Network.

Parkhurst, J. O. and L. Lush. 2004. 'The Political Environment of HIV: Lessons from a Comparison of Uganda and South Africa'. *Social Science and Medicine* 59(9): 1913–24.

Richey, L. A. and S. J. Haakonsson 2004. *Access to ARV Treatment: Aid, Trade and Governance in Uganda*. Working Paper 19. Copenhagen: Danish Institute of International Studies.

Rwabwoogo, M. O. 2002. *Uganda Districts Information Handbook*. Kampala: Fountain Publishers.

Seidel, G. 1990. "'Thank God I Said No to AIDS": On the Changing Discourse of AIDS in Uganda'. *Discourse and Society* 1(1): 61–84.

Smythe, K. R. 1999. 'The Creation of a Catholic Fipa Society: Conversion in Nkansi District, Ufipa', in *East African Expressions of Christianity*, ed. T. Spear and I. N. Kimambo. Oxford: James Currey, 129–49.

Spear, T. 1999. 'Toward the History of African Christianity', in *East African Expressions of Christianity*, ed. T. Spear and I. N. Kimambo. Oxford: James Currey, 3–24.

Talle, A. 1995. 'Bar Workers at the Border', in *Young People at Risk: Fighting AIDS in Northern Tanzania*, ed. K.-I. Klepp, P. M. Biswalo and A. Talle. Oslo: Scandinavian University Press, 18–30.

Tiendrebego, G. and Buykx, M. 2004. *Faith-Based Organisations and HIV/AIDS Prevention and Impact Mitigation in Africa*. Amsterdam: Royal Tropical Institute.

Weisner, T. S. 1995. 'Support for Children and the African Family Crisis', in *African Families and the Crisis of Social Change*, ed. T. S. Weisner, C. Bradley and P. L. Kilbride. Westport, CT: Bergin & Garvey.

Whyte, S. R. 1997. *Questioning Misfortune: The Pragmatics of Uncertainty in Eastern Uganda*. Cambridge: Cambridge University Press.

Yamba, B. 1997. 'Cosmologies in Turmoil: Witchfinding and AIDS in Chiawa, Zambia'. *Africa* 2: 200–23.

Chapter 3

'Fight against Hunger'

Ambiguities of a Charity Campaign in Postwar Croatia

Carolin Leutloff-Grandits

Introduction

In 2001, six years after the ethnic war between Croats and Serbs in Croatia that succeeded the collapse of socialist Yugoslavia in 1990, ethnic conflict was still prevalent in former Croatian war regions. At the same time, Croatia was still struggling with the consequences of postsocialist economic transition and its specific dimensions in these areas. Here, Croatian and Serbian returnees as well as new Croatian settlers from Bosnia lived a marginalised existence fraught with poverty and competed for scant economic resources. It was in this situation that the local branch of the Catholic Caritas organisation began a charity campaign for 'hungry Croats' in the town of Knin, a centre of ethnic conflict during the war and a town with one of the highest unemployment rates in Croatia in 2001.

Led by the abbot of the Franciscan monastery in Knin, the local Caritas branch addressed socio-economic and national issues in the Knin region under the slogan 'Fight Hunger in Knin'. Having gained the support of leading representatives of the Catholic Church, among them several bishops from the Croatian coastal towns, as well as local and national politicians of Croatian national parties and (former) war officers from the Croatian army, the campaign soon gathered national momentum, stretching even beyond the borders of Croatia. With the help of donations, Caritas managed to open a public soup kitchen in Knin to feed the 'poor'. This chapter will discuss the functions and

Notes for this chapter begin on page 59.

meanings of the charity campaign, critically examining its impact on the creation of social security in material, emotional and spiritual terms.[1]

Taking the ideological background to the mobilisation into account, it will be shown that the campaign relied on a charity ideology based on Croatian society's collective experience of forced migration and ethnic war in the 1990s, where Serbs were seen as aggressors and perpetrators and Croats as victims who defended themselves. These collective Croatian war experiences were instrumentalised in an attempt to mobilise national solidarity for Croats in Knin, in a nationwide, even trans-state effort to attract donors. Hence instead of overcoming the interethnic tension that had overshadowed daily life in Croatia since the early 1990s, the charity campaign set mechanisms of nation-building in motion, continuing the war policy of ethnic engineering, albeit with other means.

Looking at the establishment of the network and its effects in the locality of Knin, the quality of the social security achieved by the campaign must be examined critically. The charity campaign failed to improve the everyday life of most Serbian returnees in the region. On the contrary it was experienced as threatening. Remarkably, the campaign also had ambiguous meanings for Croats in Knin. Principally directed at Croatian settler families from Bosnia, who were under increasing economic and international pressure to leave the region again, the campaign was of no genuine assistance in making ends meet. Importantly, however, the campaign encouraged Croatian settlers to feel accepted and needed in Knin as a vital part of the Croatian nation-building project. This led to a greater sense of security and increased Croatian settler's willingness to endure the tough economic situation in Knin.

The ambivalence of the charity campaign is also evident in the structural difference between the Croatian settlers from Bosnia who had moved into the region after the war and native Croats who were in fact returning to their home region. The latter frequently saw themselves as excluded from the network, which led to a sense of marginalisation and powerlessness.

In an attempt to elaborate on these findings, the first section of the chapter will present background information on the settlement history and on social security provisioning in the Knin region. In the second section I will concentrate on the charity campaign of the local Caritas branch in 2001 and explain the process of establishing a translocal network to attract donations for and solidarity with Croats in Knin. Here I will first of all describe the activities of the local abbot to rally external support for the 'poor' in Knin. This will be followed by an account of the response of translocal Catholic organisations, Croatian politicians and former high-ranking army officers. The third section presents a more detailed description of how the various population groups reacted to the charity campaign in the Knin region: Croatian settlers, native Croats who had returned home and Serbian returnees. It should be noted that these categories are generalisations based on structural, political and historical differences, and cannot be applied to everyone in the Knin region.

Historical Background to Changing Intergroup Relations and Social Security Providers in the Knin Region

Before the war broke out in the 1990s, the population of the town of Knin was ethnically mixed, with a Serb majority and a Croat minority. Up to the Second World War, the Knin region was a poor rural area where agriculture constituted the main source of income for the large majority. Although Croats and Serbs practised different religions (Croats are Roman Catholic and Serbs are Serbian Orthodox), they had organised their daily lives for centuries in similar ways and developed a common social identity. With the rise of national movements religion gradually gained significance as a criterion among Serbs and Croats, since it became the main marker of the respective Croatian and Serbian nationalities. In the course of the Second World War, nationalist tensions had culminated in violent clashes along national lines (Grandits and Promitzer 2000).

Based on the socialist ideology of brotherhood and unity, and on the growing industrialisation in the 1960s that brought economic prosperity to the region, interethnic relations once again became harmonious, with interethnic marriages particularly common in the town of Knin. Around this time, the socialist state had become the key provider of social security. Once people were employed, they had rights to housing, health insurance and pensions. However, agriculture on private land never fully lost its meaning and became a secondary source of income as well as a means of maintaining family, kinship and community relations and practising solidarity beyond ethnic boundaries (Halpern 1968: 294; Brkić and Žutinić 1993). As a result of the political and economic crisis in the late 1980s, nationalism resurfaced, exacerbating the conflict between Serbs and Croats in Knin.

Croatia declared independence in 1991, only one year after the collapse of socialist Yugoslavia. Around that time Knin had become a stronghold of Serbian insurgents. With the frequent assistance of the Yugoslav National Army, they occupied a third of the Croatian territory and established the (internationally not recognised) 'Republic of Serbian Krajina' with Knin as its capital (Denich 1994; Grandits and Leutloff 2003). The Serbs expelled their Croatian neighbours and occupied or destroyed their houses. In 1995, this situation changed dramatically when the Croatian army succeeded in recapturing most of the Serbian-occupied regions in Croatia, thereby prompting the flight of some 200,000 Croatian Serbs – almost the entire population of the so-called Serbian Krajina – to Yugoslavia or the Serbian Republic in Bosnia

(Mappes-Niediek 1995). Hence the war ended and the Krajina region was reintegrated into the territory of the Croatian state. The town of Knin became the symbol of Croatian victory.

The Knin region was resettled by Croats soon after the victory of the Croatian army. Most of the settlers were young families with several children and came from Bosnia. War refugees themselves, they hoped to find a permanent home in Croatia and settled in abandoned Serbian houses. Socially marginalised Croats from other parts of Croatia also settled in Knin, albeit to a lesser extent. Furthermore, some native Croats originally from the region returned to their own homes, from which the Serbs had expelled them during the war years. In comparison to Croatian newcomers they were now in the minority, a circumstance that carried the seeds of conflict. The slow but steady return of native (mainly elderly) Serbs following major efforts by the international community in 1998 provoked renewed tension along national lines. Serbs began to reclaim their property, thereby putting pressure on Croatian settlers to move out of the houses (and possibly the region) again. However, implementation of the restitution policy was slow.

An added drawback to the interethnic and intergroup complications in the region was the weak economic situation. In the year 2000–01, unemployment had reached approximately 50 to 70 per cent and a large number of inhabitants in the Knin region lived in poverty. As a result of the deteriorating economic and housing situation, some Croatian settler families left the region again, while others were frustrated and considered the option. Native Croats were not enamoured of their future prospects in Knin either, as work was unavailable and predictability nigh to impossible. Many young Croats had therefore not returned home. The economic situation and future prospects of the Serbs, who made up almost half the population in the wider region in 2001, were even worse than those of the Croatian settlers or native Croats. While elderly Serbs relied on small pensions, the few young Serbs who had returned were confronted with harsh economic conditions, interethnic tension and housing problems (Leutloff-Grandits 2006).

The Creation of a Translocal Charity Network
for Croats in Knin

In February 2001, the head of the local Caritas branch in Knin, Petar Klarić, wrote an open letter to the Croatian Catholic weekly *Glas Koncila*, which was later reprinted in other Church magazines. He appealed in the letter to Croats all over the country to donate money, food and hygiene articles to the 'hungry' in Knin. The appeal was simultaneously linked to national considerations. Petar Klarić argued as follows:

Save the hungry in Knin.

As everyone knows, Knin is facing a humanitarian catastrophe with about 12,000 Croats living on the edge of poverty.... They are our decent, honest Croatian families with many children.... Are we to allow the exodus of our Croats from Knin to another European country or overseas? Of course we don't want that! That is why we invite all Croats from our homeland and all expatriates, as well as all our friends and people of good will, and those who have the interest of Croatia and Knin at heart to help immediately with money, food and articles of hygiene today, because tomorrow could be too late.

Yesterday we heard more sad news, 'Father, these are my parents. They are now planning to move to America.' Why, you ask? 'Because they cannot make a living here.' Do we want to get this kind of news every day? This is not only our concern here in Knin but that of all Croats in the homeland, and throughout the world. We all know the meaning of the Croatian flag on the castle of Knin.

Recently, one of the local inhabitants of Knin [Kninjanin – a local from Knin] said, 'Every morning when I wake up I immediately look at the castle and at the Croatian flag flying there. I implore God that I may never wake up one day to find the Croatian flag no longer in its place, because then I would move away from Knin at once. As long as the Croatian flag remains on the castle of Knin, only hunger could drive me away.'

If we do not help the hungry people of Knin now, our conscience will speak to us tomorrow. Let us awake, today.

Jesus said, 'What you do for one of my brothers, you do for me.' And I can say openly: if you have not fed your brother and sister, you have killed them. (Glasnik Sv. Ante 2001: 14)

It is evident from this public appeal by the Franciscan abbot that the 'fight against hunger' was presented as a campaign to help Croats in dire circumstances. To justify and support the charity element, however, the letter refers to Croat war experiences when Knin was ruled by Serbs and Croats were expelled. The suggestion here is that if Croats were to leave the region yet again – this time due to poverty – Knin could once more become Serbian. This is made explicit by the image of the flag flying on the castle in Knin. The Serbian flag was hoisted onto the castle during the war and then exchanged for that of the Croatians following their victory over the Serbs. The objective of the hunger scenario and the Croat exodus from Knin was to make Croats all over Croatia aware that their presence in Knin was a stronghold against the growing power of the Serbs in Knin (and accordingly in Croatia).

The abbot's allusion to the many children of the Croatian settler families was another hidden argument to create a sense of solidarity and concern among Croats all over Croatia and abroad. In fact, Knin deviated from the general demographic picture in Croatia where population figures were gradually decreasing. This was characterised by a steady decline in birth rates and a negative migration balance (Akrap and Živić 2001: 643; Gelo 2003; Živić 2003).

In the years 2000 and 2001, in contrast, Knin showed the highest birth rate in Croatia after the war, as many of the Croatian settler families from Bosnia had three or more children. Since the Catholic Church and the conservative political parties, all of whom were deeply concerned by the demographic decline in Croatia, had declared higher birth rates and the prevention of emigration as demographic goals, they disapproved of the out-migration of Croatian settler families from Knin to foreign countries. Hence assisting Croats in Knin was – at least on a symbolic level – a method of combatting Croat emigration and the worrying birth rate in Croatia.

In response to this public appeal by the local Catholic abbot, other Catholic Church congregations expressed their solidarity with the 'hungry' Croats in Knin by praying for the allegedly poverty-stricken Croatian families and their many children in Knin, collecting donations and visiting Knin to preach to the Catholic congregation. In spring 2001, when the campaign had already been launched, the demonstration of solidarity from Catholic congregations reached its peak with the presence of Catholic bishops and Franciscans from the Dalmatian towns of Split, Dubrovnik and Šibenik at Sunday mass in Knin. They preached to a crowd of a thousand Croats who had gathered in the provisional church building (a former warehouse), since the original Catholic church did not have the capacity to hold the throngs of visitors.[2] In their sermons and speeches, not unlike those of the local Franciscans, the Dalmatian bishops highlighted the situation of the many Croats who had moved to the region for the first time after the war. They interpreted the settlement of Croats in territories formerly inhabited by Serbs and their right to a minimum standard of living as the direct will of God. The bishop of the Šibenik diocese declared:

> God the Father gives his people land and a homeland where they can live freely. So that they will live honourably on their land and in their homeland.... You have the right to a worthy human life. Here in Knin in Croatia. You dear and troubled families, dear children and dear young people. Jesus Christ offers this to you, he who is the foundation of all human dignity and human rights. You have the right to a human dwelling. You have the right to a piece of land, to your free homeland, to your nation, to your language, the right to express yourself and to vote. (Glasnik Sv. Ante 2001: 17–19)

In this citation the bishop makes it clear that when he claims God 'gives his people' he means Croats and not Serbs or Muslims, and when referring to 'homeland' he means the Croatian state territory in which Croats (and not Serbs and Muslims) would be at home.[3] His sermon blends Catholic principles of humanity and Croatian nationalist ideologies; religion and nationalism are presented in union. The Catholic Church thus pursued a policy it had adopted in the late 1980s and to which it adhered in the 1990s (cf. Vrcan 2001: 7–38). It closely resembled the policies of the Croatian national HDZ (Hrvatska

Demokratska Zajednica – Croatian Democratic Union) party led by the then president Franjo Tudjman, which ruled in Croatia from 1990 until 2000. In the opinion of many Croats, the greatest achievements of the HDZ were the establishment of Croatian independence and the regaining of territories previously held by Serbs. From 1995 onwards, the HDZ supported the settlement of Bosnian Croats in the former Croatian war regions. As a result of Croatia's growing international isolation and the public recognition of vast corruption practices under Tudjman, the HDZ lost the 2000 elections to a coalition of opposition parties led by the SDP (Socijaldemokratska Partija Hrvatske – Social Democratic Party of Croatia). The HDZ was, however, still the leading nationalist party in Knin at local level, not least due to the huge support of Croatian settlers from Bosnia.

A mere ten days after the Catholic mass in Knin mentioned earlier, Caritas opened a public soup kitchen that supplied 150 meals a day for the 'hungry' (*gladne/gladnike*), as Caritas officials put it. The establishment of the soup kitchen marked a further pinnacle in the Caritas charity campaign. This time the help provided by the organisation was palpable.

The festive opening of the soup kitchen was attended by those who had given financial, logistical and/or spiritual support, including the Bishop of Šibenik; other high-ranking clergy; senior army officers who had been active in the war, most of whom were members of the Croatian nationalist party HDZ; local HDZ representatives, such as the HDZ head of the county and his deputy; as well as the president of the Club of Croatian Returnees from Abroad. The senior army officers brought with them 120 tons of flour, sugar and oil valued at 100,000 euros, and placed approximately 10,000 euros in the Caritas euro bank account in Knin. Another high-ranking officer brought 2,500 euros that had been collected by various war veteran associations ('U Kninu otvorena pučka kuhinja', *Vijesnik*, 22 March 2001). The representatives of the Croats from abroad also contributed generously to the soup kitchen.

The strong presence of HDZ politicians and distinguished army officers once again shows their extremely close relationship with the Catholic Church and their joint moral imperative to do 'God's work' and strengthen Croatian unity by combining sacred and secular forces. This added a spiritual and political dimension to the material aspect of the soup kitchen. Janko Bobetko, the highest ranking commander of the Croatian army during the war, referred to moral responsibility in his explanation of why he had attended the opening of the soup kitchen in Knin:

> What are the officers doing here today? Knin is liberated, there is no battle. So what are we doing here? I must answer frankly that we are here for our own sake, for Croatian history and the Croatian truth.... We came to Knin, the town we liberated, to the people for whom we acted as guarantors that Croats could return. Today, as

before, things are not easy for them, that is why we must be with them. (Glasnik Sv. Ante 2001: 28, 29)

Emotional appeals of this kind, for Croatian solidarity in the face of 'hungry Croats' living in one of the country's most symbolically loaded towns, did not fail to have the desired effect. The sensational manner in which the Catholic Church, leading politicians and senior army officers presented the disastrous situation of Croatian families received huge national and occasionally international media coverage. Leading Croatian newspapers soon picked up on Knin as a town where Croat settlers and native Croats who had returned there were now starving. A sense of solidarity and responsibility thus spread beyond Catholic Church congregations and nationalist-politician and army-officer circles to 'normal' Croatian citizens in Croatia and abroad. Firms, schools and individuals sent parcels and money to Caritas in Knin. Truckloads of donations arrived day after day. In Knin itself, donations were collected by the local Caritas branch and subsequently distributed to those seen to be needy. Between the beginning of November 2000 and 19 May 2001, some 2,555 families received 4,407 humanitarian parcels with groceries and hygiene articles (Glasnik Sv. Ante 2001: 14–16).[4] The head of Caritas in Knin expressed his gratitude to the numerous donors in the local church bulletin, 'We were extremely grateful for such great loving attention from our Croats in the homeland and throughout the world' (Glasnik Sv. Ante 2001: 15).

As anticipated and outlined earlier, however, reactions of the inhabitants of Knin – Croatian settlers, native Croats and native Serbs – to the charity campaign differed. Some were critical or at least ambivalent. In the next section I will present these reactions in more detail and examine the various meanings the campaign had for those concerned. To fully understand the perspectives of Croatian settlers, native Croats and Serbs on the charity campaign of the Catholic Church, I will take a closer look at the role of religious practice in everyday life.

Reactions to the Charity Campaign in the Locality of Knin

The Perspective of Croatian Settlers

A large number of Croatian settlers in Knin were enthusiastic or at least positive about the fact that the Catholic Church had finally brought their fate to public attention. Prior to 2001, the majority of the Croatian settlers who had moved to Knin and occupied Serbian property after the war were unemployed and depended for the most part on small welfare payments from the Croatian state amounting to approximately 50 euros per month for each member of the household. Furthermore, their housing rights were highly insecure. In this situation, Croatian settlers were deeply disappointed with the policy of the new Croatian government (which ruled from 2000 on) as well as with the international community, which seemed to be more interested in the return of the native Serbs than the fate of Croatian settlers in former Croatian war regions, all of which made the future of Bosnian Croat settlers in Croatia highly unpredictable. In an endeavour to grasp the implications of this disappointment and sense of insecurity, the process will be explained more systematically. As outlined briefly at the beginning, most Croatian settlers in the Knin region originally came from Bosnia and had experienced violence and expulsion during the war years as a result of their Croatian nationality. Moving to Croatia meant settling in the safety of the 'mother state', where they belonged to the national majority and not the persecuted minority. Many of those who moved to Knin benefited from the new law introduced by the Croatian state legalising Croat occupation of abandoned Serbian houses after the massive flight of the Serbs in 1995. However, the law contained not only a clearly ethnonational bias but also a social component confining occupation of Serbian houses to Croats who neither owned property in Croatia nor possessed use rights to apartments (cf. 'Law on the Temporary Take-Over and Administration of Specified Property', *Narodne Novine* 73/1995, 06/1996, 1000/1997; and 'Law on the Lease of Apartments in the Liberated Areas', *Narodne Novine* 73/1995). Consequently it primarily attracted Croats from Bosnia and other parts of Croatia, who had found themselves at the lower end of the social ladder in socialist times and/or in the war years. Most of them had merely basic education and had frequently lost their jobs and accommodation during the war and/or during the postsocialist transformation. The fact that settlers in Knin did not have to pay for housing, water, electricity or other communal services meant that the cost of living in comparison with other places was considerably less. At the time, the Croatian government declared the houses would become their property after ten years of uninterrupted settlement. It furthermore promised Croatian settlers in former war regions employment and additional economic and social benefits, assurances that were broadcast on national radio and TV stations as well as through agencies of the Catholic Church.

Following the calls of HDZ politicians and representatives of the Catholic Church, Croatian settlers were enthusiastic about coming to Knin. Although the majority lacked personal links with Knin and came as strangers after the flight of the Serbs and the reintegration of the region into the Croatian state once the war was over, they regarded it as an empty space. They assumed that settling the area with ethnic Croats was legitimate, and expected to begin a new life and create a livelihood in the Knin region. This was especially important for Croats from Bosnia, who either could not or did not want to return to their home region.

However, the positive expectations and feelings surrounding their new home, encouraged by the Croatian government between 1995 and 1997, were gradually frustrated in the years that followed. As a result of pressure from the international community on the Croatian state to revoke the property law that had granted Croatian settlers permanent use rights and even gave them the prospect of receiving property rights in 1998, and especially since the establishment of the new government in 2000, settlers found their rights diminished to a more or less temporary state of enjoying 'use rights' to the house they occupied. In the long run, they were to hand the houses back to their legal owners, the Serbs. With the gradual return of a growing number of Serbs, settlers became disillusioned and developed a sense of insecurity. There was no definite indication of when they were to move out of their accommodation; what, if anything, was to be offered as an alternative; and where. These feelings of insecurity and frustration were aggravated by the punishing economic situation in the former war regions. During the 1991–1995 war, the economy of the Knin region was almost completely destroyed. The factories, a key source of employment in the region in socialist times, were either looted or devastated, which led to high unemployment in Knin.

In this atmosphere of disappointment about the overall situation and the new political course of the reigning SDP coalition, Croatian settlers hoped that the charity campaign of the Catholic Church would contribute to improving their situation, and their fate might finally take a turn for the better. For those who received humanitarian parcels with food and articles of hygiene and/or went to the soup kitchen for lunch, the Catholic Church was seen as the sole actor that had succeeded in supporting them with concrete assistance. However, a visit to the soup kitchen was not an option for the numerous disadvantaged families with several children. Since children came back from school at different times and/or preschool children needed to be looked after at home, mothers preferred to cook for the whole household than to send three or more children to the public kitchen at different times or on their own.

Although some settlers did not profit materially from the charity campaign of the Catholic Church, most saw it as an acknowledgement of their efforts to settle in Knin, and confirmation of being a respected member of the Croatian nation.[5] The solidarity displayed by other Croats and the Catholic congregations all over the country made them feel incorporated into the Croatian national community and cared for by the Catholic Church. Many of the Croatian settlers saw the locality of Knin as Croatian territory to which Croats – natives and settlers alike – had a sacred claim. They expressed a sense of belonging to the 'family' of the Croatian people and felt that the Catholic Church had encouraged them not to lose faith in the settlement project. When all was said and done, however, the Catholic Church was unable to grant settlers permanent housing rights and there was no sign of improvement in the overall economic situation in the Knin region. In fact, the Catholic charity campaign focused on the spiritual, indicating that a sense of belonging did not necessarily coincide with an improvement in objective circumstances and that although the economic situation remained grave, psychological and spiritual support could conjure up a subjective sense of security.[6]

The Catholic charity campaign was more likely to appeal to Croatian set-tlers because most of them went to mass at least once a week. Being close to God was seen as giving a sense of personal value to their lives. Furthermore, quite a few of the settlers from Bosnia-Herzegovina had developed a special relationship with the Catholic Church in socialist and pre-socialist times, and used to attend church services regularly (Vrcan 2001: 101–54).[7] At that time, the Catholic Church was associated with opposition to socialism and was an expression of their national and cultural identity (Ramet 1992). The Francis-cans in particular played a vital role in preserving and promoting Croatian national identity in Bosnia-Herzegovina. The positive response to the charity campaign was therefore grounded on existing religious identity and the strong religious beliefs of the settlers. It was furthermore bound to their position of being uprooted and of being 'strangers' in the Knin region.

According to the narratives of Croatian settlers from Bosnia in Knin, the Catholic Church had promoted the construction of a settler community immediately after their arrival in Knin. Regular church attendance permitted the settlers, who were newcomers to the area and lacked social contacts, to meet others who shared a similar fate; they began to chat with each other in front of the church either before or after mass. These meetings became insti-tutionalised to a certain extent, allowing networks to emerge among settlers closely connected to the Catholic Church. Relatives and friends who went to mass on Sundays began to invite one another home for a cup of coffee before lunch. Couples would compare notes and discuss political and community issues, such as the new charity programme of the Catholic Church or the over-all prospects in the area. They occasionally helped each other to renovate their new homes or carry out other tasks. Thus for the new Croatian settlers in the Knin region, the Catholic Church functioned as a form of spiritual and prac-tical support. Taking over the role of catalyst for communication, it was the motor behind the creation of a social (and at the same time Catholic religious and Croatian national) network. Apart from the Caritas charity campaign, the church building(s) itself, the annual Catholic celebrations and especially the regular church services all helped Croatian settlers to develop a sense of being at home in Knin in their 'own' Croatian culture. Hence the commitment of Caritas as a Catholic organisation in 'feeding the hungry Croats in Knin' was highly appreciated by the many Croatian settlers from Bosnia because it made them feel integrated in the Croatian state and consequently secure.

The Perspective of Native Croats

Many of the native Croats, however, did not perceive recent events in the same way as the Croatian settlers, but were on the contrary critical, even negative about the actions of the local Caritas branch. Some felt ashamed that Knin had the reputation of being the poorhouse of Croatia, and saw this as tainting their home and degrading their social status. A student from Knin studying in the coastal town of Zadar about 70 kilometres away told the story of her experience in a copy shop there. Before paying for the copies she had made, she showed her student card, which indicated she came from Knin. The man in the copy shop obviously felt sorry for her, said she could have the copies for free and gave her 10 kunas (1.25 euros) to buy herself a sandwich. She felt utterly embarrassed and was unable to forgive the Catholic Church for having presented this image of Knin to the general public. She felt ashamed at the idea of being considered a charity recipient, perceiving it as socially degrading both personally and for her family.[8]

According to native Croats this picture did not represent the reality of Knin but rather the view of Croatian settlers, who claimed there were countless 'hungry' Croats in Knin. To native Croats this was a gross exaggeration. They calculated the monthly welfare payments Croatian settler families received from the state and came to the conclusion that it must be a few thousand kunas (approximately 500 euros, the average monthly income in Croatia) every month. Neither did the settlers have to pay rent for the houses they occupied. Some even received water or electricity free of charge. From this perspective, most settlers were indeed in dire straits and depended on social assistance, but starving? No!

Native Croats furthermore argued that the great majority of settlers 'who could not feed themselves' made no effort to do so, and claimed the latter were either too comfortable to budget their income or too lazy to find a way of making ends meet. In fact, native Croats were convinced that Croatian settlers from Bosnia would rather drink coffee and chat than work in the garden harvesting vegetables, or doing some other job. Some argued that the settlers from Bosnia preferred to spend their money on cigarettes, alcohol or other luxury goods than on food for their many children. An elderly native Croat woman, for example, stated that people who queued up at the Caritas office to receive free food parcels smoked cigarettes or had dyed hair, a sign that they had money to spend. Others did not come to pick up parcels of food with wheelbarrows, but arrived in Volkswagen Golf cars or bigger. Generally, native Croats saw most of the Croatian settlers as social spongers who lived off the state and the community, and were thus partly responsible for the difficult situation in the town of Knin.

The native Croats stressed that they themselves were not like that, arguing that they had not occupied former Serbian houses (which was true, as most of them had returned to their own property) and unlike the settlers, paid their water and electricity fees. Furthermore, they were not recipients of social benefits from the state. This too was true in most instances, since those who owned property were not eligible for social assistance. They did confess that the economic crisis had hit them hard and that unemployment rates were high in their ranks too. However, they made a point of saying that they had done everything possible to master the situation, working on their own and showing solidarity within the family. In the majority of cases they relied on small-scale subsistence agriculture and support from other family members, frequently the older generation, who received state pensions (see Leutloff-Grandits 2005). In fact, the percentage of older people was far higher among native Croats than Croat settlers and that of children much lower, making pensions a key source of finance for native Croats. This again also points to the fact that many of the younger native Croats have stayed in their places of exile – and often out of economic reasons, because the prospects in Knin were limited. The return of the elderly resembled in a way also a household strategy, as it meant to be eligible for reconstruction assistance and to secure the housing property or a material value for the children.[9]

Other native Croats were too proud to queue for humanitarian assistance, although they too were affected by the intolerable economic situation. It was more important for them to uphold their social position and self-esteem than to take advantage of the charity campaign, even when this meant economic hardship.

Last but not least, native Croats avoided turning to the local Caritas branch to the same extent as Croatian settlers because of their somewhat different relationship to the Catholic Church compared to their Bosnian compatriots (Vrcan 2001: 101–54). In some aspects, religion had assumed a more crucial role in their lives than before the war and was additionally seen as a marker of Croatian identity. Being a good Croat was associated with being a good Catholic (Vrcan 2001: 88–91). On the other hand, since many of the locals had never been great believers and/or gone to the church in socialist times, they had no reason to do so after the war. With regard to the contest for the 'better' Croat, native Croats disapproved of the settlers' regular church attendance and tried to set themselves apart by foregrounding differences. They drew attention to their own roots in the region of Knin and their moral superiority, describing the settlers as strangers and as morally deceptive despite their frequent visits to the church. They argued that the latter had occupied and plundered Serbian property and had no qualms about living off others. Because they felt Croatian settlers were dismissive of them, native Croats deliberately avoided going to the same church services. Some said they went to the neighbouring town of Drniš, which was inhabited almost exclusively by Croats before the war. Because no settlers had moved there after the war, the church services were attended by native Croats only.[10]

The atmosphere of competition between native Croats and Croatian settlers and the more distant relationship of native Croats to the local Catholic Church explains why the native Croats had a critical attitude towards the local Caritas branch and the Franciscans. Many of them perceived the charity campaign of the Catholic Church as helping Croatian settlers to manifest political power in Knin and thus as overruling their own interests. Indeed, since they constituted no more than 10 per cent of the population in the Knin region and Croatian settlers approximately 50 per cent (with Serbs making up the additional 40 per cent), native Croats had every reason to feel overpowered by Croatian settlers, who were already in possession of key political positions at the time. In this context, native Croats suspected the local Franciscan abbot of competing for a leading position in Knin and of using the campaign for his own purposes. The Catholic Church appeared, at least at the time, to have become a political player, although the Franciscan abbot strongly denied this notion.

Several native Croats also accused Caritas of holding on to the best donations for themselves or their friends and clients, who were not necessarily in need. One middle-aged woman highlighted, for example, that neither the soup kitchen nor the humanitarian parcels contained meat, although it was quite clear that meat had been included in the donations. Others were particularly sceptical about the cash donations deposited in the private bank account of the local Caritas branch in a nearby town. It was suspected that this money was not to be used to help the poor but to build a new Catholic church or, worse still, for private purposes. The first suspicion was not unrealistic, since the Catholic church was now too small to hold the huge crowds of new Croatian settlers in Knin who visited the church regularly, and it had long been the wish of the local Franciscans to build a church with sufficient capacity for all the faithful. Furthermore, the new church would tower above the Orthodox church building in Knin and symbolise the religious and national dominance of Croats in the Knin region, a view that would surely be echoed by the native Croats who had been at war with the Serbs. However, a church building in a prominent location in Knin with a capacity to hold the entire congregation would also give Croatian settlers a more centralised position, which in turn could produce fear and a sense of competition among native Croats. All in all, native Croats maintained that it would be better for the local Franciscans to stick to issues of faith and leave humanitarian intervention and politics to others.

The Native Serb Perspective

As expected, most Serbs responded with reservation to the Caritas campaign. They were not mentioned explicitly in the campaign by the local Caritas representatives in Knin, by the Catholic clergy who visited the community there, or by the national media, although their return to Knin was also linked to social and economic opportunities. As mentioned at the beginning, it was almost impossible for Serbs to find employment as a result of the ethnic discrimination that prevailed in the postwar region. Many of the younger Serbs had not returned to Knin for precisely this reason, leaving the average age of Serbian returnees at about sixty in 2001 (PULS 2001: 13). The latter received low pensions and/or eked out a living by working their small plots of land, not unlike many elderly native Croats.[11]

Whereas native Croats voiced their criticism of the Caritas charity campaign loudly, most native Serbs gave the impression of being completely unaffected by it. They were aware of its national dimensions, but did not dare to criticise it openly. The Catholic Church was after all a moral authority in Croatia, and native Serbs, who were still in the position of a suppressed minority in postwar Croatia, had no political voice in Knin. The campaign came as no surprise to them, since they assumed the Catholic Church would take a national view and support Croats rather than Serbs. On the other hand, they expected their own Orthodox Church to help Serbs and not Croats. The churches had been seen to defend the frontiers of different religious worlds and were the main markers of nationality. As a result they were frequently regarded as the purest supporters of the national idea (Vrcan 2001: 195–228). Last but not least, native Serbs had not anticipated receiving material support from the Catholic Church, as the Orthodox Church itself tended to focus on matters of a spiritual and missionary nature rather than on humanitarian help for Serbs after the war.

Nevertheless, when the charity campaign received national and international recognition, critical voices outside Knin could be clearly heard with regard to the national dimensions of the project. Caritas was accused of pursuing political aims instead of adhering to the Christian principles of helping those in need regardless of their religious beliefs. In response to this, the local Caritas leader expressed willingness to provide Serbs with humanitarian aid once they had proved their neediness. In this way, the Catholic Church would be seen not to have neglected Christian principles and at the same time have saved its reputation internationally, not least that of the head organisation, Caritas International. The shift in the Caritas attitude was, however, akin to cosmetic surgery and kept out of the public eye in Knin itself. Despite these Caritas assurances, only a very small number of Serbs asked for Caritas support, either because they were unaware that aid was available to them or because they were (still) convinced that Caritas was a strong ideological supporter of the Croatian settlement project. In fact, encouraged by the criticism of Caritas outside Knin, they too began to reproach its use of the charity campaign for political purposes. They kept a low profile on the matter, however, discussing it only among themselves.

Conclusion

The analysis of the charity campaign of the local Caritas branch of this Catholic organisation in Knin six years after the war was revealing in several aspects. First of all, it was identified that Caritas took responsibility for some of the basic tasks carried out by the state in socialist times, but also during and after the war, that is, looking after the impoverished in the population and providing them with material and spiritual support. Around the time Caritas launched a charity campaign and opened a soup kitchen in Knin, many in the region had felt abandoned by the state and the politicians, and were now insecure and devoid of all prospects for the future, although the settlement policy of the Croatian state had brought them to Knin in the first place.

Secondly, the charity campaign was successful because it appealed to a sense of Croatian solidarity, attracting donors nationwide and beyond the state borders. Supporters of the charity network were not merely members of the Catholic faith, but first and foremost Croats, among them national(ist) politicians and former war officers, all of whom were won over by a sense of nationalism to support their fellow countrymen in need. Here it was shown that Croatian nationalism and the Catholic notion of charity merged in many respects. Although the ideology of Christian charity applied to *all* those in need, the local Caritas branch referred to the experience of war and settlement from a Croatian point of view, thus making it clear that they intended to help Croats and not Serbs. By becoming involved in the charity network and generously donating money and food, politicians and former army officers upgraded not only the position of the Catholic Church in the Knin region but also their own. This win-win effect resulted in an overall empowering of the charity network.

Thirdly, it was verified that the charity campaign had different functions and meanings for the people of Knin. Croatian settlers, who were its main target group, displayed immense enthusiasm for the campaign. In most cases, however, the Caritas charity campaign did not effectively improve the material situation of the settlers, at least not from a long-term perspective. What came to the fore instead was the sense of spiritual and emotional security created by the Church network, frequently at the expense of achieving material security or a 'secure' future for people's families in other parts of Croatia. Native Croats were highly critical of the campaign, since they feared it would promote the power of the Croatian settlers in Knin, who were closer to the Church than they themselves were. They directed their criticism at the Catholic Church as a political player and reproached it for abusing the notion of charity. Furthermore, they rejected being labelled as a 'charity case', which was accompanied by a sense of being downgraded and humiliated. Surprisingly, the local Serbs, who were excluded from the charity network, were less critical of the campaign than native Croats. For the most part they respected the campaign as an act of charity towards disadvantaged Catholics, but clearly recognised its political dimensions.

This chapter clarified that the Caritas charity campaign had different and often ambivalent meanings for different people in the Knin region. The spiritual dimension of belonging and the position of people in the community and in Croatian society as a whole emerged as being of greater concern to people than material assistance. This was due to political claims, but also to diverse feelings of recognition and self-esteem, on the one hand, and of shame and humiliation on the other.

Notes

1. The chapter is based on fifteen months of socio-anthropological fieldwork in the region of Knin, Croatia between May 2000 and July 2001, and on shorter visits to the region in 2003 and 2006. Fieldwork was carried out within the framework of a PhD project, for which I received funding and valuable support from the Max Planck Institute for Social Anthropology, Halle/Saale.

2. The many Croatian settlers from Bosnia had stretched the capacity of the Catholic church of Sveti Ante in Knin. As an interim solution, an empty warehouse was used as a provisional church building, in addition to Sveti Ante. Sunday morning mass and festive church celebrations were held in the warehouse due to the vast crowds that attended.

3. This nationalist discourse on home and homeland is very different from the one of international organizations working in Bosnia-Herzegowina. The latter wanted to restore the prewar interethnic life and 're-make Bosnia-Herzegowina into a "home" for all its citizens' by focussing on a return policy. Cf. Stef Jansen (2006: 180).

4. A humanitarian parcel contained, for example, 3 L oil, margarine, 1 kg washing powder, 1 kg salt, 1 kg fruit, 2 L milk, 5 yoghurt cartons, 1 kg salami, 3 white cabbages, 3 savoy cabbages, 35 kg potatoes, 25 kg flour, 30 eggs and 2 kg sugar ('Kninu svakodnevno stižu pošiljke humanitarne pomoći sa svih strana', *Vijesnik*, 19 March 2001).

5. The supportive role of the Croatian Catholic Church in the resettlement of Croats from regions outside the Croatian state has also been stressed by Duijzings (2000: 60).

6. Stef Jansen, who worked on return in Bosnia, stresses that successful return depends not only on the repossession or reconstruction of housing property, but also on the possibility for a future orientation including stable employment, health care, education and social welfare (Jansen 2006: 186, 191). This is generally also the case in Croatia. Out of the lack of future orientations many refugees and internally displaced persons (Serbs and Croats) did not return to their homes, and most Croatian settlers (many of them refugees from Bosnia) who moved to the Knin region had the hope to be able to find such securities and build up a future. However, while the perspective for stable employment and housing receded more and more, spiritual and national visions became more important again. That said, it has to be stressed that many settlers hoped that the spiritual and national security would also provide them with housing and a material base for living.

7. However, not all Croatian settlers went to church regularly. Families who came from large Croatian towns such as Zagreb or Split were not particularly religious. In addition, men often stayed at home instead of going to mass, continuing the socialist tradition.

8. Compare the humiliation and shame of Sarajevo citizens during the war, who became dependent on charity and were thus socially degraded, having lived decent, independent lives before the war (Maček 2006: 41–45).

9. Compare Jansen (2006: 181), who describes similar intergenerational household strategies among returnees in Bosnia. Compare also Leutloff-Grandits (2005) for return of elderly Serbs as a strategy of social security including their children, too.

10. Competition and cultural downgrading among local inhabitants and newcomers of the same nationality after the war are not unique to Knin, but can be found in many other areas of former Yugoslavia. For post-war Sarajevo see, for example, Stefansson (2006), and for Serbian refugees and local inhabitants in post-war Belgrade, Leutloff 2002).

11. In fact, in mixed neighbourhoods of native Serbs and Croats, a certain level of interethnic cooperation became normal again after the war. This is based on the very similar way of life as well as shared values of native Serbs and Croats, which differed from that of Croatian settlers. The reconciliation between the two native groups who had been in war against each

other was also supported by the institution of *komšiluk* (neighbourhood and neighbourliness), which regulates relations between neighbours including mutual help and respect. For a detailed discussion on the meanings of *komšiluk* in Sarajevo, cf. Sorabji (2008).

References

Akrap, A. and D. Živić. 2001. 'Demografskae Odrednice i Obilježa Obiltljske Strukture Stanovništva Hrvatske', *Društvena istraživanja* 10(54/55): 621–53.

Brkić, S. and D. Žutinić. 1993. 'The Croatian Village and Family Farm under Pressure of Changes', *Poljoprivredna znanstva smotra: Agriculturae Conceptus Scientificus* 58(2): 165–76.

Denich, B. 1994. 'Dismembering Yugoslavia: Nationalist Ideologies and the Symbolic Revival of Genocide', *American Ethnologist* 21(2): 367–90.

Duijzings, G. 2000. *Religion and the Politics of Identity in Kosovo*. London: Hurst & Company.

Gelo, J. 2003. 'Demografske Promjene u Hrvatskoj oak Osnova Nationalne Obiteljske Politike', in *Nationalna Obiteljska Politika. 2. Prošireno Izdanje. Državni Zavod za Zaštitu Obitelji, Materinstva i Mladeži*, ed. V. Puljiz and D. Bouillet. Zagreb: n.p., 73–101.

Glasnik Sv. Ante. 2001. 'Glasilo Samostana i župe', *Sveti Ante Knin* 2(2).

Grandits, H. and C. Leutloff. 2003. 'Discourses, Actors, Violence: The Organisation of War-Escalation in the Krajina-Region of Croatia 1990–91', in *Potentials of Disorder*, ed. C. Zuercher and J. Koehler. Manchester and New York: Manchester University Press, 23–45.

Grandits, H. and C. Promitzer. 2000. '"Former Comrades" at War: Historical Perspectives on 'Ethnic Cleansing' in Croatia', in *Neighbors at War: Anthropological Perspectives on Yugoslav Ethnicity, Culture, and History*, ed. J. M. Halpern and D. A. Kideckel. University Park: Pennsylvania State University Press, 125–42.

Halpern, J. 1968. 'Peasant Culture and Urbanization in Yugoslavia', in *Contributions to Mediterranean Sociology*, ed. G. Peristiany, Paris: Mouton, 289–311.

Jansen, Stef, 2006: 'The Privatisation of Home and Hope: Return, Reforms and the Foreign Intervention in Bosnia-Herzegowina', in *Dialectical Anthropology* 30 (2006): 177–199.

'Kninu svakodnevno stižu pošiljke humanitarne pomoći sa svih strana'. 2001. *Vijesnik*, 19 March.

'Law on the Lease of Apartments in the Liberated Areas'. 1995. *Narodne Novine* 73. Official Gazette of the Republic of Croatia, Zagreb.

'Law on the Temporary Take-Over and Administration of Specified Property'. 1995, 1996, 1997. *Narodne Novine* 73, 06, 1000. Official Gazette of the Republic of Croatia, Zagreb.

Leutloff, C. 2002. 'Im Niemandsland. Kollektive Identitäten von Krajina-Serben in der Emigration in der BRJugoslawien', in *Umstrittene Identitäten*, ed. U. Brunnbauer. Frankfurt am Main: Peter Lang, 149–72.

Leutloff-Grandits, C. 2005. 'Return as a Strategy of Social Security? Generational and Family Based Approaches to Return of Serbian War-Refugees to Croatia', in *Generations, Kinship and Care: Gendered Provisions of Social Security in Central Eastern Europe*, vol. 17, ed. H. Haukanes and F. Pine. Bergen: University of Bergen, Centre for Women's and Gender Research.

———. 2006. *Claiming Ownership in Post-War Croatia: The Dynamics of Property Relations and Ethnic Conflict in the Knin Region*. Münster: Lit.

Maček, I. 2006. 'Imitation of Life: Negotiating Normality in Sarajevo under Siege', in *The New Bosnian Mosaic: Identities, Memories and Moral Claims in a Post-War Society*, ed. X. Bougarel, E. Helms and G. Duijzings. Hampshire: Ashgate, 39–58.

Mappes-Niediek, N. 1995. 'Ethnische Selbstsäuberung? Der Exodus der Serben aus Kroatien vom 4. bis 8. August 1995'. *Suedosteuropa*, 44. Jhg.: 9–10, 585–92.

PULS, Market, Media and Public Opinion Research. 2001. *Survey on Returnee Population in Croatia*. Zagreb. Unpublished.

Ramet, S. P. 1992. *Balkan Babel: Politics, Culture, and Religion in Yugoslavia*. Boulder, CO: Westview Press.

Sorabji, C. 2008. 'Bosnian Neighbourhoods Revisited: Tolerance, Commitment and Komšiluk in Sarajevo', in *On the Margins of Religion*, ed. F. Pine and J. de Pina-Cabral. New York, Oxford: Berghahn Books, 97–112.

Stefansson, A. 2006. 'Urban Exiles: Locals, Newcomers and the Cultural Transformation of Sarajevo', in *The New Bosnian Mosaic: Identities, Memories and Moral Claims in a Post-War Society*, ed. X. Bougarel, E. Helms and G. Duijzings. Hampshire: Ashgate, 59–78.

'U Kninu otvorena pučka kuhinja'. 2001. *Vijesnik*, 22 March.

Vrcan, S. 2001. *Vjera u Vrtlozima Transicije*. Split: Glas Dalmacije, Revija Dalmatinske Akcije.

Živić, D. 2003. 'Demografski okvir I razvoj obitelske strukture stanovništva Hrvatske 1971–2001'. *Revija za Sociologiju* 1–2 (2003): 57–73.

Chapter 4

Social Security, Life Courses and Religious Norms

Ambivalent Layers of Support in an Eastern German Protestant Network

Tatjana Thelen

Introduction

Social security is deeply embedded in the life course of the individual.[1] Expectations of future risks, the social constructions of need and the norms of caring obligations differ from one society to another, as well as among cohorts that have had crucial experiences at similar moments in their lives (Hareven 1995; see also K. von Benda-Beckmann 1994). This chapter sets out to explore the interrelation of these experiences with different layers of support in a Protestant network in eastern Germany. The mostly elderly women involved share not only a socialist past and the dramatic social changes that followed unification but also specific religious norms. The layers of support in their religious network as well as their inherent ambivalences can only be understood against the background of these personal biographies embedded in changing state policies.

Born primarily in the 1930s and 1940s, these women lived most of their adult lives in the German Democratic Republic (GDR). Given their firm connection to the Protestant Church, many of their personal social security arrangements were linked to the difficult state-church relations under socialism. Unification was to alter these patterns dramatically. Not only was there a relaxation of state-church relations, but the fundamental processes of transformation brought about manifold political, economic and social change, all of which influenced

Notes for this chapter begin on page 77.

individual social security arrangements as a result of new opportunities and new state provisions, as well as due to the emergence of new risks. Fundamental change and disruption of this kind can render former patterns of behaviour and thought, including individual life scripts, precarious. A crisis or accelerated change that has not been anticipated either in daily routines or coping strategies may challenge people's ability to construct a meaningful biography (Skultans 1998). Individuals will make huge efforts to regain a person-environment stability or ontological security, understood here as the capacity '*to keep a particular narrative going*' (Giddens 1991: 54, italics in original).[2] I argue that the breakdown of socialism in former East Germany, followed by a unification that was unexpected even for those who desired it, questioned expectations and biographical decisions previously taken for granted and thus ontological security. The efforts to reinforce meaningful biographies not only impact on individual social security arrangements, but shape specific transformation outcomes.

I will first of all introduce the ethnographic case, a café with charity status and its embeddedness in state-church relations. Then the various layers of social security within this particular network are analysed against the backdrop of the individual biographies of the actors involved.

The Elisabeth Café

The Elisabeth Café in Rostock,[3] founded in 1999, is run by a complicated Protestant network. Its organisational structure involves a legally registered association, few paid employees and a group of unpaid volunteers. Before outlining its foundation, organisation and relation to the state, I will first give an impression of the daily routine in the café.

The Elisabeth Café is located in a small house in the city centre and is open from Monday to Saturday from 11 AM to 6 PM. Volunteers serve the guests in two interconnecting rooms and there is also a small kitchen, an office, and toilets in the basement. The furniture consists of second-hand chairs and tables decorated with a candle and fresh flowers (brought in by a supporter). Usually classical music plays softly in the background.

In the two years I followed its development, the Elisabeth Café increasingly attracted more visitors.[4] It has an intimate atmosphere, where customers go to the kitchen to choose whatever cakes they want. Two women are paid for baking fresh cakes daily that are served by unpaid, mostly elderly female volunteers. The typical clientele is middle-aged to elderly women with some formal or informal bond to the church. Most guests were introduced to the café by a friend or acquaintance. Tourists occasionally dropped in, having been told about it by tourist guides at the famous church close by. In addition, the café is used as a regular meeting place for certain groups, such as the Protestant women's group or the support group for children from Tschernobyl. Sometimes private individuals (with some connection to the inner circle) rent the café for birthday parties or other festivities. Along with annual 'Thank You' outings for volunteers and more public occasions such as readings, these events constitute important activities in terms of ontological security. I will return to this point later.

The idea for the café originally came from Mrs Baum, an energetic pensioner who in 1997 convinced her friend, Mrs Scholz, to join forces with her. They acquired the premises from the parish church and received a grant from a foundation to set up the project. With a great deal of informal assistance they renovated the old building and opened the Elisabeth Café in 1999. In order for the café to acquire the status of a charity eligible for state support, an official association had to be established. Mrs Baum asked people she had known for a long time to become members and convinced fourteen people. Indicating her vast personal networks, she commented, 'If you know a lot of people, it's not a problem' (DN 22/06/2005). Although ultimately responsible, the association itself is not directly involved in the daily routine of the café. The members meet the volunteers only once a year at the above-mentioned 'thank-you' outing.

The idea at the beginning was to organise a volunteer exchange circle and mediate between people willing to do voluntary work and charitable organisations. This plan was supported by state agencies, and for the first three years the café was able to finance two people through a state work programme. Although they collected the addresses of various organisations and produced a small brochure, the plan never came to fruition. People still sometimes enquire about volunteer work, but there is no genuine information available, nor have arrangements been made with other projects. Instead, people are usually asked to volunteer at the café, which became increasingly dependent on volunteers since the expiry of state programmes in 2002.

The entire structure of the network surrounding the café is held together by the central figure, Mrs Baum, who continues to be the key figure since its founding. She knows everyone involved and is the driving force behind the commitment of those concerned. As one woman characterised her, 'Mrs Baum holds it all altogether, she keeps people going' (TI 23/2/2005). Connecting volunteers with members of the official association, she could be described as a bridge person in network terms (Schweizer 1996: 123–124).

There are no visible signs of Christianity in the café space, such as a crucifix or holy picture, and 'worldly' newspapers and magazines are available. However, its name (borrowed from the Elisabeth Church next door) and the proximity to a Christian bookstore and other church-related organisations hint at religious connections. Although not 'officially' marked as a religious enterprise, its female activists are long-standing church members. Before describing different types of provisioning of social security, I will first introduce some relevant policy changes regarding state-church relations.

The Elisabeth Café and Changing State Policies

The life courses of those involved in Elisabeth Café and the specific material and nonmaterial provisions in the network are closely linked to the changing conditions of religious life in eastern Germany. During socialism the traditionally dominant Protestant Church in eastern Germany experienced several hardships. This was particularly true for the 1950s, which witnessed two waves of intense political repression. The Protestant Youth represented one special target, and at that time the Elisabeth Café activists were in their teens or young adults. Later periods were calmer and church membership in general was no longer dangerous or a great obstacle to professional life.[5] Nevertheless active believers and especially pastor families often experienced discrimination, for example, being denied access to the desired education or subject at university. Most of the women concerned here, born into pastor families or married to pastors, again have been affected by this situation.

Moreover, the Protestant Church suffered considerable loss of membership during the socialist period. While 80.5 per cent of the population belonged to the Protestant Church in 1945, this figure had dropped to approximately 25 per cent by 1989, with an even smaller percentage (16.5 per cent) calling themselves Protestants (Pollack 1994: 271; Cordell 1995: 128).[6] Under these conditions the women discussed here belonged to a minority of active believers throughout most of their adult life. It is not surprising that in informal conversations the founders of the Elisabeth Café, Mrs Baum and Mrs Scholz, considered its mere existence and the public events that were organised as a success in itself. In fact the visibility of Elisabeth Café in a tourist area points to a shift in the public position of the Christian churches, which have been accepted and welcomed by the state since unification.

The mixed financing of the Elisabeth Café, including from state bodies, points to another feature of state-church relations, namely, the changing principle of welfare distribution in eastern Germany. Welfare during the socialist era was primarily distributed by state agencies and enterprises. Only a small number of church-based welfare institutions remained in the GDR so that the church found itself bereft of its vital role as a provider of social security. In the process of unification the West German institutional setting for the distribution of welfare was introduced in the eastern *Länder* as well. Similar to numerous other Western countries, legislation now took the charitable nature of churches for granted, and church activities were seen as contributing to the public good and thus exempt from taxation (Dal Pont 2005; Wallenhorst and Halaczinsky 2000: 99). Moreover, the close association that developed between the state and the Christian churches in West Germany, which defines them as partners in welfare deliverance, was also transferred (Thériault 2004; Sachße 1994).

The new arrangements profoundly altered the role of religion, the church and charity in eastern German society. Nevertheless, and despite the fact that the Protestant Church was highly active in the late 1980s and throughout the early period of transformation, church membership did not increase substantially after unification. Parishes where the congregation comprises no more than 10 per cent of the population are common.[7] Although recent developments have shown a new openness among the younger generation for religious issues, the Protestant Church has in particular been unable to gain from this situation (Jagodzinski 2000). The reasons for this are still under discussion. Some authors attribute it to socialist pressure, although other postsocialist countries with more restrictive policies have experienced greater religious revitalisation than eastern Germany. Others cite longstanding historical roots reaching from the Middle Ages or the Reformation to the late modernisation of Germany (Tiefensee 2002: 197–216; see also Nowak 1995). While all of these interpretations can undoubtedly explain certain elements of this development, the qualitative study of the Elisabeth Café can add some elements to the picture. Reflecting macrosociological research, the network did not grow immensely. Studying the individual biographies of those involved and social security needs reveals why there is no genuine desire to engage with the outside world, which might bring new membership.

Protestant Female Life Courses and Material Social Security

Although the Elisabeth Café maintains the official status of a public utility, the daily routine does not include any specific charitable activity. Volunteers approach customers only in the capacity of serving cake at cheap prices described earlier. They do not offer other services such as conversation or advice in crisis situations; they do not try to proselytize, nor do they engage in the distribution of material aid.

When I asked Mrs Baum how the Elisabeth Café had obtained its *Gemeinnützigkeit* status (as a public utility or charity), she replied: 'We help as well. For instance, we have this woman working here who otherwise would only get a tiny pension.' (DN 19/08/2003). At the time I found her explanation peculiar, since she made no reference to the delivery of a common good but merely pointed out the securing of one woman's income. In fact, at the time of research the café supported five women with small incomes (the former state programmes that regularly paid two employees expired in 2002): Mrs Scholz and Mrs Schneider, who carry out administrative and organisational work; Mrs Meier and Mrs Bach, the two women who bake the daily fresh cakes; and Mrs Petrowska, who has a Russian-German background and is employed as a cleaner. Once, Mrs Baum commented on the recruitment of Mrs Meier, 'I knew she had a tough life and needed it [the job]' (DN 22/06/2005). The statement suggests that Mrs Meier had experienced some (undeserved) hardship that left her in need of support. To explore this construction of need and the merit of support, I will present her biography in more detail and then compare it to that of Mrs Scholz, the cofounder of Elisabeth Café.

Mrs Meier

Mrs Meier was born into a Protestant family in the south of the GDR. As a young woman she wanted to move to Rostock. Given the socialist-era housing shortages that represented a constant obstacle to mobility (and considerably worse so for people who could not fall back on state resources), she used her church contacts. With the help of the pastor she managed to find an apartment, which she then shared with another member of the congregation. In Rostock she later married an agricultural engineer, a member and son of a pastor of the same Pietist-inspired congregation like herself. Ever since both have been active lay members in the parish community.

Educated as an office clerk, she gave up wage work when her three sons were born successively. At the time the boys were between ten and fifteen years old, the local cooperative that employed her husband offered her an employment as a milk controller. She refused to work full time but accepted a part-time job that allowed her to work in the early morning before her children woke up and to carry out the paperwork later on at home.

After unification both she and her husband lost their jobs as a result of economic restructuring. While her husband soon found a new employment in a Christian organisation for the homeless, Mrs Meier had far greater difficulty to position herself in the new circumstances. Once she had a job in a church senior project that ended after three years due to financial difficulties. Otherwise phases of unemployment alternated with jobs in several public work programmes, all of which were again mediated through her religious network. Finally Mrs Baum offered her a so-called mini-job at the Elisabeth Café. Today Mrs Meier lives with her husband and one adult son in a house with a garden in a village near Rostock.

Mrs Scholz

Like Mrs Meier, Mrs Scholz lived a life in close connection to the Protestant Church. She is a close friend of Mrs Baum and is paid for the administrative work she does. Born in 1940, Mrs Scholz went to school in Rostock and was trained as a bookseller. She married a year after leaving school and supported the family financially, while her husband continued to study theology. Later, when her husband was employed as a pastor, the couple had four children and

Mrs Scholz gave up working outside the home. She did a little part-time social work via church contacts, but never worked in her profession again. During the 1980s and the upheavals of 1989, her husband took an increasingly active role and later held various public positions. Their marriage broke up around this time and the couple separated (without divorce) in 1990.

After unification Mrs Scholz had difficulty in positioning herself on the labour market. For some time she was employed as a dentist's receptionist, but this was followed again by a period of unemployment that ended when she began working at the Elisabeth Café as one of the two employees sponsored by the state work programme that drew to a close in 2002. However, she has continued working, albeit for lower pay. When her youngest daughter left home recently, Mrs Scholz, whose husband supports her financially, moved into a smaller flat.

* * *

Despite obvious differences, the two biographies also reveal some striking similarities related to the women's long-term religious engagement and their role as mothers. Both share the experience of an active religious life in the GDR, closely connected through family relations with the church. Both have several children, whom they looked after as full-time mothers. Since unification and the introduction of a new economic system, both have had to go through phases of unemployment and are unable to position themselves permanently in the regular labour market. Both women found jobs in state-sponsored work programmes, mediated through church organisations, the last of which was the Elisabeth Café. Nevertheless, and although they are by no means wealthy, neither of them is in a situation of dire poverty. Both their husbands have good incomes that sustain most of their material needs. Still, they received their jobs at the café based on the assumption of their need. I argue that this appraisal is connected to the socialist past in which they made decisions supported by religious norms in opposition to the state. While all of the described features – life cycles, religious activities, family configurations and employment balance – might appear to be normal, seen against the backdrop of the GDR patterns, they are not.

Female Biographies and Changes in State Social Security

As in other socialist countries, the key elements of social security in the GDR were linked to employment (Adam 1991; Standing 1996; Read and Thelen 2007). This applied to both genders, and the GDR had one of the highest female employment rates even among socialist states (Einhorn 1993: 266).

Other legal structures and policies, such as differential taxation, widow's pensions and financial support following divorce, which in other countries constitute the mainstay of non–wage working women, were either abolished or considerably reduced. Accordingly the material well-being of women in the GDR was primarily based on their own wage work.

Together with policies that in a situation of housing scarcity favoured young parents, the widespread female engagement in employment and its encouragement by the state influenced the pattern of typical female life courses. As a rule women gave birth to their first child in their early twenties and had an average of one or two children. Rates of nursery attendance and employment of mothers with small children were extremely high. Part-time jobs were rare and rarely meant less than forty hours a week.[8] Contrary in particular to western Germany, the strong female orientation towards employment, positively evaluated by both genders, remained one of the few stable factors in eastern Germany after unification (Rosenfeld et al. 2004; Thelen 2005, 2006a, 2006b). Thus, while at first glance the biographies of the two women may seem quite 'normal', in the context of the GDR this was not the case. The decision to work only part-time or not to engage in wage work at all and to have more than two children excluded them from the dominant lifestyle of the GDR and several of its available resources.

On the other hand, in the context of their religious network, Mrs Meier and Mrs Scholz did not constitute an exception. Here many disagreed as they did with the state-advanced attitudes to family and gender relations and took similar decisions. During the annual volunteer 'thank-you' outing in June 2004, for example, I followed a conversation between the above-mentioned Mrs Schneider (paid to do bookkeeping) and two members of the Elisabeth Café association about their children and their employment during the socialist era. Two of the women had three children and the third woman had two. None had led the typical GDR life of a worker-mother. Two had worked part-time and one had worked at home as a translator. In the course of the conversation, Mrs Schneider recalled her numerous attempts to reduce her working hours in the GDR until she was finally allowed to work part-time. Like Mrs Meier, who was almost forced by the collective leadership to take up some kind of wage work, she had to fight for her decision. The fact that the women were not employed full-time of course meant a reduction in family income. However, income gaps in the GDR were generally low and labour shortages persistent, so that when women decided to work, they were usually successful, as in the case of Mrs Meier. In addition they frequently received support from West German relatives or parishes.

While the decision to reduce their working hours considerably and concentrate on mothering may have had only marginal consequences in terms of material security, it was significant for their social integration. A great deal of female social life in the GDR took place at the workplace. Workplaces were key sites of communication and friendship, and the generally long daily and weekly working hours enforced this aspect.[9] In addition, socialist enterprises distributed and channelled child care, leisure and holiday facilities. One of women in the conversation above commented on her part-time working compared to working at home: 'I must say I would have missed the collective. Ninety per cent of all women were working at the time' (DN 14/06/2004). This indicates that the decision for full-time motherhood would have meant a certain degree of loneliness in a society where nearly everybody was working full-time. Indeed the mothers who took that decision were obliged to organise their own life with their children, surrounded by neighbouring families who led quite a different life. Mrs Becker, another member of the Elisabeth Café association, recalled how she used to jointly manage her daily life as a housewife and mother of two with a friend in the same situation, remarking, 'We did lots of things together with the children' (DN 19/03/2003).

Not only might one miss the social life of work teams, but full-time mothers sometimes also experienced direct disaffirmation. Mrs Becker remembers how she 'had to listen to two young women on the stairwell landing below talking [about me], saying, "She's too lazy to work"' (DN 19/03/2003). Thus, the decision to be a full-time mother had to be taken consciously and often in the face of resistance by local authorities, especially superiors at the workplace. It also meant a social distancing from more informal networks such as neighbourhoods and work teams.

After Unification

Unification, although generally welcomed by these women who saw themselves as opposing the socialist state, was accompanied also by new risks. Eastern German society was now confronted with unemployment almost overnight, and unemployment rates have remained high in most regions ever since. As elsewhere, people over fifty, women, the poorly educated and those with interrupted work biographies are at greater risk than others. As seen above, many of the women involved in the Elisabeth Café, including Mrs Scholz and Mrs Meier, share these features. These women are over fifty years of age and, because of their decisions regarding mothering they have little experience with employment and interrupted work biographies. As a result of their life decisions, their chances of employment on the regular labour market are very slight.

Along with establishing the market economy and its inherent risks in the former East Germany, the West German state also introduced its welfare structures and institutions. This involves, for instance, various types of state-sponsored work programmes, pension schemes and family policies. As mentioned earlier, Mrs Scholz and Mrs Meier had found jobs solely through these programmes. With regard to pension schemes, the state assumed responsibility for pension claims accumulated in the former GDR, guaranteeing a relatively safe passage for the older generation, who are perceived in general to be the beneficiary of the unification process (Geißler 2002: 275). Consequently, most older women in eastern Germany receive a reasonable pension even compared to their female co-citizens in the rest of the country, who suffer from interrupted work biographies as a result of the different political strategies involved. The women of the Elisabeth Café, however, who had not accumulated long years of pension entitlements during the socialist period, were unable to enjoy this benefit to the same extent.

Due to labour shortages in socialist times, re-entering employment after a prolonged absence would not have been a major problem in the GDR. Moreover differences in pensions were comparatively low. In the new system, however, these women now face the same problems as their counterparts in the rest of Germany as a result of former decisions taken in relation to mothering. The introduction of West German family policies favourable to full-time mothers and those employed part-time came too late for them, as their children were now grown up. The only policy to their financial advantage is the increased monetary value of the widow's pension. In sum, the Protestant women belonging to the religious network of the café were and are more disadvantaged than their nonbelieving co-citizens in eastern Germany in terms of state-organised social security. However, while their religious-based convictions and life decisions exposed them to certain insecurities, their religious networks provided them at the same time with support.

Support for Life Decisions within the Religious Network

The Protestant mothers received moral and practical support through the church. Generally speaking their decision for more concentration on motherhood found moral reinforcement by the churches that judged what they saw as the antagonistic influence exerted by the socialist state on families in negative terms. More specifically, families in Rostock were able to find additional support in church family programmes. Church employees organised family gatherings as well as play groups for preschool children – one of which, for example, took place on Thursday mornings when other mothers would work. Mrs Fuchs, who was responsible for these activities in the 1980s, commented, 'They were children who did not go to kindergarten.' She declared that the decision of the children's parents was based on the assumption that 'we are a family and certain years belong to the children' (TI 22/07/2005).

As these women had only limited access to workplace-organised holidays, the church also offered alternative programs. In the 1980s Mrs Baum was in charge of the family work of the church. Each summer she organised three family camping trips to neighbouring countries (Poland and Czechoslovakia) with more than a hundred participants each. Several of the women working at the Elisabeth Café had availed of the trips more than once. Mrs Scholz, for example, went along with all her four children, and later her eldest son went with his own family. The summer camps were popular and mentioned often by former participants during my fieldwork. One woman claimed, 'Her family camps had regular fans' (TI 22/02/2005). During these trips, with the countless joint activities that took place people got to know one another well and lasting relations developed, so that some still go on holiday together. Mrs Baum claims she consciously organised the camping trips as opportunities 'for families to do something together' (DN 04/03/2004). She saw this approach in opposition to the official socialist programmes, which in her view aimed at dividing families into various leisure activities. She spoke enthusiastically of her own trips: 'The camps were a form of freedom', because 'it was unheard of for families to participate all together' (DN15/06/2004). Asked if she thought her work supported the decision of some women to stay at home and look after their children, she replied, 'Yes indeed, you just had to support them because they felt so at odds' (DN 19/08/2003). Hence these church activities were designed to reinforce family and child-rearing values.

Through contacts with West German branches of the Protestant Church, Mrs Baum came into contact with West German pedagogical literature and some of the approaches used in social work. She stated that spreading information on educational concepts to parents in the GDR was vital because 'they had no idea about them' (DN 19/08/2003). She applied this literature and methods to the summer camps, at group meetings and in counselling families. Thus the East-West connection meant material support on the one hand, and an opportunity for nonmaterial exchanges on the other. As western Germany followed quite different polices regarding mothering and employment, these contacts might also have strengthened the moral convictions concerned here.[10]

While the decision against employment led others to regard these women as outsiders, economically they were not much worse off than their co-citizens. This changed dramatically with unification and the introduction of the West German system, which rendered their situation more vulnerable. The Elisabeth Café gives a few of them material security, and by the same token shows recognition for their decision during socialism to opt for the role of mother rather than worker. The emotional quality of this recognition reinforces their biographical continuity, a component that is not unimportant for other actors in the network.

Protestant Female Biographies and Ontological Security

In order to understand the emotional quality of the security created by the activities at the Elisabeth Café, we must take a closer look at the gendered biographies of those concerned and the set-up of the café. As mentioned earlier, with one exception these women are all over fifty, have little experience of the labour market and even less in the professions they once trained for. Instead they dedicated themselves to their families. From this perspective the café can be seen as a space in which their gendered activities as housewives and mothers are extended to the public.[11] Producing and serving food to guests in a comfortable atmosphere closely resembles the activities in their own homes. Indeed this is the tenor of the flyer about the Elisabeth Café, which describes its history in a poem-like format:

> Women are sitting around the kitchen table.
> Conversation topics?
> There is no shortage: work, family,
> Time management, money, friends, the church –
> In short, the world and his wife [Gott und die Welt]
> Suddenly the idea came up. We want to give
> these conversations more space. Initiate meetings.
> Create a field of activity for women with the time and
> The interest to become involved in a meeting point.
> The idea of a café with a noncommercial character
> was born and infected others.

The scenario begins with the typical situation of women chatting around the table in the kitchen, the private space where food is prepared for the family. The idea of creating a 'field of activity for women' apparently emerged in conversation and eventually turned into a café, a public place where food is prepared for customers. The flyer explicitly mentions transferring a private activity to a public space: 'We want to give these conversations more space.'

The flyer first and foremost speaks of wanting to create a field of activity for women, thereby confirming the notion that the café is more about those who actually run it than about the customers it accommodates. On another occasion Mrs Baum stated that working in the café 'puts meaning back into these women's lives' (DN 19/08/2003). Providing women with emotional security and giving them confidence was a vital factor from the start. Some volunteers are in typical biographical crisis situations (health problems, death of a partner or becoming a pensioner), and their commitment helps them to cope.

Notwithstanding these classical crisis situations of volunteers, the 'kitchen talk' can also be interpreted as having a second meaning. During socialism dissidents frequently met at private homes and the kitchen table became the place for political debates (Ries 1997). In this perspective the activities can be seen as not only as an extension of female activities into the public but also an extension of socialist opposition into the postsocialist environment. To explore this layer, a closer look at the biographies as connected to political events is needed.

Church Engagement and Ontological Security after Socialism

The members of the official Elisabeth Café association, including Mrs Baum, and many of the volunteers, have long been associated with the Protestant Church in a variety of ways. Most of them were raised in Protestant families and frequently have close relatives who are pastors. Many were educated in church-based schools and training colleges, and had spent their entire professional life working in church organisations. The majority of women involved in the Elisabeth Café had known each other at various stages of their lives and shared each other's experiences in the socialist past. The majority had led their lives in more or less open dissent from the socialist state and many had experienced discrimination or spying as a result of their church activities. Since they all knew each other, this involvement created strong bonds of trust. Mrs Weiss, for example, recalled how she had exchanged books printed in West Germany with the Scholz family. Under these conditions the upheavals of 1989 meant the turning point when all hopes finally seemed to materialise and not few of them made a move to public engagement. The biography of Mrs Baum, the founder of the café, sheds some light on the significance of the life courses of these women and their political engagement.

Mrs Baum

Mrs Baum was born into a Protestant pastor's family with several children. She never married and has no children of her own. She was trained in community work in a religious institution and worked throughout her professional life within the framework of the Protestant Church. In later years she was primarily responsible for so-called family work in Mecklenburg-Vorpommern, where Rostock is located, including the organisation of the aforementioned family camps. She was highly active during the events surrounding 1989 in Rostock and was linked to the nascent political group Neues Forum (New Forum).[12] She subsequently became a member of the local parliament and was officially honoured after unification for her political engagement.

* * *

Although Mrs Baum as a single woman was exceptionally active, politics played a key role in the lives of most of those involved in the Elisabeth Café, particularly in the turbulent years of 1989–90. During the revolutionary days, all of the women had taken part in demonstrations and public discussions. Some printed and distributed leaflets, and organised the New Forum and the occupation of the secret police headquarters.

These convictions and events resonate with the public gatherings organised by the Elisabeth Café. The place was completely overcrowded on these occasions.

Most of the guests were female and over fifty, and knew each other. Often members of the official Elisabeth Café association also joined in. All the speakers in 2003, for example, were former pastors or people who had been active in the revolutionary events leading up to unification. On one occasion a former pastor who had become a local politician read a humorous story about a difficult mother-daughter relationship, but most of the discussions afterwards again focused on the turbulent events of 1989–90.

The constant reiteration of these events reveals their vital significance as a point of reference in the lives of those engaged in the Elisabeth Café and their wider network. Given their high level of commitment and prominence in socialism and the tumultuous times around unification, the lives of some of the protagonists seem to have quietened now. As the political role of the Protestant Church faded, some of their endeavours also failed. Projects such as the New Forum almost vanished in unified Germany. Meeting at the Elisabeth Café allows these former actors to reinforce their meaningful biographies.

Former activists also visit the Elisabeth Café during its normal opening hours. A former minister for social affairs, for example, came with his wife and some friends. He exchanged memories with Mrs Baum and Mrs Schneider of their political activities as active participants in the historic upheaval and the founding of the New Forum (DN 01/07/2003). Likewise when Mrs Weiss celebrated her seventy-fifth birthday at the café, about thirty guests served by volunteers spent time chatting about old times and recounting stories. There was talk of who went to what demonstration and who held what speech where. Other topics were the rejection of the then popular so-called *Ostalgie* programmes on television[13] and the much-wanted free access to secret service files. Similarly, these topics were prevalent during the annual outings organised for association members and volunteers. Apart from several successes, for example, entering the building of the former secret police (*Stasi*), people also recalled threatening situations during that time. Mrs Scholz remembered how men in black coats (presumably the secret police) constantly stood outside her family home, and how one of them had once indicated he was carrying a gun. She remembered being extremely frightened in this situation, at home with her children alone.

Having experienced considerable social exclusion and sometimes even fear, the desire to mix with those who had been on the other side was limited after unification. When I was walking with Mrs Meier through her neighbourhood one evening, she pointed to a particular house and said:

That's one of those ones. He was a policeman and all that. His wife joined our singing group after unification and said they had to do what they did [during socialism] with the Pioneers [socialist youth organisation], and I said: 'That's not true at all, you didn't have to do that. You just had to take the consequences.' Anyway, she never turned up again. (DN 09/12/2004)

Obviously the policeman symbolised the socialist state power and Mrs Meier seemed quite content that his wife had not tried to contact their religious circle again.

But unification also cast doubts on previous relationships of trust. Some people had read the secret police files on their activities and were now aware who had spied on them. Other relationships became insecure as new political conflicts arose. On the 2004 outing, for example, three women agreed that relationships had become more precarious and less stable after unification. One of them explained:

> You knew where to look for friends and everyone in the church council knew that the state was crap. Then the turnaround [*Wende*] came and all of a sudden half of them joined the CDU [Christian Democratic Union] and the other half joined the SPD [German Social Democratic Party]. The former said: How can you do that? You've always been against it. And the latter: How can you do that? We always thought we're all going to join the SPD. (DN 16/06/2004)

Social relations and the moral values attached were taken for granted during socialism but became precarious after unification. The shared normative assumptions with regard to the socialist state had to be reinforced so that what was thought and done in the past would not turn out to have been an illusion. Activists from the past who meet at the Elisabeth Café regain the ontological security of biographical continuity by retelling each other their life stories.

Conclusion: Layers of Support Embedded in Religious Life Courses

The case study presented here focused on individual biographies surrounding the Elisabeth Café, a charity in eastern Germany. The women within the network are active believers and belong to a cohort that share specific historical experiences of socialism and its aftermath. Generally the conditions for social security changed dramatically in eastern Germany after unification. Individuals gained religious freedom and the church gained as an actor in the provision of welfare. These developments made the founding of the Elisabeth Café and its status as a charity possible. The café, however, does not so much deliver a universal social good but rather contributes at different levels to the social security of those engaged in it. All of these levels are embedded into the changing state-church relations, and the life decisions taken by the women engaged at the Elisabeth Café.

In the course of transformation, the women involved in the café are confronted with a shift in risk structures. Many of them led lives in more or less open defiance of state ideology in the domain of motherhood. Contrary to the dominant model of worker-mother during the socialist period, they decided to work part-time or become exclusively housewives and mothers. The decision put them at a disadvantage in relation to state social security in the GDR as well as unified Germany. As they have difficulties finding employment, work programmes and mini-jobs created at the café provide some of them with material security. The café represents a recognition for their decision and an extension of their private activities of caring and feeding into the public arena. But it also represents an extension of the socialist dissident 'kitchen talk' into the postsocialist present that allows for another layer of social security.

As a result of their religious affiliation, these women during their life-courses experienced marginalisation and discrimination by the state, as well as considerable upheaval when their lifelong endeavours turned into public political actions. After unification, however, they witnessed the petering out of interest in their projects, and at times even their failure. In addition, newly emerging political differences among church members and the hitherto-forbidden access to secret police files made relations generally more precarious and may have led these women to question the significance of their previous activities.

Within the network the creation of meaningful biographies is neatly linked to the remembrance of the socialist past and the following upheavals from the perspective of opponents. Enlarging religious networks by allowing former opponents to enter their intimate social sphere could well have cast doubts on their own convictions. The alternative was to look for a reinforcement of established social relations and create a space for biographical continuity. The cultural activities of the café reassure them of their identity as former GDR dissenters, thereby contributing to their ontological security. The Elisabeth Café is merely one example of keeping that particular narrative going – to borrow a phrase from Giddens. Assuming the existence of similar tendencies elsewhere, the search for ontological security could be interpreted as a contributing factor in shaping the outcome of transformation in eastern Germany, where despite its new recognition by the state and reinstitutionalisation as a major welfare provider, the Protestant Church has not managed to increase its membership significantly.

Notes

1. The research for this chapter was supported by the Max Planck Society. I would like to thank Franz and Keebet von Benda-Beckmann, Frances Pine, Rozita Dimova and the participants at our conference in 2005 and those at the research colloquium of the MLU in Halle for comments and language corrections to earlier versions.
2. The concept of ontological security has been fruitfully employed in several areas. Nettleton and Burrows (1998), for example, argue that housing policies have undercut many people's ability to maintain the dominant notion of self in British society, and Kinnvall (2006) analyses

the relation between globalisation and the search for ontological security with regard to religious nationalism in India.

3. Rostock is a city of approximately 200,000 inhabitants in the northern part of eastern Germany on the Baltic Sea. For reasons of anonymity, all names have been changed.

4. Fieldwork lasted from 2003 to 2005. During a stationary phase (March until the end of September 2003), I worked with increasing regularity the late shift from 2 PM to 6 PM once a week. Later I worked at irregular intervals until the end of April 2004 and came back for interviews and other occasions until late 2005. In the course of later stays my host was usually one of the women I had frequently worked with. My tasks entailed preparing and serving beverages and cakes, usually with one other female volunteer. Apart from participant observation, my fieldwork included taped informal and semistructured interviews with members of the wider circle. In the following I mark quotations from the field with DN for diary note and TI for taped interviews.

5. On relations between the state and the church in the GDR see, for example, Fulbrook (1990), Gerlach (1999), Graf (1994) and Pollack (1994a).

6. The situation in Rostock was similar. In 1946, 83 per cent of the population were church members, dropping to 43 per cent in 1964 and a mere 28.7 per cent in 1982. The authors of a 'church study' commissioned by the state considered these figures too high and counted only those who paid church taxes as 'real' members – arriving instead at 11.1 per cent in 1984. Moreover, only 5.6 per cent of all children were baptized in 1982 (Schäfer 1996: 18–19). This development did not lead to the more active participation of the remaining members of the congregation that some theologians had hoped for (Henkys 1988). Although church membership in the GDR required an active decision, engagement in church rituals and activities based on individual piety was no higher than in West Germany, where adherence to the religious community was almost automatic (Pollack 1994b: 280–88).

7. According to church statistics in Mecklenburg-Vorpommern, 18.9 per cent of the population are church members, including 10 per cent from Rostock. Figures for other eastern *Länder* of unified Germany are similar, with Thuringia displaying the highest figures at 26.5 per cent (http://www.ekd/statistik/kirchenmitglieder). The café is located in a parish of 2,700 members.

8. In 1989, 80.2 per cent of all children in the GDR in the respective age group were cared for in so-called crèches, compared, for example, to 4.4 per cent in Poland or 8.6 per cent in Hungary (Einhorn 1993: 262). For more details on the influence of changing social policies and on female life course models in the GDR see, for example, Merkel (1994), Gerhard (1994) or Tippach-Schneider (1999).

9. The average weekly, annual and lifetime workloads in the GDR were higher than in other European (socialist and nonsocialist) countries (Winkler 1990: 202–3).

10. In contrast to the socialist family policies that guaranteed work as well as public child care, the West German conservative model of a welfare state generally favours child care at home (Esping-Andersen 2003; on West German ideological notions regarding motherhood, see Vinken 2002). Varying policies during the last decades have enlarged parents' entitlements to parental leave, an opportunity mostly taken by mothers. These policies of enabling child care at home are further supported by tax policies that tax a second income severely and are accompanied by a chronic shortage in public child care facilities.

11. I would like to thank Haldis Haukanes for drawing my attention to this fact.

12. The New Forum was the first independent party founded by GDR dissidents involved in the events of 1989.

13. The so-called *Ostalgie* shows, prominent in 2003 and 2004, revolved around lost GDR symbols and consumer goods, and were accused of transporting a false nostalgia for the socialist past.

References

Adam, J. 1991. 'Social Contract', in *Economic Reforms and Welfare Systems in the USSR, Poland and Hungary: Social Contract in Transformation*, ed. J. Adam. Basingstoke: Macmillan, 1–26.

Benda-Beckmann, Franz von and Keebet von Benda-Beckmann. 1994. 'Introduction', in *Coping with Insecurity: An "Underall" Perspective on Social Security in the Third World*, ed. F. von Benda-Beckmann, K. von Benda-Beckmann and H. Marks. *Focaal* 22/23: 7–34.

Cordell, K. 1995. 'The Church: Coming to Terms with Change', in *Between Hope and Fear: Everyday Life in Post-Unification East Germany*, ed. E. Kolinsky. Keele: Keele University Press, 123–34.

Dal Pont, G. E. 2005. 'Charity Law and Religion', in *Law and Religion*, ed. P. Radan, D. Meyerson and R. F. Croucher. London and New York: Routledge, 220–43.

Einhorn, B. 1993. *Cinderella Goes to Market: Citizenship, Gender and Women's Movements in East Central Europe*. London and New York: Verso.

Esping-Andersen, G. 2003. *The Three Worlds of Welfare Capitalism*. Cambridge: Polity Press.

Fulbrook, M. 1990. 'Protestantismus und Staat in der DDR', in *SOWI* (Sozialwissenschaftliche Informationen), *Deutschland '90: Ein Staat – Zwei Gesellschaften*, ed. A. Lüdtke, 19(3): 143–52.

Geißler, R. 2002. *Die Sozialstruktur Deutschlands*. Wiesbaden: Westdeutscher Verlag.

Gerhard, U. 1994. 'Die staatlich institutionalisierte "Lösung" der Frauenfrage. Zur Geschichte der Geschlechterverhältnisse in der DDR', in *Sozialgeschichte der DDR*, ed. H. Kaelble, J. Kocka and H. Zwahr. Stuttgart: Klett-Cotta, 383–404.

Gerlach, St. V. 1999. *Staat und Kirche in der DDR: War die DDR ein totalitäres System?* Frankfurt am Main: Lang.

Giddens, A. 1991. *Modernity and Self-Identity: Self and Society in Late Modern Age*. Stanford: Stanford University Press.

Graf, F. W. 1994. 'Eine Ordnungsmacht eigener Art. Theologie und Kirchenpolitik im DDR-Protestantismus', in *Sozialgeschichte der DDR*, ed. H. Kaelble, J. Kocka and H. Zwahr. Stuttgart: Klett-Cotta, 295–321.

Hareven, T. 1995. 'Changing Images of Ageing and the Social Construction of the Life Course', in *Images of Ageing: Cultural Representations of Later Life*, ed. M. Featherstone and Andrew Wernick. London: Routledge, 119–34.

Henkys, R. 1988. 'Thesen zum Wandel der gesellschaftlichen und politischen Rolle der Kirchen in der DDR in den siebziger und achtziger Jahren', in *Die DDR in der Ära Honecker: Politik, Kultur, Gesellschaft*. Opladen: Westdeutscher Verlag, 332–53.

Jagodzinski, W. 2000. 'Religiöse Stagnation in den neuen Bundesländern: Fehlt das Angebot oder fehlt die Nachfrage?' in *Religiöser und kirchlicher Wandel in Ostdeutschland 1989–1999*, ed. D. Pollack and G. Pickel. Opladen: Leske + Budrich, 48–69.

Kinnvall, C. 2006. *Globalization and Religious Nationalism in India: The Search for Ontological Security*. London and New York: Routledge.

Marcus, A. 2006. *Where Have All The Homeless Gone? The Making and Unmaking of a Crisis*. New York and Oxford: Berghahn.

Merkel, I. 1994. 'Leitbilder und Lebensweisen von Frauen in der DDR', in *Sozialgeschichte der DDR*, ed. H. Kaelble, J. Kocka and H. Zwahr. Stuttgart: Klett-Cotta, 359–82.

Nettleton, S. and R. Burrows. 1998. 'Insecurity, Reflexivity and Risk in the Restructuring of Contemporary British Health and Housing Policies', in *Postmodernity and the Fragmentation of Welfare*, ed. J. Carter. London and New York: Routledge, 153–67.

Nowak, K. 1995. 'Historische Wurzeln der Entkirchlichung in der DDR', in *27. Kongreß der Deutschen Gesellschaft für Soziologie. Gesellschaften im Umbruch: Kongreßband II*, ed. H. Sahner and S. Schwendtner. Opladen: 665–69.

Pollack, D. 1994a. *Kirche in der Organisationsgesellschaft: Zum Wandel der gesellschaftlichen Lage der evangelischen Kirchen in der DDR*. Stuttgart: Kohlhammer.

_____. 1994b. 'Von der Volkskirche zur Minderheitenkirche. Zur Entwicklung von Religiosität und Kirchlichkeit in der DDR', in *Sozialgeschichte der DDR*, ed. H. Kaelble, J. Kocka and H. Zwahr. Stuttgart: Klett-Cotta, 271–84.

Read, R. and T. Thelen. 2007. 'Social Security and Care after Socialism: Changing Notions of Need, Support and Provision'. *Focaal* 50(2): 3–18.

Ries, N. 1997 '*Russian Talk: Culture and Conversation during Perestroika*', Ithaca, NY: Cornell University Press.

Rosenfeld, R. A., H. Trappe and J. C. Gornick. 2004. 'Gender and Work in Germany Before and After Reunification', *Annual Review of Sociology* 30: 103–24.

Roth, C. 2005. 'Threatening Dependency: "Limits of Social Security, Old Age and Gender in Burkina Faso"', in *Ageing in Insecurity/Vieillir dans l'insécurité*, ed. W. de Jong, C. Roth, F. Badini-Kinda and S. Bhagyanath. Münster: Lit, 107–38.

Sachße, Ch. 1994. 'Subsidiarität: Zur Karriere eines sozialpolitischen Ordnungsbegriffes', *Zeitschrift für Sozialreform* 40(1): 717–38.

Schäfer, B. 1996. 'Die KPD/SED und ihr Umgang mit religiösem Brauchtum und kirchlichem Leben im Alltag von SBZ und DDR – unter besonderer Berücksichtigung Mecklenburg-Vorpommern bzw. der ehemaligen drei Nordbezirke', in *Religiöses Brauchtum und kirchliches Leben im Alltag der DDR – zwischen Anfechtung und Behauptung*. Gutachten für die Enquete Kommission des Landtages von Mecklenburg-Vorpommern, http://www.hti-schwerin.de/publikationen.

Schweizer, T. 1996. *Muster sozialer Ordnung: Netzwerkanalyse als Fundament der Sozialethnologie*. Berlin: Reimer.

Skultans, V. 1998. *The Testimony of Lives: Narrative and Memory in Post-Soviet Latvia*. London and New York: Routledge.

Standing, G. 1996. 'Social Protection in Central and Eastern Europe: A Tale of Slipping Anchors and Torn Safety Nets', in *Welfare States in Transition: National Adaptations in Global Economies*, ed. G. Esping-Andersen. Thousand Oaks, CA: Sage, 225–55.

Thelen, T. 2005. 'Caring Grandfathers: Changes in Support Between Generations in East Germany', in *Generations, Kinship and Care: Gendered Provisions of Social Security in Central Eastern Europe*, ed. H. Haukanes and F. Pine. University of Bergen, Centre for Women's and Gender Research, 17: 163–88.

_____. 2006a. 'Lunch in an East German Enterprise: Differences in Eating Habits and Their Interpretation as a Symbol of Collective Identities', *Zeitschrift für Ethnologie* 131: 51–70.

_____. 2006b. 'Experiences of Devaluation: Work, Gender and Identity in Eastern Germany', *Working Paper No. 85, Max-Planck-Institut für ethnologische Forschung*, Halle/Saale, http://www.eth.mpg.de/publications.

Thériault, B. 2000. 'Die "Professional Guardians of the Sacred" und die deutsche Verfassungsgebung', in *Religiöser und kirchlicher Wandel in Ostdeutschland 1989–1999*, ed. D. Pollack and G. Pickel. Opladen: Leske + Budrich, 186–205.

_____. 2004. *"Conservative Revolutionaries": Protestant and Catholic Churches in Germany After Radical Political Change in the 1990s*. New York and Oxford: Berghahn.

Tiefensee, E. 2002. 'Homo areligiosus. Überlegungen zur Entkofessionalisierung in der ehemaligen DDR', in *Gottlose Jahre? Rückblicke auf die Kirche im Sozialismus der DDR*. Leipzig: Evangelische Verlagsanstalt, 197–216.

Tippach-Schneider, S. 1999. 'Sieben Kinderwagen, drei Berufe und ein Ehemann. DDR-Frauengeschichten im Wandel der Sozialpolitik', in *Fortschritt, Norm und Eigensinn. Erkundungen im Alltag der DDR*, ed. Dokumentationszentrum Alltagskultur der DDR e.V. Berlin: Links, 129–50.

Vinken, B. 2002. *Die deutsche Mutter. Der lange Schatten eines Mythos*. Munich: Piper.

Wallenhorst, R. and R. Halaczinsky. 2000. *Die Besteuerung gemeinnütziger Vereine und Stiftungen*. Munich: Vahlen.

Winkler, G. 1990. *Sozialreport der DDR: Daten und Fakten zur sozialen Lage in der DDR*. Stuttgart, Munich, Landsberg: Bonn Aktuell.

Chapter 5

Longing for Security

Qigong and Christian Groups in the People's Republic of China

Kristin Kupfer

Introduction

In the late evening of 24 April 1999, followers of Falungong, a religious network combining aspects of Qigong,[1] Buddhism and Daoism, assembled at various spots around the Chinese central government district of Zhongnanhai in Beijing to protest against the imminent criminalising of the network. By noon on 25 April, 10,000 participants sat calmly and silently all over Zhongnanhai. After thirteen hours of silent protest and a pledge by the Chinese authorities to negotiate with representatives of Falungong, the protesters dispersed in the same orderly fashion as they had appeared. However, negotiations never took place. Confronted with a highly organised opponent, the Chinese government declared Falungong illegal and an 'evil cult'; a policy of brutal repression and propaganda against the group began (Malek 1999: 66–72).

The case of Falungong is merely the most prominent example of a more far-reaching dimension of religious networks. In the rapidly changing China of today, where competition for status and power has intensified and socio-economic disparities are increasing, disillusioned party cadres and intellectuals and marginalised sections of the population long for a spirit of community and mutual assistance to help them overcome material and idealistic hardships.

This chapter will argue that religious networks provide notions and practices of social security that fill the gap left by the organisational and ideological withdrawal of the state since 1978. Religious networks utilise or reinterpret the

---

Notes for this chapter begin on page 98.

concepts abandoned by the government, while Christian networks in particular also refer to resources of traditional Chinese secret societies.[2] Drawing on nostalgic feelings in current Chinese society about state care and comradeship during the Mao era, these religious networks incorporate the longing for paternalistic guidance and communal support. The position of religious networks in relation to the second major provider of social security – family and kinship networks – is twofold.

Due to work migration of young adults and a growing lifestyle gap between the generations, provision of social security based on family and kinship has weakened. Children living far away from their parents still may support them financially. But because of geographical distance, limited holidays and lifestyle priorities, many children do not provide their parents with the emotional support the elderly long for. Religious networks help their members to deal with feelings of loneliness and insecurity. Still, some Christian networks tend to pressure their followers into severing their personal relationships; although reinforcing notions of security, they evoke at the same time threats of insecurity should followers leave the network.

I use the term *religious network* to indicate the multilayered organisational structure and multiple activities of these groups, which are dependent on the social, economic and political circumstances in which they operate.

Effects of Socio-economic and Political Change on Religious Life in China

The late 1970s in the People's Republic of China witnessed a strong and diverse awakening of spiritual/religious life, which had been forced underground during the Cultural Revolution (1966–1976). As a result of the ideological and organisational retreat of the Chinese Communist Party and of rapid socio-economic change, both triggered by Deng Xiaoping's economic reform and open-door policy, official and unofficial religious communities,[3] folk religious practices and various 'Great Masters' of Qigong have been able to attract a growing number of people in search of ideological orientation and communal support.[4]

Religious networks have experienced a dynamic development within the religious realm. Characterised by charismatic leaders, hierarchical and flexible organisations, and teachings of healing and salvation, they combine resources from folk religion and evangelical movements, as well as from traditional Chinese secret societies, and even the Communist Party itself.

Offering material and idealistic assets couched in a familiar, highly appealing form, networks draw followers easily. Disappointed or marginalised sections of the population responded to the promise of a new spirit of community and attitude to life based on mutual assistance in overcoming material and idealistic hardship, often conjuring up ideas of the ostensible security of Maoist paternalistic guidance and the imagined community. Opinions such as 'During the Mao era, you could leave your door open and people looked after each other', or 'When Mao was still with us, we were all poor, but we were all worth the same', are heard frequently in China today.

Since 1978, two types of religious networks in particular, one based on Qigong and the other inspired by the Christian faith, have attracted a substantial number of followers. Their individual structures, teachings and activities differ greatly due to their specific resources and awkward relationship with the Chinese state, which for the most part supported Qigong networks but persecuted those that were Christian-based during the 1980s and 1990s. On the other hand, both types of networks developed strikingly similar features that were linked to ideological and organisational resources in the Chinese political, socio-economic and cultural system. Consequently, the notions and practices of social security provided by these groups should be analysed in the context of a lessening in the capacity of the Chinese state and of social institutions such as kinship networks to provide social security.

Economic Reforms and Social Security in China since 1949: From State Supply to Self-Support

Prior to 1978, China developed a two-tier social security system based on the administrative separation of urban and rural areas, coupling social security with registered residence status. Social security in the cities was closely associated with the work unit (*danwei*), for example, a state institution, a state or collectively owned enterprise. These units provided workers and their families with a broad variety of social services. Besides lifelong job assignments, workers and their families were granted free access to pensions, medical services, cheap housing and care institutions for their children. Foodstuffs and other goods, such as grain, cooking oil and clothes, were subsidized and distributed at low cost. A social benefit system for those unable to seek employment or obtain family-based support was put in place.[5]

Although Mao Zedong initially identified peasants as the driving force behind revolution, economic development demanded the creation of (heavy) industry. Hence, all state resources were directed at securing the social needs of skilled urban workers as a precondition and incentive to hard work. In the rural areas, state-initiated social benefits were limited to social relief, the so-called 'five guarantees': social assistance in the form of food, clothing, fuel, children's education and funeral expenses, which were distributed to orphans, widows/widowers, the sick and people without children via the respective production institutions (collectives, reorganised in the early 1960s into production teams). In addition, a basic collective health care system was built up during the 1960s; peasants paid a small fee to the collective, supplementing the common welfare fund for free medical services, often carried out by itinerant 'barefoot doctors'. The collective could therefore be considered by the peasants as a distributive agent of state-initiated social relief and a self-reliant mechanism of social support (Chang 2006).

Despite various attacks on the concept of the family, especially during the Great Leap Forward (1958–1960) and the Cultural Revolution (1966–1976), kinship networks remained the second major source of social security. Children were responsible for taking care of their parents and contributing towards special medical treatment and other needs. Informal, non-kinship-based networks that subscribed to social security in the pre-Mao era, such as religious associations, occupational guilds or burial societies, disappeared or were forced underground in order to survive. Similar to the religious networks mentioned earlier, they re-emerged on a small scale after 1978.

Although people were expected to treat one another equally as 'comrades', personal relations (*guanxi*)[6] based on kinship, places of origin, school attendance or acquaintances were viewed as informal social capital. Faced with limited access to resources (e.g. coal, marriage licenses), a rigid bureaucracy and political campaigns with varying focus, *guanxi* contributed to people's survival. Cultivating and broadening their personal networks enhanced their sense of security.

In summary, the level of social security provided by the state in the urban areas was quite high prior to 1978, particularly compared to other developing countries. In the rural areas, on the other hand, people were accustomed to relying on family ties, other personal relations and the collective to secure social needs.

Economic Reforms and the Restructuring of Social Security Provision

The reforms of the social security system introduced in 1978 were largely a response to the changing economy. Major reforms began in the countryside. The communes (pooled collectives) had proved to be economically ineffective and were disbanded, often on the peasants' own initiative.

The Household Responsibility System – the farming of land leased by individual households from the village collective – consequently became the national policy in 1983. Once the collective had lost its role as the basic economic and social unit, social services collapsed, health stations were abandoned and itinerant doctors left for the cities to make money. Whereas in 1970, 85 per cent of the rural population had access to medical services, only 7 per cent received health care in 1990 (Heberer 2004: 81). Health personnel decreased from 206 per 10,000 in 1978 to 146 per 10,000 in 1990 (Wu 2005: 193).

The government only began to revive the system of collective social services at the beginning of the 1990s, albeit mostly in villages of China's more prosperous eastern provinces. On the other hand, this move did not serve as a forerunner to its becoming state policy. By 2003, only some 20 per cent of the rural population was covered by collective medical services, as the system lacked public funding or did not enjoy the trust of the peasants (Hussain 2005). Although the state-owned Chinese People's Insurance Company began to operate in some areas, peasants still regarded illness as a major source of insecurity (Schädler 2001: 287). In 1993, some 24.5 per cent of peasants said that they could not afford to see a doctor, a figure that had risen from 13.4 per cent in 1985. In the poorer provinces, the figure increased in the same time frame from 72 per cent to 89 per cent (Wu 2005: 194). Because the population has increased, and environmental problems have destroyed arable land, the amount of land for each family has decreased. The Chinese government is reluctant to allow peasants to own (or sell) land, since family land is seen as a basic insurance for the survival of the peasants. Other state-led social security projects, such as the voluntary pension insurance system, still suffer from obscure management, and hence a lack of trust.

The shift in social security provision in the urban areas is related to the decoupling of state enterprises from government financial systems. Enterprises were no longer required to carry out a productive plan, but to make profits instead. The associated costs that work units were obliged to pay for workers and their families hampered their capacity for economic performance. This led the government to introduce a contract employment system in the mid-1980s. In response to the new risk of becoming unemployed, an unemployment insurance system was set up in 1986. Based on the Labour Law passed in 1995, the state committed itself to the establishment of social insurance systems that would cover pensions, health, unemployment, accidents and pregnancy. All insurances have a dual structure. The health insurance system, for example, includes a private account funded by employee contributions (2 per cent), and a solidarity account based on the employer share (6 per cent). 'Minor illnesses' were to be covered by the former and 'major illnesses' by the latter; definitions, however, may differ according to the province. Furthermore, if medical costs exceed certain national or local limits (e.g. hospital fees in Beijing), and individual funds are not available, patients must pay for their own treatment. This explains why many of the elderly are afraid of not being able to pay hospital fees (Darimont 2004).

Although the scope of some insurance systems was extended to joint-venture and private companies, only 45 per cent of urban workers are covered by the social security insurance scheme (Social Security Online 2004). A series of setbacks, such as insufficient capital or varying degrees of legal enforcement in different provinces and companies, still have to be resolved.

A Pluralistic Concept of Social Security

Since the state has partially withdrawn from the provision of social security, it is fostering a more pluralistic approach that contains several components: the establishment of a private insurance market (China Daily 2004), the restructuring of urban residence committees as providers of social security, the engagement of nongovernmental organisations (NGOs)[7] and the development of the charity sector (CASS 2006).

The government interpreted the Falungong incident as an indication of the need for renewed social control of China's citizens. The work unit (*danwei*) system began to erode as the reform of state-owned enterprises got underway in the latter half of the 1990s. Faced with growing unemployment and urban poverty, people are obliged to change accommodation more frequently. Former homogeneous residential areas now consist of a floating and more diverse population, and have consequently lost their function as social networks. To counteract the attraction of religious networks, the government offered a variety of activities and participation channels. This strategy has had only moderate success, as many residents no longer identify themselves with where they live and are reluctant to take an interest or engage in communal activities (BASS 2002; Heberer 2003).

Both national and international NGOs contribute to a broad range of social projects, in particular those dealing with unprivileged sections of the population, such as the handicapped, the old and the long-term ill (Hamrin 2003). Although the Chinese government praises the 'social services' of faith-based NGOs and religious groups (e.g. those addressing leprosy or relief to poor families), it is still reluctant to offer a broader legal framework to religious groups as providers of social security (SARA 2003; SARA n.d.; Malek 2005).

After 1978, the state altered the idea of social security as being provided and guaranteed, converting it into a marketable commodity subject to economic efficiency. This caused widespread grievance about the above-mentioned degeneration and rising costs, and led to protests by laid-off state workers and pensioners over social services, which although promised had not been forthcoming. A psychological factor produced a further blow to the growing sense of insecurity. Peasants began to feel discriminated against by urban citizens. Whereas they had been applauded as the 'revolutionary base of the Communist Party' during the Mao years, they now felt betrayed by this same party. Since the mid-1980s, the state has plainly focused on urban modernisation at the expense of rural development.[8] State workers, who had enjoyed privileged social service provision up to 1978, are also beginning to feel cast aside by a state perceived as using money for its own ends (corruption) and as willing to sacrifice social equality for the goal of economic efficiency. The rising number of migrant workers in the urban areas has added to the workers' sense of insecurity, as they now fear they may have to share the already tight social and economic resources.[9]

The Most Vulnerable Sections of the Population: Migrants and the Elderly

Migrant workers form one of the most vulnerable groups in relation to social security. Having come from the countryside, they are mostly registered as rural residents, and are in possession of either a temporary urban residence permit or none at all. Hence they are largely excluded from the provision of urban social security. In constant danger as a result of frequently illegal residence status, they run the risk of having an accident or being deprived of payment after months of work. Although they may be able to send most of their revenue back home to support their families, long-distance assistance cannot compensate for the loss of the intimate atmosphere of conversation and mutual support.

The elderly are in a likewise vulnerable position. Young adults often leave their homes for educational reasons or to seek a job in larger cities and enjoy a modern lifestyle. Although the latter may support their parents financially, elderly members of the family frequently long for emotional support and care. Due to geographical distances and limited holidays, and the growing gap between the generations and between urban and rural values, many children do not meet their parents' expectations (Li 1999; Wong 1998).

Rapid economic development and social change have generally affected personal relationships, which represent vital social security capital in Chinese society. The need to communicate with people outside personal networks has increased, and relations have become more temporary. Faced with rising competition for goods and services, which became highly diversified commodities of huge demand and limited supply at the high-quality end of the chain (e.g. placing a child in a top school as the most suitable preparation for university entrance examinations, obliging nurses to look after patients particularly well or securing an appointment for an operation at a well-known hospital), the need to secure resources through *guanxi* became more pressing. When exploitation of personal relationships began to dominate numerous aspects of life, Chinese society increasingly suffered from what several scholars call a 'crisis of trust' (Peng 2006; Qin 2005: 273–316; Hamrin 2006).

Against this background of changing social security concepts in China, the resources of religious networks have been able to draw on people's longing for renewed concepts of social security, both in the material and the idealistic sense.

Social Security Provided by Religious Networks

Analysing three Qigong and three Christian networks, the following section reflects on various aspects of the notion and practice of social security, both at the materialistic and idealistic level in reference to the definition presented in the introduction to this volume. The analysed Qigong networks are 'National Gong' (*Guogong*), 'Flagrant Gong' (*Xianggong*) and 'Chinese Gong' (*Zhonggong*); the three Christian networks are 'Society of Disciples' (*Mentuhui*), 'Teachings of the Soul' (*Linglingjiao*) and 'Teachings of the Supreme God' (*Zhushenjiao*).[10]

The analysis is based on literature research only (official and semi-official publications of religious groups and state agencies, as well as scientific literature from Hong Kong), as the field proved to be too sensitive to carry out systematic interviewing. Not only were people unwilling or afraid to talk to me, but I also received warnings from police agencies.

Social Security and the Organisational Structure of Religious Networks

All of the above-listed religious groups are characterised by a hierarchical structure with headquarters and layers of sub-branches from the provincial down to the village level. The structure clearly resembles the cell system of the Chinese Communist Party (CCP), and the Christian networks are even reminiscent of 'traditional' secret societies.

Qigong. All of the Qigong groups established a three-tier organisational structure, with 'research societies' as the core element. They were named after the national roof organisation for Qigong, the 'Chinese Qigong Scientific Research Society', under which the networks had been registered. The positions in a research society include director, vice-director, secretary-general, secretary and office worker. Their titles correspond to designations in the Communist Party structure and are thus familiar. An indication of power for many people, they may specifically appeal to party cadres and those with reservations about religious titles. At the middle organisation level, the Qigong groups set up schools offering classes with trained teachers. The position of 'promoter', marked out from the average teacher by being authorised to heal others or lead 'promotion sessions or lectures', required graduation from special training courses (ZGXG n.d.; ZGQG 1998). Information on salaries could not be obtained from the present sources.

'Guidance stations' formed the third organisational layer or ground level, the principal meeting point for practitioners of Qigong. These guidance stations, normally overseen by a 'head of station', were less formally organized. They provided a lively venue for networking, resembling the old concept of neighbourhood committees at their best: not surveillance, but care. As one follower of National Gong wrote:

> [The guidance stations] became a warm home.... If someone was ill, station leader Cao would visit them in hospital; if someone was unable to pay the doctor, she convinced people to donate some money. If a family was in trouble, she would advise them patiently, and help them to solve things. If a student was disrespectful to his elders, she convinced him that caring for the elderly was the duty and a virtue of the younger generation. Lots of people went to Cao, she became a confidante.... Some of the elderly played *Majiang* to relax, they had nothing else to do. Now that they have something to do, they are laughing again. (Wang 1997)

National Gong even took over the Communist fashion of 'modelling', assigning outstanding guidance stations as 'model stations'.

Chinese Gong developed an organisational structure similar to a business conglomerate. Its founder, Zhang Hongbao, had studied economic management and was keen to develop a 'Qigong enterprise'. His entrepreneurial skills and specific 'Qigong business culture' was based on a 'middle way system', which combined marketing features such as competition, efficiency and chain sales, with an ethical code of conduct (focusing on self-restraint) in relation to his employees. The organisation is made up of five industries: life-care training (3,000 schools and almost a million chain guidance stations), life-care products (120 articles), life-care bases (hotels, shops, restaurants and various services), research facilities and education. In 1995, Zhang Hongbao founded the Kylin Group conglomerate with the intention of placing the companies and stores from all five industries, including almost 10,000 employees, under one roof (WA 2001a; Zhang 1994; Sun and Li 2003).

Christian Networks. The structure of the Christian networks is more complex than those of Qigong, and can be attributed to state persecution, which demanded a greater degree of secrecy. In addition, they clearly put more emphasis on attaching religious names to the ranks, and on incentives for advancement within the group.

The leaders of all three religious groups claimed absolute authority, although the Society of Disciples does have a 'Main Assembly' consisting of twelve members (paralleling the twelve apostles), three of which form a core known as the 'three limbs' or 'three pillars'. While there are some similarities to Christian concepts, the overall structure is again reminiscent of secret societies and composed of a hierarchical system referred to as 'Seven Seven', which relates to the number of levels and the number of organisations at each level.

In the 'Supreme God' organisation, the 'God Mother' instructs the Supreme God in theoretical concepts and scriptures as preparation for his teachings. The 'Four Living Things' formulate the 'interior policy' and teachings of the group, and function as 'Standing Companions' of the Supreme God. The hierarchical stages from 'Same (Level) as the Supreme' to 'Seven Angels' represent certain developments in Teachings of the Supreme God.[11] Similar positions assigned to specific tasks such as evangelising, responsibility for holding meetings, receiving followers from other provinces and taking care of finances is also found in the organisational structure of other networks (Jiang 2000; Li 2000).

At the level directly below the leading male figures, almost all of the higher positions were or still are occupied by young women. One example is eighteen-year-old Li Ping, whose case is described in several monographs written by Chinese scholars. Although detailed footnotes are not provided, the authors mention reports of police interrogation as a general source of information at the end of the book. All of the accounts tend to portray Li Ping as a victim rather than a criminal, although she did get arrested. Within the space of a few months, she rose to the third-highest rank of the Supreme God organisation to become the 'Goddess of Fine Gold', responsible for compiling documents and lecturing other core members. Li is cited as always having been confident about her own skills; on the other hand, she was perceived as being looked down upon because of her modest economic background. Forced to leave school for cheating at an exam, she joined Teachings of the Supreme God, where, seizing the opportunity to develop her skills, she gained a sense of being 'worthy' and 'successful'. In 1995, she was in charge of organising and presiding over the first 'National Representative Congress' (Wang 2000: 183ff.; Chen and Zhang 2001: 112ff.; Wu 2005: 210f.).

Her example clearly demonstrates the ambivalence of social security provided within the confines of the network. On the one hand, Li's career was surprisingly successful, providing her with spiritual security, and with social and financial prestige – a rare occurrence for women, at least in rural Chinese society. One could speculate, on the other hand, about the personal sacrifices involved, considering that the leader of her group was sentenced to death for rape. In addition, when state agencies became suspicious of her position, she was interviewed by the police.

One of the most vital tasks of Christian networks was proselytising. The assignment of different posts to a particular region is a common feature of network organisation. The organisational structure of Teachings of the Soul is closely related to their missionary work. They divided Chinese territory into three 'pieces' or 'parts'. The appointed heads of pieces are responsible for the establishment of smaller administrative units for the purpose of evangelising.

Christian networks also offer material incentives to potential followers. This takes the form of a pledge that 'donations' or 'offerings' made by followers will reap a hundredfold in the next life. Followers were furthermore supplied with mobile phones or a 'salary' containing a bonus for each new recruit (Li 2000: 231). The Society of Disciples, for example, promises to pay 50 yuan for each new recruit, 500 yuan for each new Youth League member, and as much as 1,000 yuan for a police officer or a district or town cadre who joins the ranks (Jiang 2000: 68).

Apart from a complex hierarchy, codified behaviour and disciplinary measures are key elements of these religious groups, highlighting their social ethics. Christian networks are more tightly controlled organisations in comparison to the loosely knit Qigong networks based on voluntary participation.

There are two reasons for this. Firstly, the illegal status[12] of Christian groups forced them to develop measures to avoid being discovered by the police, and to sidestep the spying activities of the government. Teachings of Supreme God, for example, ordered their followers not to stay in hotels, to speak Mandarin only, and not to carry identity cards (Wu 2005: 229). Secondly, codes of behaviour reinforce identification with the group and its leader, keep followers in check and mount the pressure not to leave. With their peculiar mixture of 'enforcing security in an insecure (hostile) environment', while at the same time evoking fear of being expelled from the group or of not fulfilling requirements and thus remaining isolated with no hope of 'salvation', the networks managed to bind followers over a considerable period of time.

To strengthen the internal organisation, the Society of Disciples pursued a highly exclusive marriage policy, whereby group members were only permitted to marry among themselves. Non-members were referred to as 'people outside the gang' (Li 2000: 19; Tan and Kong 2001: 256). They also set up special 'Truth Groups' or 'Small Control Groups' to investigate violations of their highly detailed rules, a practice also common in Teachings of the Soul. The respective document titles, such as 'Temporary Rules for Administration of the Renaissance of All Things', resemble the language of the Communist Party (Jiang 2000: 132f., 157). In contrast, the Qigong groups were based on voluntary participation, where people could leave of their own accord. The Chinese Gong website declares that 'if you don't want to continue [after the second of three course levels] you will still have gained' (WA 2001e). Flagrant Gong states that changing over to another style of Qigong is possible, should Flagrant Gong turn out to unsuitable (ZGXQ n.d.: 9).

However, Flagrant Gong has laid down detailed 'regulations' for practitioners, which are closely related to their strong moral thrust and will be analysed below. A set of moral standards and objectives can also be found in the teachings of Chinese Gong and National Gong, but have not yet been codified. The eight rules of Flagrant Gong aim at shaping followers into good citizens in a Communist and Confucianist sense. Although no indication is given of the consequences of violating these rules, the specific disciplinary measures developed by Flagrant Gong reflect the language of the CCP, and are similar to those of the Christian networks (WA 2002). Asked what would happen to someone who turned 'bad', Tian declared that he or she could be expelled by the Flagrant Gong conference, 'stripped' of certain 'skills' or dealt with internally (ZGXQ n.d.: 68).

The regulations touch on three topics. Obedience to the political principles of the Communist Party policy ('love socialism ... support the four basic principles of the party') is stressed first and foremost. A second topic instructs students to advocate the science of Qigong and fight against superstition. Described virtues – a third topic of the regulations – praise the Confucian values of self-discipline and tolerance towards others, piousness towards parents and respect for the elderly, and love for children. Other values referred to are closely associated with the desire for a social utopia often nostalgically linked with the era of Mao Zedong, such as to act in the interests of society, to be united, to work hard regardless of criticism, to be modest and honest to other people, to protect the common good and not to bet or steal. Lei Feng[13] is quoted among others as a role model for social behaviour.

Here, Qigong groups again reveal structures parallel to those of Christian groups. The Society of Disciples, for example, issued principles in the form of warnings, such as 'Do not use money to make friends', or 'Do not depend on connections or bribery'. Likewise, the rules of Teachings of the Soul, which were referred to as the 'Ten Commandments', order followers to 'love God Jehova, not to worship other idols, to praise the name of God, not to make false declarations in the name of God, to respect the Sabbath day, to be filial to mother and father, not to kill, not to rape, not to steal, not to make false testimony, and not to be greedy for money' (Jiang 2000: 135, 160).

Based on the above-mentioned principles, the religious groups project a past utopia based on humanity, honesty, self-sacrifice in the service of others and justice. They appeal to those who experience a sense of disorientation and insecurity in a rapidly developing and somewhat-ruthless capitalist society.

Ideational Social Security Resources Provided in the Religious Groups

The issues addressed by the Qigong and Christian groups primarily concern illness and visions of the future or of spiritual security. The teachings of religious groups are centred on the task of physical and spiritual healing, and to a certain extent the salvation of their followers through (a reunion with) a higher moral authority. Healing is understood in both network contexts as a process related to both the body and the mind. The causes of illness are therefore diverse, and interpreted as signs of an ailing society doomed to failure and annihilation. For this reason, religious groups provide their followers with an exclusive vision of survival and a more promising future.

Healing. Christian groups spread the notion that illnesses or unfortunate incidents are the result of possession by 'evil spirits' or 'demons', and could be related to sinful conduct as defined in the code of behaviour for adherents described earlier. Hence, people who have already tried various hospitals and treatment in an effort to cure their illness or have experienced a number of 'unsatisfactory events' are more disposed to believing in the help of spiritual powers. Mrs Cai, a forty-five-year-old follower of Teachings of the Supreme God is cited as follows:

> When I was twenty I had heart disease, and at twenty-nine, arthritis. I often had broken bones, I had headaches and stomach pains, and my whole body was diseased. The sickness just wouldn't leave me. I went to Gulou Hospital ... but they

never really cured me. My mother told me one day that 'Mr Cai from our village said believing in Jesus can cure disease and asked if the family were believers. If you're cured, you don't have to sit at home'…. The elderly women in the group said I just have to pray with all my heart and the illnesses will go away. They also said God created mankind, so he must be able to cure disease. You have to have faith and keep God in your heart. (Wu 2005: 195f.)

Another follower of Teachings of the Supreme God, 44 year-old peasant Mr Tian, was portrayed as saying:

My wife said that believing in God [Society of Disciples] is good. It makes you safe. You don't need cash, you only have to pray. I didn't believe this in the beginning. One of our pigs was sick once. I had no money to pay for treatment, so I went to Mr Chen's place to borrow some money. He wasn't there, but then I met a man called Zhou, who was about forty, and he said, 'One of your pigs is sick because you had no regrets and didn't change. The sick pig is male.' I was surprised because I didn't know that. He also said if I prayed to God I'd be safe. When I came back I found that the sick pig really was male. That's when I began to believe. (Wu 2005: 200f.)[14]

Treating ailments as an element of degenerated social and economic circumstances, Teachings of the Soul and the Society of Disciples proclaim illness to be a sign of approaching 'doomsday': 'Doomsday has come, epidemics will descend on the world, and there will be hunger, floods and locusts' (Wu 2005: 43, 55). The SARS lung disease that raged in China in 2003 was also used by the Society of Disciples as proof that the end of the world was nigh. Prior to this, the turn of the millennium had inspired Teachings of the Supreme God and the Society of Disciples to declare the approach of doomsday. The forthcoming end of the world not only caused current illnesses, but was also responsible for the exodus of large sections of the human race and their descent into hell.

Qigong groups, on the other hand, did not relate illness to a doomsday scenario, although National Gong was accused by a Chinese newspaper of having spread 'doomsday theories' (SWB 1999). This cannot be confirmed by the present sources. Similar to Christian networks, the Qigong ones closely associate the condition of the body with that of the mind. One National Gong follower cited the explanation of a teacher at the central school in Sichuan: 'If someone does something wrong, they'll be on tenterhooks. There'll be a lot of tension and their heart will grow heavier with the burden. Their energy levels drop, their heartbeat is irregular, and their immune system suffers. That's when disease strikes' (Ren 1996). Zhang Hongbao, the founder of Chinese Gong, integrated questions on the relationship between morale and illness into his 'Principle of Cause and Effect', as one of eight assumptions that make up his highly comprehensive 'Kylin philosophy'. Similar to the Society of Disciples, Zhang places illness in a larger social context. Interestingly, the last lines of the following have a strong parallel with the Old Testament:

Mao Zedong said, 'There is neither love nor hate in this world without a reason'....
Continuing to practise hard at Qigong is the cause, for example, and a healthy body
is the effect; doing good for society is the cause, widening your gong abilities and
increasing your wisdom is the result.... Harming the interests of the state is the
cause, punishment is the effect. Chen Yi [a famous revolutionary and a general in
the 1930s and 1940s] said that good would be rewarded with good, and bad with
bad. If there is no retribution, then the time has not yet come; when the time comes,
there will be retribution. (WA 2001b)

The above paragraph points to a basic method of healing central to all three
Qigong networks. The head of Flagrant Gong, Tian Ruisheng, framed this in
the concept of 'merits and virtues'. Everybody is obliged to do good for society
as a means of healing illness: 'The more [good] you do, the faster you will be
healed.' Tian links charity to a positive, physical stimulus to the brain, a form
of 'massage' (WA 2001c).

Dualistic Worldview. But who is to be the judge of 'good' and 'bad'? For the
Christian groups, the answer is 'God' or 'God incarnate', the respective leader
of each network. Hence, both the Society of Disciples and Teachings of the
Supreme God practise so-called demon punishments or healing through exor-
cism to cure illness. Medicine or regular treatment in hospital was considered
unnecessary. The exorcizing of demons could be induced through prayer and
'soul dances' or 'soul songs' 'inspired by the soul', and is related to free forms of
praying and speaking in tongues known from evangelical movements (Jiang
2000: 161, 165). Qigong practitioners meet to attend courses or to exercise
collectively as an effective method of self-healing. Qigong groups were subject
to fierce intergroup competition during the 'Qigong fever'[15] of the 1980s and
1990s, with each one presenting their Qigong method as easy to learn, a valuable commodity suitable to modern life and well worth the money:[16] 'Anyone
can learn National Gong. There are no taboos, it should just proceed naturally.
It can be practised sitting down, standing up, asleep or on the bus.... Some
diseases cannot be cured with contemporary medicine, but we have a method
of curing them' (Liu 1998; Rui 1998).

Visions for Survival and a Better Future. With regard to the above-mentioned
vision of 'doomsday', all three leaders of the Christian groups propagate that
only their followers will survive the exodus of mankind and escape being
condemned to hell. Consequently, belonging to such a group is tantamount to
being 'good'. Furthermore, the Society of Disciples painted a utopian picture
of life, juxtaposing it to the reality numerous followers face. In this 'new era
of God', a time of eternal sources of wealth and food, 'what is asked for will be
received, what is sought will be found'. In a 'world of equals', poverty, injustice
and falsehood would no longer exist (Li 2000: 221).

Liu Jineng, the founder of National Gong, also gives an account of another world, associated with his theory of 'one centre, two worlds'. Whereas one world is reality, visible to the naked eye, the other is invisible and can only be perceived after cultivation to the highest level. Reaching this physical and mental state is to 'merge' with the 'centre', which is the universe, or nature itself. Nature is not only understood as pure energy, but as 'just and upright, fair and compassionate, dignified and not evil' (Rui 1998). Nature is in itself 'good' and a moral authority. All living things are a 'small universe' and must obey the moral principle of nature: 'if you perform well, you will rise, if not, you will fall' (Rui 1998). Although the philosophy of Chinese Gong portrays the universe in morally neutral terms, influenced by the constant interchange of the 'visible and invisible elements' of yin and yang, it also features the 'principle of self-control and adjustment of the universe'. All things are subject to the above-mentioned interchange, and healing or achieving a balance can be brought about by pursuing a 'middle way' (WA 2001c).

The leaders of Qigong groups regularly conducted 'assemblies to bring skills'. Accounts of physical healing are well documented by testimonies and eye-witness reports of participants and followers: for example, that deaf mutes could speak, those who were paralysed could walk, tumours were 'removed', the blind could see and organic stones were 'beaten down' (Zhuo 1992; Ren 1994).

Contrary to Chinese Gong and National Gong, Flagrant Gong does not allow pupils to use their skills to heal others, as it would harm the 'fundamental qi' (ZGXG n.d.: 57). They thus favour 'long-distance healing'. Handkerchiefs belonging to those who participated in a Tian Ruisheng study session can also carry qi; when touched, for example, they can heal smallpox. Drinking 'information' water, that is, water that has absorbed Tian's energy, can also improve health (WA 2001d). Chinese Gong sold various articles that contained 'received skills' and thus the energy of Zhang Hongbao. Zhang was reported to have demanded large 'donations' for activities such as having his picture taken or eating a meal in his company (Sun and Li 2003). This is reminiscent of holy water, baptism and even relics in the Christian context. However, the Christian groups analysed do not make use of these concepts, at least according to the present sources. On the other hand, the issue of 'donating', as advocated by Teachings of the Supreme God and Teachings of the Soul, was linked to the Christian concept of salvation (Jiang 2000: 71, 140; Wu 2005: 252f.).[17] In the biographies of the founders of the Christian groups, constant references are made to the mystical or miraculous events that enabled them to develop exceptional abilities. The biographies also emphasised the hardship their life entailed.

Hua Xuehe refers to the 'Second Jesus'. With the exception of one character, his name resembles the Chinese translation of 'Jehova' (Hua Xuehe and Ye Hehua). Hua, like Jesus, was born in the winter and suffered in a similar manner. He calmly withstood police beatings and healed a great many people (Deng 1996; Wu 2005: 80f.).

Among the Qigong groups, only Zhang Hongbao, the master of Chinese Gong, heavily promoted the acquisition of 'exceptional skills' beyond healing, such as 'heaven eye ability' (e.g. to have a penetrating or long-distance view) or 'Buddha eye ability' (the ability to alter other people's lives, values and aims, or to redeem them) (WA 2001d).

All group founders speak highly of 'exceptional skills' or healing powers, which they allege to be the result of a cultivation process available in principle to everyone. They provide followers with the opportunity of acquiring 'mystical powers' to deal with various challenges. The founders themselves are willing to act or become God-like, and at the same time to present themselves as human-like figures of public admiration and hope.

Concluding Remarks

As a product of the Chinese transformation process driven by economic growth, the context of social security politics and practices has undergone a tremendous change since 1978. Having once enjoyed secure social services provided by the state, urban dwellers now had to cope with the risk of unemployment and were obliged to pay for social security. Collective mechanisms of social security deteriorated in the countryside, and kinship ties as supportive social security networks altered with growing migration. Social ethics under Mao Zedong aimed or were perceived as aiming at social equality and mutual assistance, also experienced change as the new competitive society fostered diversity and individualism, seized on by many as the key reason for widespread rudeness and corruption.

Thus, disillusioned cadres, disappointed urban workers, desperate peasants and disoriented migrants began to long for organisational and/or spiritual support in dealing with their sense of insecurity.

Religious groups have proved particularly adept at catering for people's needs, providing access to material and spiritual resources in a community of followers, based on commitment and idealistic efforts. They succeed in incorporating a sense of dissatisfaction, even despair, into the framework of their teachings. They present explanations for the perceived state of society, validate them and indicate ways of overcoming hardship and suffering. Importantly, they place their teaching in a frame of reference that is familiar in both organisational and idealistic terms.

The Qigong groups are loose networks based on voluntary participation. They offer organisational support that does not interfere with existing personal ties. The Christian groups, however, possess a tight-knit hierarchical structure that binds members, occasionally even fostering the break-up of existing personal relations.

Both networks have designed a utopia to cover the spiritual dimension of security. The Qigong groups offer a glorious past based on the spirit of Lei Feng and Mao Zedong as their vision of the future. Disappointed party cadres, scientists and people with a Qigong background seem predisposed to join Qigong groups. The Christian utopian vision is that of a 'heavenly kingdom', a complete break with the past and the worldly sphere. People with a Christian background and a strong desire for community and spirituality opted to become followers of the Christian groups. Since lack of adequate data prevents an insight into the composition of these followers, the availability factor – followers join a group because no other religious networks are available – cannot be ruled out.

Despite their differences, both Christian and Qigong networks clearly reflect the organisational principles and ideological orientation of the Chinese Communist Party. They make use of concepts that the party is no longer able or willing to offer its people, but that are retained by some sections of the population as memories of the 'good old days'. The language of the teachings frequently resembles that of the Communist Party, while the core of the respective group reference system reverts to the era of Mao Zedong, symbolising social equality and justice. Thus, the religious groups described in this chapter incorporate a longing for paternalistic guidance and communal support.

Without justifying the repressive policy of the Chinese regime, an evaluation of the contribution of the religious networks to social security must bear several critical issues in mind. Firstly, while many members joined these groups on a kinship basis, belonging to Christian networks occasionally created tension between family members as a result of the group principles of inclusion and exclusion. Secondly, with the exception of Flagrant Gong, all networks favour their concept of healing over medical treatment, and even advise followers not to see a doctor. Failure to be cured while belonging to the group is blamed on the followers' own lack of commitment and effort. Thirdly, hierarchical group organisation and a charismatic leader are indicative of paternalistic structures. The teachings reflect an overzealous, nonpluralistic approach to reality and change, which obfuscates the past by neglecting critical accounts of the Mao Zedong era. Hence beyond individual membership, these religious groups do not present a sustainable and comprehensive strategy for the solution of social security issues. They have nevertheless driven the Chinese government to reconsider the social and spiritual needs of the population, and to give way to a more pluralistic society, allowing a variety of actors to shape China's development.

Notes

1. *Qigong* could be translated as 'energy work'. It refers to a set of exercises that coordinate different breathing patterns with physical movements of the body, all of which is aimed at physical and spiritual cultivation. Up to 3,600 styles of Qigong were practised during its surge of popularity (*Qigongre*) in the 1980s and 1990s. Most of these were new creations and not registered with the state (Chen 1995).

2. For more information on Chinese secret societies, see Chesneaux (1971); de Groot (1903); ter Haar (1992, 1993).

3. The Chinese government officially recognises five religions (Buddhism, Daoism, Islam, Protestantism and Catholicism) and has installed five patriotic religious associations as roof organisations under state administration. All local religious congregations and communities must apply for registration and submit to administrative control. If they refuse to register, the respective groups are considered illegal and frequently persecuted by the authorities on these grounds.

4. According to the Government White Paper of April 2002, more than 200 million people in China adhere to various religious beliefs and practices. The country is said to possess more than 100,000 sites for religious activities, 300,000 clergy, more than 3,000 religious organisations, and 74 training centres for the clergy. The paper puts the numbers of Buddhists at 100 million, and refers to 20 million Muslims, 5 million Catholics and 15 million Protestants. With regard to the latter two, academics calculate that there are at least 10 million Catholics in the combined official and unofficial churches. Researchers estimate the number of Protestant adherents, including those of nonregistered congregations, as varying between 30 and 90 million people.

5. The Chinese government did not include 'social support' (or personal savings) in the official social security concept until 1993. Social security now comprised 'social insurance; social relief; social welfare; work of *youfu anzhi* (providing preferential treatment to families of soldiers, martyrs, and proper arrangements for the placement of demobilised soldiers); social support; and personal savings' (Wang 2006: 2).

6. *Guanxi* can be traced to the Confucian concept of portraying human beings as part of reciprocal relationships based on moral obligation. Hence, Chinese society tends to be separated into several 'small societies' or 'circles', used to divide other people into those who are related to their *guanxi* network and those who are not. *Guanxi* includes the principle of mutual assistance based on expectations and moral obligations, and combines exploitation with sentiment, depending on the scope, content and purpose. It should be viewed as a dynamic concept, closely linked to other components of Chinese sociality, such as 'face', 'human feelings' or 'reciprocity'. For a good overview of *guanxi*, see, for example, Chen and Chen (2004) and Gold et al. (2002).

7. Since larger NGOs are obliged to affiliate themselves to a state institution in order to be registered, they are often referred to as nonprofit organisations or government-organized NGOs. Numerous small-scale NGOs operate illegally or are registered as a company. On NGOs in China, see Lehrack (2005).

8. As of late, the government has begun to emphasise rural development. However, without major changes to land ownership and residence status, or the establishment of peasant associations, improvements cannot be expected (Asia News 2006).

9. 'Social security' (*shehui baozhang*) has figured in the ranking of the six top urban resident concerns since 1995. It scored second in 1996, as in 2002 (34 per cent), 2003 (32.1 per cent) and 2005 (35.7 per cent) (Liberation Daily 1998; Run 2005: 65).

10. For more information on the Qigong networks, see Guo (2003), Liu (1998), Ren (1994), Rui (1998), SWB (1999), WA (2001e). For Christian networks, see Wu (2005), Chen and Zhang (2001), Jiang (2000), Li (2000), Wang (2000).

11. A more detailed investigation of name sources would be of great value. 'Four Living Things' and 'Seven Angels' could be derived from the Revelation 4:7 and 8:2.

12. As a nonregistered Protestant community, Christian groups were considered illegal even before they were banned for promoting 'heretical teachings'.

13. Lei Feng (1940–1962) was a soldier of the People's Liberation Army of the PRC. Characterised as a selfless and modest figure, he became an idol to many after his death. Since then, the CCP has frequently initiated 'Study Lei Feng' campaigns, designed to portray Lei as an example of selflessness to the Chinese people, and to encourage them to give priority to others.

14. A sick pig is considered a crucial event in the rural areas, since pigs symbolise good fortune (Chang 2006: 24).

15. According to official estimates, more than 2,000 Qigong groups with some fifty million practitioners existed at the end of the 1990s (see AP 2000; Chen 1994: 347).

16. Judging from the present sources, fees for courses and study material were quite modest. However, all three groups had alternative means of finance. Chinese Gong built up a conglomerate, while Xianggong seems for the most part to have made money on tickets for mass study sessions. National Gong conducted naming ceremonies, where companies were either named or had their names changed; it also issued work licenses to Qigong doctors. Still, Liu Jineng and Tian Ruisheng were said to have regularly donated money to the poor or to social welfare organisations (Sun and Li 2003; WA 2001a; Guo 2003; Zhuo 1992; ZGXG n.d.: 4; Dian 1999).

17. It is on these grounds that Chinese authorities accuse the groups of 'swindling money' from their followers and 'deceiving' them. Tian Ruisheng's daughters and Liu Jineng were sentenced to fixed-term imprisonment for illegal financial activities.

References

AP. 2000. 'China to Scrutinise Spiritual Groups Similar to Falun Gong', *China Study Journal* 3 (December 1999): 83.

Asia News. 2006. 'New Agricultural Development Ignores Farmers' Problems', 3 January. http://www.asianews.it/view_p.php?l=en&art=5025. Accessed 21 May 2006.

BASS/Beijing Academy of Social Science. 2002. 'Jiaqiang shequ jianshe, sheli zhili xiejiao de changxiao jizhi de dianxing moshi' (Strengthen Communal Construction, Build up a Type Model of a Long-Term Mechanism for Managing Heretical Teachings), http://www.bjpopss.gov.cn/bjpopss/xzlt/xzlt20021129.htm.zh. Accessed 12 May 2006.

CASS (Chinese Academy of Social Science). 2006. 'Cishan yu shehui gongyi. Xueshu taolun di shi qi' (Charity and Public Interest of Society. Academic Discussion Series No. 10), http://www.sociology.cass.cn/shxw/xstl/default.htm. Accessed 7 May 2006.

Chang, X. 2006. 'Lishang Wanglai: Social Support Networks, Reciprocity and Creativity in a Chinese Village' (PhD diss.), 3, http://personal.lse.ac.uk/changx/PhD%20Thesis.htm. Accessed 6 May 2006.

Chen, N. 1995. 'Urban Spaces and Experience of Qigong', in *Urban Spaces in Contemporary China: The Potential for Autonomy and Community in Post-Mao China*, ed. Deborah P. Davis et al. Cambridge: Cambridge University Press, 347–61.

Chen, X. and C. C. Chen. 2004. 'On the Intricacies of the Chinese Guanxi: A Process Model of Guanxi Development'. *Asia Pacific Journal of Management* 21: 305–24.

Chen, Z. and X. Zhang. 2001. *Xiejiao Zhenxiang* (*xia*). *Yiguandao, Huhanpai, Beiliwang, Zhushenjiao, Mentuhui* (*Truth of Heretical Teachings, Part 2. All Pervading Principle, Shouters, Anointed King, Teachings of the Supreme God, Disciples Society*), Beijing.

Chesneaux, J. 1971. *Secret Societies in China in the 19th and 20th Century*, trans. Gillian Nettle. Hong Kong, Singapore, Kuala Lumpur: Heinemann Educational Books.

China Daily. 2004. 'See China's Insurance Sector Grows Amid Ups and Downs', http://english. people.com.cn/200410/07/eng20041007_159214.html, 7 October. Accessed 5 November 2005.

Darimont, B. 2004. 'Antworten aus Beijing: Die Sozialpolitik der chinesischen Regierung', in *Sozialer Sprengstoff in China? Dimensionen sozialer Herausforderungen in der Volksrepublik*, ed. Kristin Kupfer. Essen: Focus Asien, 67–78.

De Groot, J. J. M. 1903. *Sectarianism and Religious Persecution in China: A Page in the History of Religions in Two Volumes*, vol. 1. Amsterdam: Johannes Müller.

Deng, Z. 1996. 'Recent Millennial Movements on Mainland China: Three Cases'. *Qiao* (*Bridge*) 80: 17.

Dian, L. 1999. 'Guogong zhi hun. Liu Jineng dashi Beidaihe chuangong sanji (Spirit of Guogong. Sketches of Great Master Liu Jineng's Passing of Skills at Beidaihe)'. *Zhongguo Qigong* (*Chinese Qigong*) 4: 22.

Gold, T., D. Guthrie and D. Wank, eds. 2002. *Social Connections in China: Institutions, Culture, and the Changing Nature of Guanxi*, Cambridge: Cambridge University Press.

Guo, Z. 2003. 'Xianggong toumu Tian Ruisheng si le, qi zi xing pian bei kuan (The Head of 'Xianggong', Tian Ruisheng is Dead, His Daughter Cheated and Was Punished)', *Zhongguo Qigong* (*Chinese Qigong*) 5: 63.

Hamrin, C. L. 2003. 'Faith-based Organisations: Invisible Partners in Developing Chinese Society, Oral Presentation for the Issues Roundtable 'To Serve the People': NGOs and the Development of Civil Society in China', The Congressional Executive Commission on China (CECC), http://www.cecc.gov/pages/roundtables/032403/Hamrin.php. 24 March. Accessed 1 November 2005.

_____. 2006. 'China's Social Capital Deficit', http://www.chinabalancesheet.org/Documents/ Papers_Social_Capital.pdf. Accessed 6 May 2006.

Heberer, T. 2003. 'Die Reorganisation städtischer Wohnviertel im Lichte kommunitaristischer und partizipativer Vorstellungen'. *China aktuell* 11: 1223–40.

_____. 2004. 'Soziale Frage und soziale Sicherung im urbanen Raum China', in *Sozialer Sprengstoff in China? Dimensionen sozialer Herausforderungen in der Volksrepublik*, ed. Kristin Kupfer. Essen: Focus Asien, 79–96.

Hussain, A. 2005. 'Rural Social Security – Current Situation and Trends', Stanford Center for International Development, Conference Paper, http://scid.stanford.edu/events/China2005/ Hussain.pdf. Accessed 25 April 2006.

Jiang, J. 2000. *Duliu – Dangjin Zhongguo xingxing sese de xiejiao zhuzhi* (*An Ulcer – All Kinds of Heretical Groups in Present Day China*, Beijing.

Lehrack, D. 2005. Neue Regulierungen für den zivilen Sektor – Fortschritt oder Rückschritt?', http://www.asienhaus.de/public/archiv/neue-regulierungen.doc. Accessed 3 November 2005.

Li, L. 1999. 'Family Insurance or Social Insurance? Policy Options for China's Social Security Reforms'. *International Journal of Economic Development* 1: 431–50.

Li, Z. 2000. *Xiejiao, huidaomen, heishehui. Zhongwai minjian mimi jieshe zonghengtan* (*Heretical Teachings, Societies, Ways and Schools, Mafia: Discussion on Popular Secret Associations in China and Abroad*), Beijing.

Liberation Daily. 1998. 'Survey of Urban Chinese – How are You Doing in 1998', http://www. usembassy-china.org.cn/sandt/survery98.html, 5 December. Accessed 3 November 2005.

Liu, J. 1998. 'Guogong yu zhong bu tong de tedian (Characteristics of Guogong that Distinguish It from the Mass of Qigong Styles)', *Zhongguo Qigong* (*Chinese Qigong*) 12: 45.

Malek, R. 1999. 'Falun Gong: Chronik der Ereignisse, Restriktionen, Dokumente', Meinungen. *China heute* 3–4: 66–72.

———, trans. 2005. 'Neue Vorschriften für religiöse Angelegenheiten in der Volksrepublik China'. *China heute* 1–2: 22–31.

Peng, S. 2006. 'Wo pin shenme xinren ni? – dangqian de xinren weiji yu duice (What Do I Lean On to Trust You – Current Crisis of Trust and Countermeasures)', http://www.sociology. cass.cn/shxw/shgz/shgz9/PO2041026314516562394.pdf. Accessed 6 May 2006.

Qin, J. 2005. *Xinrenwenhua de duanlie – dui chongchuanzhen minjian 'biaohui' de yanjiu (The Breaking Apart of the Culture of Trust – Research on a Popular Credit Association in Chongchuan Township)*, Beijing.

Ren, W. 1994. 'Tian Ruisheng yu Zhongguo Xianggong (Tian Ruisheng and Chinese Xianggong)'. *Zhonghua ernue (haiwaiban) (Chinese Children, Overseas Edition)* 3: 73ff.

Ren, Y. 1996. 'Women suo jianshi de Guogong. Lai zi Zhongguo ziran teyi gong di shi jie shici peixunban de baodao (The Guogong We Experienced: A Report from the Tenth Teacher's Qualification Training Class of Chinese Natural Extraordinary Skills)'. *Zhongguo Qigong (Chinese Qigong)* 10–11.

Rui, M. 1998. 'Ziran de jindan (Natural Golden Cinnabar)', *Zhongguo Qigong (Chinese Qigong)* 9: 16.

Run, X., ed. 2005. *2006 nian: Zhongguo shehui xingshi fenxi zu yuce (2006: Analysis and Forecast of Condition in Chinese Society)*, Beijing.

SARA (State Administration for Religious Affairs). 2003. 'Guan ai ruoshi qunti, gong jian xiaokang shehui (Love the Weak, Together Build a Well-Off Society)', http://www.sara.gov. cn/GB/xwzx/ztbd/zjyhxsh/edb0c2c6-5644-11da-9bfd-93180af1bb1a.html. Accessed 13 May 2006.

———. n.d. 'Zongjiao shehui fuwu de linian yu shixian (Theory and Practice of Religious Social Service)', http://www.sara.gov.cn/GB/xwzx/ztbd/zjyhxsh/9c8b3236-4aa8-11da-a1dd-93180af1bb1a.html. Accessed 13 May 2006.

Schädler, M. 2001. 'Im Angesicht von Arbeitslosigkeit und Depravierung – Gegenwart und Zukunft der chinesischen sozialen Sicherung', in *China: Konturen einer Übergangsgesellschaft auf dem Weg in das 21. Jahrhundert*, ed. Gunter Schubert, Hamburg: Institut für Asienkunde, 267–95.

Social Security Online. 2004. 'International Update: Recent Developments in Foreign Public and Private Pensions, China', http://www.ssa.gov/policy/docs/progdesc/intl_update/2004-10/2004-10.htm. October. Accessed 7 May 2006.

Sun, Y. and N. Li. 2003. 'Zhang Hongbao de 'qian shi jin sheng' (Zhang Hongbao's Previous Life and Current Existence)'. *Xinwen zhoukan (News Weekly)*, no. 19, 2 June, http://www. chinewsweek.com.cn/2003-6-06/1/1532.html. Accessed 8 June 2005.

SWB. 1999. 'Sichuan cracks down upon Guo Gong sect', translated from *Sichuan Ribao*, 29 October 1999, 30 October, 3679.

Tan, S. and S. Kong. 2001. 'Dangdai zhongguo xiejiao gailun (Introduction to Modern Heretical Teachings of China)', in *Lun xiejiao. Shoujie xiejiao wenti guoji yanjiu taolunhui lunwenji (Collection of the Contributions for the first International Research Symposium on Questions of Heretical Teachings)*, ed. Shehui yanjiu congshu bianji weiyuanhui (Editors of Collection on Social Research). Nanning, 251–65.

Ter Haar, B. J. 1992. *The White Lotus Teachings in Chinese Religious History*. Leiden, New York, Cologne: Brill.

Wang, Y. 2000. *Shijiao xiejiao. Renlei de gongdi (Heretical Teachings Worldwide. Public Enemy of Mankind)*. Zhuhai.

Wang, Z. 1997. 'Guogong fudaozhan de tiexinren (Intimate Person of Guogong Guidance Station)'. *Zhongguo Qigong (Chinese Qigong)* 3: 9.

WA (Web Archive). 2001a. 'Jilin shengmin kexue (Kylin Life Science)', http://web.archive.org/web/2001/0519212451/http://members.nbei.com/kylin. Accessed 4 July 2005.

_____. 2001b. 'Jilin wenhua jianjie' (Short Introduction to Kylin Philosophy)', http://web.archive.org/web/2001/0519212451/http://members.nbei.com/kylin. Accessed 5 July 2005.

_____. 2001c. 'Tian Ruisheng dashi xueshu baogao (luyin gao) (Study Report of Great Teacher Tian Ruisheng [Transcript of Recording])', http://web.archive.org/20011011164222/http://www.zhgxg.com/wen/xgbg.html. Accessed 25 August 2005.

_____. 2001d. 'Zhang Hongbao xiansheng jianjie (Short Introduction to Mr Zhang Hongbao)', http://web.archive.org/web/2001/0519212451/http://members.nbei.com/kylin. Accessed 3 July 2005.

_____. 2001e. 'Zhonggong gongfa jianjie (Short Introduction to Way of Zhonggong)', http://web.archive.org/web/2001/0519212451/http://members.nbei.com/kylin. Accessed 5 July 2005.

_____. 2002. 'Xiangong xueyuan shouze. Zhongguo guonei xueyuan shiyong (Regulation for Xiangong Students. For Use in Mainland China)', http://web.archive.org/web/20020206052853/http://www.zhgxg.com/wen/xgxysz.html. Accessed 15 August 2005.

Wong, L. 1998. *Marginalisation and Social Welfare in China*. London, New York: Routledge.

Wu, D. 2005. *Xiejiao de mimi – dangdai Zhongguo xiejiao juhe jizhi yanjiu (The Secrecy of Cult. A Study on the Regime of Evil Cult Assembly in Today's China)*, Beijing.

ZGQG (Zhongguo Qigong – Chinese Qigong). 1998. 'Renren neng xue hui Guogong, renren neng chuanshou Guogong, renren dou neng wei ziji taren zhibing zhanggong (People Can Learn Guogong, People Can Pass on Guogong, All People Can Heal Themselves and Others and Improve Their Skills)'. *Zhongguo Qigong (Chinese Qigong)* 12: 4.

ZGXG (Zhongguo Xianggong – Chinese Flagrant Gong). n.d. 'Zhongguo Xianggong dangdai chuanren Tian Ruisheng da Xianggong aihaozhe wen. 1–70 wen (Modern Transmitter of Chinese Xianggong, Tian Ruisheng Answers Questions from Friends of Xiangong. Questions 1–70)', http://web.archive.org/web/20011219205725/www.zhgxg.com/tdsdw.html. Accessed 10 August 2005.

Zhang, P. 1994. 'Zhonggong shiye de qiye wenhua tezhi (Special Business Culture Quality of Zhonggong Enterprise)'. *Zhonggong qinnian keji* 6: 23.

Zhuo, Q. 1992. 'Shenqi de Zhonggong (Mysterious Zhonggong)'. *Zhongguo Qigong (Chinese Qigong)* 4: 5.

PART II

Ambivalences of Religious Gifting

Chapter 6

Questioning Social Security in the Study of Religion in Africa

The Ambiguous Meaning of the Gift in African Pentecostalism and Islam

Mirjam de Bruijn and Rijk van Dijk

Introduction

The two Abrahamic traditions of Islam and Christianity, which are becoming more widespread in Africa, are marked by extensive ideological notions and practices surrounding the giving of gifts in cash and/or in kind. The followers of these traditions give gifts to religious bodies and leaders, but also give to others in the form of charity in and outside of the communities. This giving can be substantial and involve gifts of great value, representing a typical form of religious accumulation. The aim of the present contribution is to explore the relationship between religion and the provisioning of social security by looking at the meaning and significance of the gift in terms of security and insecurity, and to examine whether giving provides genuine security. This may appear to be the case when we take an objective standpoint – an etic view – where the definition of social security is taken for granted as something that is both positive and necessary. However, an emic approach reveals a different picture. From the perspective of the local, an automatic relationship between religion and social security does not exist per se. While from an outsider's perspective religious networks can provide security even if it is not their explicit aim or they can be seen to produce insecurity while propagating security (cf. this volume's introduction), the question this contribution explores is whether religion can be addressed in these terms of (in)security at all. The problematic is the possible superimposition of a set of interpretative ideas (security versus insecurity) onto a range of religious ideas and practices that may actually bear no relevance to the ways in which these ideas and practices are understood locally. A superimposition of an analytical dichotomy between religious behaviour classified as either leading to security or to insecurity may become a dangerous undertaking if this becomes part of a North-Atlantic and academic invention of the 'Other'.

In recent debates on social security, the definition of the term has changed. It now includes the informal and, explicitly, the social, moving away from institutional definitions based on the meaning of the term *social security* that date from the 1930s, when the concept was introduced as an institution in the United States:

> Social security as the dimension of social organization dealing with the provision of security not considered to be an exclusive matter of individual responsibility....

> Social security is seen as a quality of social relationships and institutions, ideologies, philosophies, ethics, policy programmes and sets of rules. It can also refer to human interactions through which plans are made to have them transferred in the future. It can further be used to indicate the relative state of security, thus referring to the economic and social position of actual persons. Finally it refers to resources used for the purpose of reducing insecurity. (F. von Benda-Beckman and K. von Benda-Beckman 1994: 14, 15)

Moving away from an institutional level of analysis, this etic definition of social security still harbours normative notions that may not exist at the emic level of understanding. The most elementary of these is that social security implies a Durkheimian perception of society as leading by definition to the well-being of its members. Implicit in this understanding is the idea that societies strive towards a minimisation of risk, uncertainty and vulnerability by creating structures, such as the state, to take responsibility for the provisioning of security.

It is assumed in this interpretation that people and social formations regard vulnerability and insecurity as something to be avoided as far as possible (Alwang et al. 2001). Very little of the literature pursues the study of vulnerability and insecurity in the positive, that is, the attempt to arrive at an understanding of how and why certain groups and societies may not perceive these things to be solely negative, but view them as a normal, perhaps even desirable state. In poor or high-risk environments characterised by war, climate change, drought, HIV/AIDS or lack of access to resources, for example, people live in a permanent state of crisis or insecurity. Crises and related insecurities are experienced daily, and thus become accepted and integrated into their social structures (see, e.g., de Bruijn and H. van Dijk 1995). In such situations, the notion of social security becomes obsolete, as the distinction between security and insecurity is harder to identify.

Furthermore, the nature of the social security concept is ideological and serves to obscure realities on the ground. The concept should be scrutinised more in terms of what it hides than what it reveals about these social realities and the workings of power. Linking religious practices to the process by which people and societies try to manoeuvre out of situations of vulnerability and insecurity – for example, by organising systems of charity and gifting – is a research question, not a fact. Religions may contain elaborate ideologies that emphasise the bliss of suffering as indispensable to religious salvation (for Africa, see Werbner 1997). However, both views are linked to a utilitarian perspective of religion that does not always fit African realities, since it is based on an often normative and etic understanding of these relations.

In exploring a possible relationship between religion and the gift as social security provisioning, can we assume this normative understanding of how religion functions as operating for the greater good of all? A second question is whether religion should be understood ambiguously as creating security and insecurity at one and the same time. Can we assume a sense of optimism in the ways, albeit religiously based, in which the social provides people with the means to cope with these insecurities? The third fundamental question is whether religion and its practices can be linked to coping – that is, whether religion is a tool that allows people to cope or one with which they are obliged to cope.

The underlying problematic is how we consider religion. If we view it as part of, or even productive of, social organisation, how should this be understood in an African context? Both perspectives – religion as coping/creating security and as being coped with/creating insecurity – commonly assume an etic and objectifying position, whereby religion remains at a distance, distinguishable from the social in that it becomes either an instrument for utilitarian purposes or a *Fremdkörper* (outside entity) through which the social could suffer. We cannot assume that religion in Africa has taken the institutionalised forms it frequently has in the West (Müller 2000). The extent to which this institutionalisation has taken place differs considerably across the continent and from one religion to another. With state formation, religion has come to belong to a separate domain in the West, particularly in its organised and institutionalised forms, a process that has taken quite a different trajectory in Africa, and from an emic and subjectifying position must take into account the fact that religion is deeply embedded in the patterns, structures and sentiments of everyday life. This makes it hard, for instance, to discern whether the power to deal with situations is political or religious in nature, as these two are often conflated. In this contribution we look at the relationship between religion and social security, moving beyond an instrumentalised and etic notion of religion. It is vital to understand that there are varying degrees to which religion is set apart from society in an African context, and that consequently religion is not merely a tool with 'functions', but to a great extent inherent in people's daily lives and their ideas about the future. As such, it can be considered emically as a philosophy of life that guides people's actions and thoughts.

To understand the emic view of the relationship between religious thoughts and social security, we must step outside the etic view and its underlying normative assumption that religion exists to serve the common good. This problematic has also been noted in the study of social capital (see Fine 2002), where religion is investigated under the aspect of how it produces associational life, trust, confidence and reciprocities that tend to obfuscate many of the other tendencies religion may espouse to, particularly the way they are understood at the emic level. On the one hand, contradicting tendencies may exist in how religious forms and organisations foster and produce inequality, exploitation and oppression, that is, in the way religion is also the bearer of insecurities. The question remains as to how these situations are experienced and explained by the people themselves.

Certain activities undertaken by religious groups in Africa can produce security, no matter how rudimentary, in an emic understanding of things. The most obvious are gift-giving relations, which sometimes take the form of charity, whereby religious bodies organise the collection of money or donations in kind, and arrange for a form of sharing among those most in need. This can range from alms-giving to the poor and needy to the establishment of religious associations that play a role in organizing funerals, weddings or birth rituals, occasions when members may need additional support. Unlike social security, people/members cannot presume a *right* to these reciprocal relations (which contradicts the notion of social security that defines itself as a system of rights and obligations). The question remains as to whether, perceived emically, one can speak of a rudimentary type of social security in these forms of support. In the context of Islam and Pentecostalism, we will examine below the extent to which relations emerge from the process of gift giving and shed light on their provisioning of security or insecurity in the social and cultural domain.

We propose a comparison between a specific form of Christianity, Pentecostalism, and Sufi Islam as is common in West and Central Africa. The religious ideology of Pentecostalism emphasises (critical) distance to cultural traditions – unlike Islamic religious forms, which are deeply embedded in the local cultural and social fabric, and pursue a project of profound integration into society. Pentecostalism may even urge its members to sever linkages with forms of social security that exist locally, proclaiming to develop alternative social security arrangements through systems of gift giving and reciprocity. Does this in fact take place and if so, does it improve the situation of the needy? Does it intend to do so, and is it obliged to in an emic perception of the role of religion in society? In the case of Islam in the Sahelian countries of

Africa, social security mechanisms in gift giving appear to be deeply engrained in the social fabric, not with the aim of replacing customary and cultural forms of social-security provisioning but as ideological and practical forms for those in need. Here again the question is whether it achieves its ideological goal or whether there are hidden transcripts that indicate otherwise, once the etic is shifted to the emic understanding of these relations.

The two case studies demonstrate that vulnerability and suffering are valued highly in these ideologies. From a utilitarian perspective, that is, foregrounding how these religions diminish or foster securities or insecurities, we need to explain how local people are 'realising' instead of 'using' religion. By concentrating on gift-giving practices and their social and institutional frameworks, we will show that although we might share the perception of a social security function in these religious practices, it seems in reality not to be the case. Even in situations where social security appears to be the hidden moral force behind religious gift giving, we can not superimpose an utilitarian and instrumentalised perception in the local people's understanding of their involvement in emic terms. While the aim of gift giving may not be to reduce suffering, vulnerability or insecurity, the subjective view might, on the other hand, be to prolong this state in the pursuit of religious truths.

Gifting as Security in Pentecostalism?

In considering whether practices of giving, money collection and reciprocities lead to forms of social security in African Pentecostalism, we should bear in mind the following warning by Taussig (1995: 393):

> And while the devil contract can be seen as a striking, if morbid, confirmation of the gift principle as balanced exchange, the gift of largesse being paid for by the dissemination of barrenness and death, what I now see as special to it and deserving emphasis is its sheer excessiveness … the overflowing 'too-muchness' of its key terms … and the dreadful proximity here of the gift to death, of creation to destruction.

Although not referring to Pentecostalism as such, he makes the point that in studying religion in Latin America and how certain gifts are meant to produce devil contracts, the gift cannot a priori be seen as producing reciprocities or other securities. Contrary to Mauss, there is nothing inherently secure in the way gifting leads to the reproduction of society or the preservation and continuation of the social body, since gifts can result in illicit accumulation, excess and even death. These considerations are particularly relevant to understanding the significance of gifting in African Pentecostal circles, where the centrality of giving money and other items has been noted by many (see Maxwell

1998; van Dijk 1999, 2002, 2005; Meyer 1999). These studies highlight the fact that giving, and giving abundantly to the church even in circumstances of dire poverty, is a key ideological and ritual practice of the numerous Pentecostal churches that have sprung up all over sub-Saharan Africa. However, few studies have investigated whether this can be seen as a form of social security provisioning. These churches thrive on their gifting practices, and the enormous amount of money involved occasionally makes them vulnerable to the public criticism that they are simply money-making enterprises. This also relates to their predominantly social image of being churches for groups in society that have middle-class aspirations or already belong to the emerging urban middle classes of professionals, white-collar workers and business men and women in the rapidly expanding cities of sub-Saharan Africa.

A wide range of fellowships and ministries in these churches generate money for specific purposes with the practice of gifting. Some of these have burial societies or offer support to their members in times of financial need. While all of this could be described from the perspective of a social security paradigm, the real question is what precisely is the relationship between giving and social security. If social security is understood as the ways through which certain social practices become functional and are constituent of societal continuity, reproduction, order and survival, we may need to recall Taussig's caveat that the gift does not necessarily coincide with this; if it leads to discontinuity and failure of reproduction and order, why then should the gift be understood as spawning social security in the first place?

The dimensions of gifting money in African Pentecostalism extend from the moral and the spiritual to the economic and the political. Hence, giving in the context of ministries and fellowships that offer support to church members is merely one of many possible contexts in which the gift emerges as a vital element of this ideology. The significance and implication of the gift is different in each context, particularly with respect to its 'security outcomes', if they exist at all.

The Gift Economy and Morality in Pentecostalism

Broadly speaking, there are two separate contexts surrounding the giving and collecting of money in Pentecostal churches. The first is the collection at church meetings, the second is the ministry and fellowship networks that fulfil specific functions on behalf of the church membership and thus act as support associations.

The three main types of giving are tithing, offering, and harvesting, all of which are contributed by members and visitors at the Sunday church meetings. Tithing is the process by which people donate 10 per cent of their net income to the church on a monthly basis and is regarded as the scriptural law to which all Bible-believing Christians must adhere. It consolidates a person's status as a confirmed believer and full member of the church. Churches keep records of tithing and urge their members to be faithful, a task they are reminded of almost every Sunday.

While tithing provides churches with regular financial resources, the second context of giving also occurs during the central Sunday meetings and is referred to as 'offering'. In Pentecostalism from Malawi to Ghana to Botswana (van Dijk 2001, 2003a, 2003b), the general pattern confirms much of what has been written about the accumulation that takes place at these moments. A power play typically evolves in how members and visitors alike are encouraged – if not pressurised – to give freely to the church, with the pledge that God will repay these gifts bountifully. Due to their elaborate healing practices, these churches receive frequent visitors who maintain clientelist relations without becoming full members or participating in networks. While members are expected to comply with the law of tithing, they also take part along with non-members in large gifting 'tournaments' (Appadurai 1986), where competition in giving is promoted. During these collections, pastors shout at their audiences to come forward with as much money as possible. Dancing and singing, the entire congregation – sometimes a crowd of thousands – moves forward to put money into the bowls near the pulpit. Coins are not considered acceptable, and since these public offerings are visible to all, most people contribute banknotes.

The third and most important form of giving in terms of the amount collected is the 'harvest', when members are expected to give generously for specific goals decided upon by the church leadership. This symbolic harvesting is significant in that it enables members or visitors to gain a certain status in the community, as competitiveness in giving is encouraged. It commonly takes the form of the 'highest bidder', where the pastor demands an exorbitant sum of money, thereby exhorting the audience to come forward. Whoever does so is applauded and publicly acclaimed. The pastor then lessens the amount slightly and a new round begins until the sums requested are so low as to no longer warrant public respect.

The amount of money collected in this manner is substantial, and perceived as a sign of the strength of the church and its leadership and the benevolence of the heavenly powers. Church leaders frequently enjoy a life of luxury on the basis of this accumulation, something that is essentially expected of them and interpreted as a sign of divine benevolence, although part of the money is used for church spin-off activities. Investments are made in books, pamphlets, videos, and technical equipment, for example, and in church buildings or Bible schools. Numerous activities in the gift economy serve to reinforce the church's position in the public domain. For the members, however, the act of giving, offering and harvesting is to be understood as linked to the process of making meaning, which will be explored in the next section.

The second context of giving, that is, offering, in the Pentecostal church involves the ministries and fellowships organised in its network. These organisations usually operate with a specific purpose, such as to give members moral instruction and support in male and female fellowship groups, or to establish marriage and funeral committees (van Dijk 2004). As a rule, donations are given on a monthly basis and systems specifying when members can draw on their (financial) support are in place. Contributions tend to be smaller than those made at gifting tournaments, and membership varies considerably. Members who do not contribute cannot expect assistance, since there is a strong sense of reciprocity. This may, however, depend on the status of the person in the church or community. Support tends to gravitate towards people of higher status, whereas those of lower status may find it harder to count on reciprocities.

The many ways of giving and the crucial importance of a gift economy for these churches begs the question of why people engage in these diverse forms of giving, of the type of social security elements attached, and the meaning of the gift economy in cultural terms from the perspective of the members and visitors.

Meaning and Message in Pentecostal Giving

Many aspects of the tournaments of excessive gifting extend beyond expectations of reciprocity, as evidenced in the way members literally speak to the banknotes they put in church envelopes. They imbue their gifts with messages and sentiments with the intention of 'personalising' the money that would otherwise remain impersonal (van Dijk 2005). In Ghana, this act relates above all to expectations of prosperity. Described as a 'prosperity gospel' by some (see Gifford 2004; Ter Haar 1998), and often interpreted as an escapist religion in the socio-economic context of poverty, political instability and impeded development, the promise of prosperity made by these churches is believed to be of a strictly personal nature. Giving money with the hope of becoming prosperous refers to an ideology in which the onus of mollifying the powers above to bestow bounty on the giver is placed firmly on the individual. Hence these contexts of giving are embedded in the 'prayers for a million' that require certain bodily postures representing the symbolic receipt of vast sums of money from heaven. Lengthy ecstatic prayers, for which the Pentecostals have become renowned, are meant to create a 'breakthrough' in personal circumstances and the spiritual forces that block the arrival of such prosperity. The fact that the latter frequently fails to materialise and a breakthrough is nowhere in sight is explained by the leadership in terms of moral laxity and spiritual weakness on the part of the respective Pentecostal believer.

This produces a context of direct contestation and rivalry with the many other contexts and conditions of belief that exist in a society where gifts also impinge on the sense of well-being and the world of spiritual forces. Excessive giving in the context of these Pentecostal meetings and the breakthroughs they are deemed to summon act in confrontation with and in contestation of the world of deities, which the Pentecostal ideology tends to demonise. In other words, by giving excessively, believers can demonstrate that they are free or are vying to free themselves of 'entrapment' by greedy forces from the realms of the ancestors and deities that inhabit the rivers and the sea. The idea behind the public testimonies of individual members is to attest to this success; the relations with ancestral and other deities have been successfully severed, relations that would otherwise have kept the believer bound to gift-giving relations to their shrines. Overindulgent gift giving thus breaks with other relations, as it refutes responsibilities vis-à-vis kinship relations, the wider family and its ancestral guardians. The simple logic here is: what is given in the church cannot be spent elsewhere; neither can it be used to meet family obligations or for practices of ancestral veneration.

This is of concern for the messages that gifts carry. Van Dijk (1999, 2002, 2005) has analysed how and why Pentecostals view gifting as inherently dangerous. If giving involves the obligation to receive, the money and objects Pentecostals receive from outside the immediate Pentecostal context could cause danger as a result of the intentions imbued. Examples abound of how giving and reciprocity have led to increasing uncertainty as to the danger gifts can harbour. The most common response is for gifts to be consecrated during the process of acceptance and receipt, mostly through intense prayer (*nteho*). To use Pentecostal rhetoric here, the 'blood of Christ' must be poured over the gift to neutralise the potentially harmful powers it may have been infused with. The most suspicious gifts are those that come from the immediate family circle and kin, since danger of bewitchment in this form is not unlikely, and is greatly feared. Moments of gift giving are therefore accompanied by prayers, which are considered the most effective method of calling on the assistance of the powers above. Pentecostal leaders are true 'men of God' in the sense that although they are the receivers of the gifts offered, they appear not to be immune to the potential harm these gifts might cause.

While an all too easy interpretation of this position of ordinary members vis-à-vis the Pentecostal gift might argue that the Pentecostal churches afford greater security from danger, the opposite is true in reality. The Pentecostal ideology fosters insecurities, and as a result of the massive Pentecostalism of the public domain in many parts of Africa, much of its rhetoric and practices produces uncertainties. On the one hand, Pentecostal leaders claim that they merely make their members aware of the many dangers that exist and of the requirements for the receipt of heavenly benevolence in the form of prosperity. They warn members of the 'generational curses' ancestral spirits use to entrap living descendants and keep them in bondage, enforcing their veneration on the living and ensuring thereby an entanglement of the believer with the family and the kinship obligations this entails. The Pentecostal demonisation of the world of spirits – with the exception of the one true Holy Spirit – is a vital aspect of the ritual practice of 'deliverance', whereby ancestral bonds are broken, or as a popular slogan in Pentecostal circles emphasises, 'Make a complete break with the past' (see Meyer 1998). The effect is a profound reduction of dependencies within the family structure, leading to a further breakdown of the reciprocities and mutual support that exist at kinship level, since the genuinely devoted Pentecostal believer stands alone.

The consequences for the rudimentary forms of mutual support and security through the family system are enormous, not so much for the up-and-coming middle classes that have belonged to the Pentecostal movement since its inception in the early 1960s, but for the lower socio-economic strata who have gradually begun to jump on the bandwagon of Pentecostalism. Their vulnerable position in comparison to the more prosperous middle classes makes the risks they take in severing family ties far greater.

Since insecurities only seem to have increased at this level, the question is what kind of security, if any, is gained by becoming a member of a Pentecostal church? Hope of prosperity at the individual level is something akin to a lottery. As Comaroff and Comaroff (2000) indicate, the prosperity gospel of the Pentecostal churches in the current context of the neocapitalist restructuring of African societies adopts many of the features witnessed, for example, in pyramid games, sweepstakes or stock-market speculation, where the potential gains are high but the chances of winning almost nil. The Comaroffs attribute current African interest in taking chances in the face of limited opportunities to the mystified workings of global capital and the hidden sources of unbelievable wealth African populations are exposed to via the media, albeit without hope of participation. We cannot assume that this pursuit of uncertainty lies in a misconception of the capitalist order. Neither are we convinced that the ordinary church member's hope for prosperity is basically informed by an imperfect understanding of the whimsical nature of the global capitalist system or the market, where only the chosen few become inconceivably rich, while the majority are forced to watch from the sidelines. Many Pentecostalists have a consummate understanding of the market and capitalist systems of profit making, and display entrepreneurial skills in organising their affairs, most of which are copied from Western, particularly American, Pentecostal churches. They belong to a global religious structure in which the leaders set an example by becoming religious entrepreneurs par excellence. They run their churches as businesses and view their religious ventures as operating in the national or even international religious market (see van Dijk 2001, 2003a).[1] It is difficult to see 'prayers for a million' as a capitalist delusion, as a form of false consciousness or exotic mystification of the market (Meyer 1999, 2004).

More and more people face insecurities and uncertainties, which are now more prevalent than ever (Durham 2002; for the insecurity of the African middle classes, see Mbembe 2000), and the vagaries of the market and the world capitalist system are hitting local economies as never before. The question is whether becoming a devout member of the Pentecostal church was instigated by a concern or pursuit for greater security. This problematic exists not only in the eyes of the academic beholder of Pentecostalism, but is reflected in how members deal with the choices they have in spending their limited resources. The 'millions' are rarely forthcoming, and as accumulation on the part of the leadership continues to increase, the resources of the church members are gradually dwindling. There are no grounds for the argument that these vast gift-giving economies are locally perceived as working towards greater social security; neither is there a sense of individual security, let alone one of working towards the greater common good.

At first sight, ministries and fellowships, welfare societies and marriage and funeral committees active within the structures of these churches appear to have the function of generating a lively discourse and practise that relate to notions of support. These associations can loosely be defined as a network, albeit the clientelist nature of such relations should not be misunderstood (i.e. people 'activate' them only in times of need). Yet here again it is difficult to see how these church-based associations produce greater security, since their support in financial terms is usually minimal. The latter tends to be biased towards those who have higher status in the church (leading to even greater inequality).

Studying how marriage committees in Accra, Ghana, function, for instance, revealed that the reciprocity they offered in the form of financial donations and specific gifts to the family of the bride on behalf of the prospective husband's church seemed in reality to sanction inspection and moral supervision of the marriage relationship by the church leadership. The vast amount of money required for weddings and funerals (in Ghana often running to millions of cedis) to cover large parties, expensive clothes, gifts for important family members etc. reduces the contribution from church coffers to little more than a token. An ongoing public debate in Ghana addresses the mounting cost of these life-changing events, which deplete family resources significantly. It can be read as a debate on risk-taking and entrepreneurship, but the real issue is how to make a profit despite the huge investments required for such extensive gift-giving practices.

While these events take on a form reminiscent of a potlatch, the contribution from church associations is negligible, and does not genuinely produce 'security'. Nevertheless, it does place them under Pentecostal scrutiny (see Van Dijk 2004). Alcohol is not served, the pouring of a libation in honour of the gods does not take place, there is no indecent dancing, and drunkenness or

immoral behaviour is considered unacceptable. This church allows for implementation of a moral regime, a critical approach to culture and the pursuit
of modernity, which in itself is difficult to capture in a security vs. insecurity
dichotomy. The latter two aspects are either diminished or increased, as the
Pentecostal message, ideology and practice is neither informed nor geared
towards such considerations.

Hence while the institutional features of Pentecostalism can certainly be
explored, allowing for a straightforward study of how it relates to social security
in an African setting, the findings indicate the problematic of the social security concept. This conclusion must take into account the features of the type of
religion under review, and perceive them as deeply engrained in society and
less focused on creating distance. They are also less preoccupied with replacing existing cultural forms, since religion itself has become the cultural form
through which key aspects of everyday life are organised. Islam in the Sahelian
areas of Africa provides for such an example. The question is whether religion
has penetrated society to such an extent that its social security endeavour war-
rants greater functionality. In other words, does it produce social security, and
does it produce social security more effectively and more meaningfully?

The Gift in Islamic Sahelian Societies

This section looks into the signification of the gift for people defined as vulnerable in an Islamic and Sahelian context. The practices of giving and begging are
explained in religious terms in these Sahelian-Islamic cultures. The Sahelian
economy is poverty ridden, and many people in this zone face severe economic struggles. Illiteracy rates are high, official health care is almost nonex-
istent, while state provision of aid and social security is entirely lacking. This is
a region where informal social security could be expected to flourish and societies to have developed systems of mutual aid. However, as shown in earlier
studies of this region (de Bruijn and H. van Dijk 1995; de Bruijn 1999, 2000),
informal social security is merely rudimentary and can be explained by the
covariance of risk (Platteau 1991): it is difficult to share nothing. People asking for alms are commonly seen in this area and begging has adopted almost
institutional forms, for example, among the old or the Koranic students.

The manner in which Islamic practices have become an integral part of
society makes gift giving appear a manifestation of religious duties, initially
at the level of doctrine. Giving to the needy is a central theme in Islamic texts
and rules, and constitutes one of the five pillars of Islam. The payment of *zakat*
and *sadaqa* is the most prominent gift form in the Islamic system. *Zakat* is
the obligatory annual head tax to be equally divided across society. *Sadaqa*,
a smaller gift, is given by the rich to the poor on a daily basis. The rich are

also called upon to give on numerous other occasions, for example, *zakat al fiti/adahi al hajj, al wasiyya* and *al waqf*.[2] Al-Marzouqi (2000) explains these Islamic gifts and taxes as elements of Islamic ideology that address charity, giving and sharing. He argues that in Islamic theories, economic rights and social security rules are clearly defined. The Koran states that 'unemployment and begging are considered unlawful unless there is a justifiable excuse' (Al Marzouqi 2000: 295). Directing man's natural temperament towards developing human welfare, (Al Marzouqi 2000: 310) where kin are central, is a strong feature of Islamic economic regulations: 'Kin have rights to maintenance of their family. The economic regulations ... lead to a financially self-sufficient family. This in its turn reduces the financial burden of the state in providing people with social security benefit, and *zakat* replaces social security of the state' (Al Marzouqi 2000: 311). This official 'translation' of the Islamic rules for a broader public describes the importance of giving and of the assistance received. What the gift entails for the receiver, however, is not discussed. Is giving, and thus the act of giving, more significant than the effect the said gift has on those at the receiving end?

Benthall (1999) concludes from an anthropological analysis of *zakat* and *sadaqa* that the gift in Islam presupposes inequality and is ideologically beneficial to both parties. While the benefit to the poor is adequately explained above, the advantage to the giver is less obvious. Gilliard (2005: 48) explored 'giving' and 'begging' in Islamic societies in Niger, and presents the following observation on the act of giving:

> Acte purificatoire, dépense noble dans l'islam, l'aumône est la manifestation de l'établissement d'un système spirituel opposé aux formes de dons ritualisés. Avec l'Islam comme avec la modernité on assiste au passage d'une société de tradition axée sur la circularité des biens de l'échange entre le donateur et le donataire, avec une création de lien social à une société axée sur le don démonstratif basé sur la seule intention spirituelle du donateur indifférent au donataire. Raffirmé sa conscience ou son statut auprès de la divinité.[3]

He goes on to explain that structural inequality is seen as indispensable to realising Islamic expectations of bliss, arguing: 'L'importance de l'aumône est fondamentale pour les croyants, car elle débarrasse en eux l'égoisme et permet de nourrir certaines qualités nécessaires que développement spirituel' (Gilliard 2005: 50).[4] This again stresses that the significance of giving in these Islamic contexts is greater for the giver – who receives *baraka*[5] – than the effect such a gift might have on the receiver, although gifts may generally provide relief and contribute to the alleviation of poverty. This, however, may not be the ultimate meaning of the gift for believers. As Aminata Sow (2001) so eloquently put it: 'Non, mes amis, ils s'en foutent. Notre faim ne les dérange pas. Ils ont besoin de donner pour survivre et si nous n'existions pas, à qui donneraient-ils? Comment assureraient-ils leur tranquillité d'esprit? Ce n'est pas pour nous qu'ils donnent c'est pour eux! Ils ont besoin de nous pour vivre en paix!'[6] Despite a ban on begging in the official doctrine, the rich seem to have an urgent need to give to the poor, that is, if there is a need, then begging is allowed (Al Marzouqi 2000). These observations guide us to the core meaning of the gift in Muslim societies in the Sahel, which may not fit the social security model but should be primarily considered as a pathway to Allah.

Islamic Gift Practices in the Sahel

Social hierarchies in the Sahel have a grounding in Islamic belief and practices. Hierarchies between masters and slaves are not condemned by Islam, nor have they been abolished in Islamic beliefs and practices. On the contrary, it seems that hierarchies are accepted as part of life and related to the interpretation of insecurities as they exist in the region. Beck (1992) felt that risks were unevenly distributed across the population and that some people carried more than others. Hierarchies of insecurity keep certain people at the deep end of the insecurity burden, that is, the slaves of the past are the penniless of today (de Bruijn and H. van Dijk 2004). The explanation of *zakat* and *sadaqa* as given in Muslim law subscribes to this hierarchy: what the rich give to the poor will never be enough to escape poverty. Since Islamic welfare requires a hierarchy based on wealth differences, inequality is accepted and has become an integral part of the ideology of social order. Begging is an institutionalised form of survival fully sanctioned by society and simultaneously a prerequisite for wealthy Muslims to become 'good' Muslims.

The meaning of Islamic gifts in Central Mali among the pastoral Fulbe (who consider themselves Muslim) has been widely documented. Nonetheless, it should be explored how these gifts are given and to what extent they fit the religious model sketched above: the *zakat* and *sadaqa* gifts are often engrained in personal relations, and were mostly given to a poor mother and the old aunt in the next hut (de Bruijn 1994). On the other hand, because poor people in this society have a sense of shame, they may decide to leave the area altogether despite the possibility of help from their kin in the form of Islamic gifts (de Bruijn 1999).

The dynamics of the gift described in the paragraph above point to a complexity in the relationship between Islam and social security similar to that noted in the previous section for Pentecostalism. This relationship is not automatic or self-evident and could well turn out to be contrary to what is expected, if seen from an emic perspective. While help and support in the first instance seem indeed to be the meaning of gift giving or the desired effect of the religious gift, it should be considered subjectively as a religious endeavour, a pathway to God and the reflection of a specific social order, and not as the provision of social security in an etic understanding of the term. Similar to Pentecostalism, gift giving in the Islamic context appears to operate at the level of individual control and supervision of a moral position in society, of moral behaviour in the pursuit of both heavenly bliss and comfort, as well as this-worldly prosperity and fortune. In these religious-cum-moral perspectives, inequalities and insecurities should not be resolved but instead fostered and accepted as a natural and God-given way of life in pursuit of a future state of benevolence. The improvement of social security is, as such, contradictory to the systems of *zakat* and *sadaqa*, and therefore not a desirable objective.

This is particularly striking when we take a closer look at the world of the child, and the way in which Islam in these societies cannot be seen to produce greater security, not even for those who need it most. Here again, the way in which religion produces insecurities is fundamental to understanding how systems of gift giving work. While religion thus simultaneously produces securities and insecurities, even in the context of the most vulnerable in society, it once more demonstrates that in an attempt to gain greater insight in the nature of such systems, the analytical value of the social security concept becomes obsolete.

Gifts and Vulnerable Children

Koranic schools are a prominent manifestation of Islam in the Sahelian region, and a study of these schools can lead to a better understanding of the specific role of the gift in these societies.

Early in the morning, travellers gather around the coffee stands of the bus stations, while traders drink coffee at similar stands in the markets of small Sahelian towns and cities. They are, however, not the only ones who congregate at these spots. As soon as the sun begins to light up the sky, unwashed children in worn-out clothes, some of them extremely undernourished, others obviously ill, come here to try their luck with the customers, who are eager to begin their day with a gift to someone needy and fulfil Allah's daily quota. The children carry small buckets with them, sometimes containing the remains of last night's meal from the households they visit in the morning, to which some coins or crusts of bread are now added by the customers at the coffee stands.

Once their baskets are filled, the children return to their master, an Islamic scholar and their teacher, and share the food and coins with him. Having completed their first round of begging in the morning, their studies begin. They will now learn another Koranic verse in a further step towards becoming wholly proficient in their knowledge of the Koran; this helps them to feel closer to Allah and to fulfil their parents' wish that they, too, will eventually become Islamic scholars. They travel with their teacher from town to town, occasionally leaving after a few months, sometimes staying for a few years. During the rainy season the teacher may decide to return to the village with his students to work in the fields. The itinerant schools are quite small, varying from one teacher and one pupil to one teacher with eighteen to twenty pupils. As a rule, some of the students are related to the teacher via kin or neighbourly relations.

The children frequently come from families in the countryside whose grandparents had converted to Islam. Although Islamic beliefs were introduced less than two generations ago, its customs and practices and the accompanying new social order have already been internalised. Sending a child to a Koranic school, preferably where the child has to beg and travel, is intrinsic to this practice. The suffering and endurance entailed helps children to pursue the right path and allows them to come closer to Allah. The 'gift' of a child to an Islamic scholar is a gift to God, who will take care of the child (Troch 2006; Keja 2006; de Bruijn 2006).

Villagers who send their children to these schools are often confronted with shortages. The Sahelian environment is frequently hit by drought, harvests are poor and hunger is a constant threat. Recent decades have seen no improvement in the economies of rural Sahelians. On the contrary, impoverishment has forced countless rural inhabitants to move to the urban centres and join the armies of the poor. As Gilliard (2005) described for Niger, Seeseman (2002) for Sudan and de Bruijn (2006) for Chad, numerous families among the urban poor are simply unable to feed their children. Many of these children join Koranic schools and survive by begging for alms and submitting themselves to the school regime. Iliffe (1987) indicated that schools of this kind were also part of Sahelian Islamic societies in the past, and that one of their functions was to sustain these children. At a certain level, the schools provide a form of social security, both for the children as well as for the families who can barely feed them (Seeseman 2002).

From a local perspective, however, Islamic teachers in northern Mali deny that these schools are a fallback system for poor families, declaring them to be first and foremost of religious significance. What children endure as a result of being separated from their families, and the hunger they experience are all part of the suffering to be borne in pursuit of Allah's path (Troch 2006). Daily begging is based on the exchange of gifts and blessings (*baraka*). The child who receives a gift blesses the donor, an act that brings the recipient closer to God.

Zooming in on itinerant schools in Chad, where poverty is widespread and children are among the most vulnerable, reveals how these schools produce social (in)security and religious (in)security and deal with their negotiation. The following case makes it particularly clear that the schools should be regarded as a social institution that socialises children into a Sahelian way of life on a moral and normative basis, without necessarily improving their 'security' status.

Mongo, a town of some 20,000 inhabitants in central Chad, hosted at least ninety itinerant Koranic schools in the dry season of 2003 (April), whose teachers and students came from villages of up to 200 kilometres away. Approximately 1,000 children from impoverished rural areas attended these schools. Harvests in recent decades have been less than meagre, while the deprivation that followed Chad's long civil war (1965–1990) has become the rule. Mongo itself is by no means a rich town, but has a regular economic life, with traders and a weekly market. Koranic students are frequent visitors to the market, not as buyers but as beggars. In addition, they make their way from house to house mornings and evenings requesting food or other gifts. However, their physical condition clearly betrays that they are undernourished. Our involvement with these schools in Mongo drove us to the hospital, to the cemetery and gradually to despair. In discussions with teachers (often Western-educated people working in the social sector of the town), this practice was defended, not condemned. The teachers were adamant that it was their responsibility and not that of the community to look after the children, although the onus to give did lie with the community. They stood by their system of schools and gifts, and despite their shock at the children's plight, they did not condemn the situation. As a doctrine of Islam, they found it perfectly acceptable.

This state of affairs was categorically condemned by the imam at the main mosque in Mongo. A modern man, he teaches at the French-Arabic school *medersa*, which has much in common with Western-based schools. The children who attend these schools do not go out begging. The imam regarded the itinerant school as part of the traditional past, and his critique focused on teachers who allow children to live in such conditions, and less on the system of learning itself. He did not mention the word *begging* during the interviews. As an imam, on the other hand, he cannot exclude this phenomenon from his modern outlook, since begging appears to be accepted in the vicinity of his own mosque during and after Friday prayers. The beggars, the old, the young, the sick and the handicapped, all come and sit in front of the mosque. Those who attend prayers and hear the imam's words ringing in their ears donate their share of *sadaqa*. The food that is prepared for the poor and needy in the courtyard of the mosque every Friday also benefits the children of the itinerant Koranic schools.

A conference in Mongo in 2004 discussed the position of these schools and their students. Meetings were attended by NGOs, Islamic teachers from various Koranic schools, the imam of the large mosque in Mongo and various Koranic students. Discussions centred on the conditions under which students are obliged to live and on their poor physical condition. The various opinions voiced made it clear that there was no one version of how Koranic schools should be run, and no explanation given as to the significance of begging and suffering. It did, however, transpire that begging *is* allowed under all circumstances. It was also explained that the wandering student is a reference to the prophet himself, who travelled when he was young. Travelling was perceived as bringing believers closer to God. The participants agreed that the Muslim community should take care of these children, that is, give them food. The gift is therefore a key element of the system. If it does not suffice, who is to blame?

These discussions demonstrate that, from a local perspective, practices of gift giving and begging, institutionalised as they may be in the context of Koranic schools, do not relate to social security and how it can be obtained and structured, whom it is to serve and whether or not security objectives have been achieved. Security is simply not part of the ideology, practice or rhetoric; neither is it the aim of this embedded local practice. Although it does not suggest a lack of concern by local people, such as teachers and imams, for the predicament of these children, the system of gift giving simply serves other (and in the local view, more important) goals.

While an exploration of the relationship between Islam and social security provisioning might lead us at first sight to consider Koranic schools as one of the most vital if not obvious methods of providing security, the reality is quite different. The idea of security operates here solely on an ideological, moral level, providing an impetus for gift giving in a context that might best be framed as purely ideological security. Similar to Pentecostalism, the pursuit of security in ideological and moral terms, which these systems of gift giving appear to foster, renders a modernist dichotomy between security and insecurity meaningless. In the context of Islam, the safeguarding of moral and ideological principles is likewise considered more crucial to and directive of such practices than any real or imagined need to reduce insecurities. In other words, the driving force behind these systems is not informed by a desire to reduce insecurity in exchange for greater social security in our common understanding of the term.

Conclusion

Despite the differences between the two cases, with Pentecostalism described as placing itself in a position of critique vis-à-vis cultural traditions and Islam in the Sahel as far more engrained in traditions, they reveal a similar picture with regard to the relationship between the religious gift and social security. Both cases make it clear that although people live in problematic circumstances, that is, in the Sahel with the vagaries of ecology and the economy, and in the case of Pentecostalism with the economic insecurities and uncertainties of neoliberalism, the distinction between security and insecurity is of no great analytical value. The religious practice of the gift prepares people to accept the religious moral order as it is, instead of placing this practice in an insecurity versus security dichotomy, which would make the gift subject to a project of moving as far as possible away from insecurity in the direction of security. A project of this kind does not exist, however, nor can it be seen as an unintended spin-off or side-effect of these systems of gift giving in the eyes of the etic beholder.

Social security may not be the principal significance members of these societies attach to gift giving in an emic understanding of the practice. It appears that although a religion may be close to the people, embedded in the cultural and social norms of a specific society, it does not lead to a better provisioning in terms of social security. Although a gift might signify relief for the receiving party, which is frequently kin in the case of Islam, the Sahelian example has shown that this can hardly be labelled social security, as it is always partial. In African Pentecostal churches, the religious emphasis on gift giving is not geared to furthering the common good, but primarily serves the purpose of accumulation in the interests of its leadership.

Yet, if we take an etic position, there is little room for naivety about the aims and purposes of charities, however much they may focus on strengthening the position of the poor or other marginalized groups in society. While their ideologies may be discursively formulated and legitimised in terms of creating social security, where other institutes (the state, the family, traditional leaders) have failed in this context, the underlying aims of such charity serve other goals. If we accept this etic perspective, both cases show that the religious gift explicitly condones or maintains social inequalities and insecurities precisely because they are believed to be part of a 'natural' or God-given order of society, whereby the rich give to the poor and in exchange receive heavenly salvation. Here, religion does not venture to reverse the inequalities and insecurities of society, but instead produces an ideology that explains this order in religious terms, attaching meaning and significance to it for the spiritual salvation of its members. These societal processes and structures will never be detected by employing the concept of social security. Our point is that these religious groups we are talking about do not maintain an 'agenda', a 'project', an 'idea' of social security and there is no reason to superimpose that notion when it does not lead to greater analytical clarity. These groups may give to and lend support to the 'very poor', yet may not have ideas, structures or ideologies that would enhance a notion or practice of 'social security', nor ideas of how 'giving' may or may not contribute to social security. We are not arguing that these groups have no role for social security nor do we propose that these groups lack social security. Instead we demonstrate that we are not able to structure our interpretation of practices of giving/reciprocity around the concept of social security because of the superimposition of a particular interpretation this implies. Our point is therefore that the paradigmatic point of departure of social security remains problematic.

For the Pentecostal style of individuality, giving is an avenue for the expression of messages, sentiments and intentions, whereby the question of more or less security for the members and their social environment is not a priori relevant. Through giving, members are able to express a sense of individuality that aspires, on the one hand, to participation in modern domains of life in urban places, in transnational connections, in entrepreneurial activity and so forth, and, on the other hand, qualifies and critically approaches socio-cultural aspects of identity that relate to the family, tradition and the world of the ancestors. In this sense the discourse is not about security, despite the hardships a country like Ghana is facing as a result of a declining economy and the impact of World Bank/IMF-induced Structural Adjustment Programmes that seem to be hitting the middle classes hardest.

In Sahelian societies the gift serves as a 'pathway to Allah', both for those who give and those who receive. The issue of security for children was raised by people confronted with a modern discourse on aid and children's rights. Nevertheless, they frequently adhere to giving as a means of being closer to God and of being modern. For people living with uncertainty and the vagaries of the climate, striving for security is an accepted phenomenon. Since the situation seems irreversible, it is more preferable to strive for a place in paradise nearer to God. The term *ideological security* can be applied to Islamic societies in the Sahel, albeit with the realisation that this implies the continued existence of hierarchies in society.

These reflections on religion and social security lead us to conclude that there is no automatic marriage between the two, especially not when we take the emic view. Implicit in the social security concept that is mainly etically defined, is the modernist assumption of progress, that is, the endeavour of societies to improve the well-being of their members. This developmental belief does not grasp the realities of the societies we have discussed. The very fact of an implied dichotomy between insecurity and security prevents the concept of social security from grasping realities on the ground in the analysis of the relationship between religion and society.

Notes

1. In so doing, these Pentecostal churches contradict many of the ways in which earlier Christian missions organised local churches and congregations. The Christian mission churches did not exist in isolation but were part of a larger, overarching church structure, in which pastors did not act independently, since they were seen to occupy an 'office' and not their own 'enterprise', as is the case in Pentecostalism. This difference in church structure and authority between mainline Christian churches and Pentecostalists is crucial to understanding the innovation this entrepreneurial style of Pentecostal religious organisation represented in Africa.

2. *Zakat al fiti/adahi al hajj, al wasiyya* and *al waqf* are different forms of Islamic taxes.

3. As an act of purification and a noble spending in Islamic customs, the gift is a manifestation of the establishment of a spiritual system as opposed to the ritualised gift. Comparable to transformations related to modernity, with the coming of Islam we observe the transformation of a traditional society in which the circulation of goods between giver and receiver is central to a social relation in which the demonstrative gift is the main intention of the giver irrespective of the position of the receiver. An act that confirms the status of the giver vis-à-vis the holy God/divinity.

4. The gift is of fundamental importance for the believers, because it permits them certain egoism to nourish qualities that are deemed necessary for their spiritual development.

5. *Baraka* means 'blessing', comparable to 'benediction' in a church context, but here blessings that come from Allah.

6. No, my friends, they do not care. Our hunger is no problem for them. They need to give in order to survive and if we did not exist, to whom would they give? How would they ascertain their spiritual tranquillity? It is not for us that they give but for themselves! They need us to live in peace!

References

Al-Marzouqi, I. A. 2000. *Human Rights in Islamic law*. Abu Dhabi: n.p.

Alwang, J., P. B. Siegel and S. L. Jorgensen. 2001. 'Vulnerability: A View from Different Disciplines', *Social Protection Discussion Paper* no. 0015. Washington, DC: The World Bank, http://www.worldbank.org/sp.

Appadurai, A. 1986. *The Social Life of Things: Commodities in Cultural Perspective*. Cambridge, Cambridge University Press.

Beck, U. 1992. *Risk Society: Towards a New Modernity*. London: Sage Publications.

Benda-Beckmann, F. von and K. von Benda-Beckmann. 1994. 'Introduction', in *Coping with Insecurity: An 'Underall' Perspective on Social Security in the Third World*, ed. F. von Benda-Beckmann, K. von Benda-Beckmann and H. Marks. *Focaal* 22/23: 7–35.

Benthall, J. 1999. 'Financial Worship: The Quranic Injunction to Almsgiving', in *Man, Anthropological Institute* (N.S.) 5(1): 27–42.

Comaroff, J. and J. Comaroff. 2000. 'Privatizing the Millennium: New Protestant Ethics and the Spirits of Capitalism in Africa, and Elsewhere'. *Afrika Spectrum* 35(3): 293–312.

De Bruijn, M. 1994. 'Coping with Crisis in Sahelian Africa: Fulani Pastoralists and Islam', in *Coping with Insecurity: An 'Underall' Perspective on Social Security in the Third World*, ed. F. von Benda-Beckmann, K. von Benda-Beckmann and H. Marks. *Focaal* 22/23: 47–65.

———. 1999. 'The Pastoral Poor: Hazard, Crisis and Insecurity in Fulbe Society in Central Mali', in *Pastoralists Under Pressure: Fulbe Societies Confronting Change in West Africa*, ed. V. Azarya, A. Breedveld, M. de Bruijn and H. van Dijk. Leiden: Brill, 285–312.

———. forthcoming. 'The Itinerant Koranic School and Deprivation in Central Chad'. *African Affairs*.

De Bruijn, M. and H. van Dijk 1995. *Arid Ways: Cultural Understandings of Insecurity in Fulbe Society, Central Mali*. Amsterdam: Thela Publishers.

———. 2004. 'Risk Positions and Local Politics in a Sahelian Society: The Fulbe of the Hayre in Central Mali', in *African Environment and Development Rhetoric, Programs Realities*, ed. W. G. Mosely and B. I. Logan. Hampshire: Ashgate, 140–60.

Dijk, R. van. 1999. 'The Pentecostal Gift: Ghanaian Charismatic Churches and the Moral Innocence of the Global Economy', in *Modernity on a Shoestring: Dimensions of Globalization*,

Consumption and Development in Africa and Beyond, ed. R. Fardon, W. van Binsbergen and R. van Dijk. Leiden/London: EIDOS, 71–89.

_____. 2001. 'Time and Transcultural Technologies of the Self in the Ghanaian Pentecostal Diaspora', in *Between Babel and Pentecost: Transnational Pentecostalism in Africa and Latin America*, ed. A. Corten and R. Marshall-Fratani. London: Hurst Publishers, 216–34.

_____. 2002. 'Religion, Reciprocity and Restructuring Family Responsibility in the Ghanaian Pentecostal Diaspora', in *The Transnational Family: New European Frontiers and Global Networks*, ed. D. Bryceson and U. Vuorella. Oxford: Berg, 173–96.

_____. 2003a. 'Beyond the Rivers of Ethiopia': Pentecostal Pan-Africanism and Ghanaian Identities in the Transnational Domain', in *Situating Globality: African Agency in the Appropriation of Global Culture*, ed. W. van Binsbergen and R. van Dijk (ASC African Dynamics Annual Series no. 3). Leiden: Brill 163–89.

_____. 2003b. 'Localisation, Ghanaian Pentecostalism and the Stranger's Beauty in Botswana'. *Africa* 73(4): 560–83.

_____. 2004. 'Negotiating Marriage: Questions of Morality and Legitimacy in the Ghanaian Pentecostal Diaspora', in *Uncivic Religion: African Religious Communities and Their Quest for Public Legitimacy in the Diaspora*, ed. R. van Dijk and G. Sabar. *Journal of Religion in Africa, Thematic Issue* 34(4): 493–522.

_____. 2005. 'The Moral Life of the Gift in Ghanaian Pentecostal Churches in the Diaspora: Questions of (In-)dividuality and (In-)alienability in Transcultural Reciprocal Relations', in *Commodification, Things, Agency, and Identities: The Social Life of Things Revisited*, ed. W. M. J. van Binsbergen and P. L. Geschiere. Munster: Lit-Verlag, 201–24.

Durham, D. 2002. 'Uncertain Citizens: Herero and the New Intercalary Subject in Postcolonial Botswana', in *Postcolonial Subjectivities in Africa*, ed. R. Werbner. London: Zed Books, 139–70.

Fine, B. 2002. 'It Ain't Social, It Ain't Capital and It Ain't Africa'. *Studia Africana* 13: 18–33.

Gifford, P. 2004. *Ghana's New Christianity: Pentecostalism in a Globalising Economy*. London: Hurst & Company.

Gilliard, P. 2005. *L'extrème pauvreté au Niger, mendier ou mourir?* Paris: Editions Karthala.

Iliffe, J. 1987. *The African Poor: A History*. Cambridge: Cambridge University Press.

Keja, R. 2006. '"Ne tourne pas le dos à l'avenir", de confrontatie van het internationale kinderrechtendiscours met het dagelijks leven van bedelende talibés in de stad Thiès, Senegal'. Masters thesis, Utrecht University.

Maxwell, D. 1998. 'Delivered from the Spirit of Poverty? Pentecostalism, Prosperity and Modernity in Zimbabwe'. *Journal of Religion in Africa* 28(3): 350–73.

Mbembe, A. 2000. 'Everything Can Be Negotiated: Ambiguities and Challenges in a Time of Uncertainty', in *Manoeuvring in an Environment of Uncertainty: Structural Change and Social Action in Sub-Saharan Africa*, ed. B. Berner and P. Trulsson. Ashgate: Aldershot, 265–75.

Meyer, B. 1998. '"Make a Complete Break with the Past": Time and Modernity in Ghanaian Pentecostalist Discourse', in *Memory and the Postcolony*, ed. R. P. Werbner, Postcolonial Identities Series. London: Zed Books, 182–208.

_____. 1999. 'The Power of Money: Politics, Occult Forces and Pentecostalism in Ghana'. *African Studies Review* 41(3): 15–37.

_____. 2004. 'Christianity in Africa: From African Independent to Pentecostal-Charismatic Churches'. *Annual Review of Anthropology* 33: 447–74.

Müller, H. P. 2000. 'The Invention of Religion: Aspects of the South African Case'. *Social Dynamics* 26(1): 56–75.

Platteau, J.-P. 1991. 'Traditional Systems of Social Security and Hunger Insurance: Past Achievements and Modern Challenges', in *Social Security in Developing Countries*, ed. E. Ahmad, J. Dreze, J. Hills and A. Sen. Oxford: Clarendon Press, 112–71.

Seeseman, R. 2002. 'Sufi Leaders and Social Welfare: Two Examples from Contemporary Sudan', in *Social Welfare in Muslim Societies in Africa*, ed. H. Weiss. Uppsala: Nordiska Afrika Institutet, 98–112.

Sow Fall, A. 2003. *La grève des battu, ou, Les déchets humains*. Dakar: Les nouvelles éditions Africaines du Sénégal.

Taussig, M. T. 1995. 'The Sun Gives Without Receiving: An Old Story'. *Society for Comparative Study of Society and History* 37(2): 368–98.

Ter Haar, G. 1998. *Halfway Paradise: African Christians in Europe*. Cardiff: Cardiff Academic Press.

Troch, H. 2006. 'Een zoektocht naar kennis, God en levensonderhoud. Leren en leven in de koranschool in de Haayre'. MA thesis, University of Leiden.

Werbner, R. P. 1997. 'The Suffering Body: Passion and Ritual Allegory in Christian Encounters'. *Journal of Southern African Studies* 23(2): 311–24.

Chapter 7

Nuns, Fundraising and Volunteering

The Gifting of Care in Czech Services for the Elderly and Infirm

Rosie Read

Introduction

This chapter is concerned with the ways in which formal and institutionalised forms of social security are made meaningful in daily life, and in particular with the processes by which they are related to or seen as separate from 'the state'. I refer to 'the state' in quotation marks here since, as much work in anthropology and related disciplines attests, it cannot be seen as a singular entity, but instead as comprising a shifting conglomeration of agencies, bureaucracies, laws and policies, whose combined effects are frequently contradictory (Herzfeld 1997; Gal and Kligman 2000; Mitchell 1991; Scott 1998). At the same time, it is recognised that states mediate the reproduction of culture. States are 'powerful sites of symbolic and cultural reproduction that are themselves always culturally represented' (Ferguson and Gupta 2002: 981; see also Herzfeld 1997; Scott 1998). Thus, within popular discourses and everyday practices states are imagined, essentialised, socially constructed and thereby rendered culturally recognisable. In Europe, as in other parts of the world, state bureaucracies regulate and assume significant responsibility for the maintenance of frameworks for social security (Benda-Beckmann et al. 2000: 12), and these frameworks are also channels for the reproduction of cultural notions of 'the state' as an agent in everyday life. However, in current global economic conditions, particularly those that require reductions in national expenditure on social security and welfare, states increasingly form alliances or partnerships with a range of other bodies, such as charitable institutions, voluntary bodies, NGOs and profit-making or commercial organisations, in order to deliver care and social security. These developments raise questions about how the giving and receiving of social security is experienced. In the context of what Illana Silber calls the 'increasing intermingling of the three sectors' (i.e. the market, the state and the 'third' or nonprofit sector), how are institutionalised, state-regulated forms of social security connected to or disconnected from notions of the state (1998: 146)? What cultural processes facilitate those connections or disconnections in everyday life?

These questions are addressed here through examination of a particular type of social security, namely, care services for the elderly and infirm, provided in a Czech nursing home run by Borromean nuns. This nursing home receives significant public funding in various forms, but is also the focus of several philanthropic activities. The Borromean nuns' participation as health care providers has been shaped by the liberal political and economic reforms of the 1990s, following the collapse of socialism in 1989. What I seek to reveal are the subtle ways in which the nuns and various networks of supporters operate within the confines of state-regulated health care, whilst at the same time seeking to eclipse the significance of their location within and dependence upon such a system. Particularly in the course of their philanthropic activities, their services for the elderly and infirm are instead strongly linked to the congregation and its charitable work. Focusing on two sets of activities – fundraising and donation, and volunteering – I explore how each uses notions of the gift to animate and define ideas about care and carers. As has often been noted, the gift and giving frequently play a central role in making care meaningful (Allahyari 2000; Kittay and Feder 2003; Hochschild 2003; Read 2005; Russ 2005). Here, I stress how a much-discussed aspect of the gift, its personal and personalising qualities, are appropriated by the nuns and their supporters in order to represent the care of the nursing home as distinct from, and clearly superior to, state sector care. At the same time, however, the nursing home is a context that brings the religious network face to face with those who would question and challenge its conception of caring work. Indeed, it is precisely the location of the religious network within broader, secular, state-dominated structures of health care provision that creates different ways of understanding and valuing care in the nursing home, thereby placing limits on how far the nuns and their supporters are able to represent care in their own terms and to their own ends.[1]

Social Security, the Church and the Borromean Order: Historical Perspectives

The involvement of the Catholic Church in the provision of social security, as elsewhere in Europe, stretches back many centuries in the Czech context.

Through the course of the nineteenth and the first half of the twentieth century, local and regional governments and municipalities gradually secured stronger ownership, influence and control over church and charitable care institutions, such as hospitals, schools, orphanages and alms houses (Frič n.d.: 602–3). However, religious orders and the clergy remained a significant presence, often working in alliance with municipal authorities and directly with the needy. The Merciful Sisters of Charles Borromeo (Milosrdných sester Karla Boromejského) were no exception. The first Borromean sisters came to Prague from France in 1837, and set about founding a hospital and an orphanage in the city. The defining feature of the congregation – the vow to provide merciful love and service to those most in need – led to the nuns' active involvement in the provision of institutionalised social security in various forms, and the work of the order was located in a range of schools, hospitals, orphanages and care homes across the country in the course of the next century. At the end of 1945, the congregation managed seventy-five institutions in Czechoslovakia, including thirty-three hospitals, twelve old people's homes, eleven kindergartens, one primary school, two secondary schools, one home for the blind and a women's prison.

The consolidation of communist power after the end of the Second World War had profound implications for churches and religious orders. The communist government sought to break the power of the Catholic Church (and its Protestant counterparts), appropriating its property and removing clerical and religious influence from public spaces. Moreover, the postwar state increasingly assumed exclusive responsibility for maintaining frameworks for social security in a wide range of areas, such as health, education, housing, etc. (Nash 2003). Having occupied a prominent position in the provision of support and care for those in need for many centuries, the clergy and religious orders in the postwar socialist era were quickly marginalised in the new discourses on need and the material frameworks for social security, assistance and care. In the period from 1948 to the mid-1950s, most of the institutions owned or run by the Borromeo congregation were nationalised. Borromean nuns were repeatedly forced to leave these establishments at short notice, or to continue their work in a climate of growing suspicion and hostility towards the church and religious orders produced by senior managers. For most of the socialist period, Borromean sisters were required to live in remote rural areas. Whilst there were periods when the political repression of religious congregations eased (such as the Prague Spring in the late 1960s), when the sisters were able to fulfil their vows and practise their spiritual vocations more openly, on the whole convent life remained a closed, quiet, inner world largely hidden from public view. Nuns did, however, continue to work in a caring capacity in institutions specialising in care for 'unproductive' members of the population, such as the mentally ill, the physically disabled, the elderly or the terminally ill, who were often accommodated in large state care institutions (*ústavy*) and whose susceptibility to religious indoctrination was of less concern to the state than that of the 'productive' public. Some sisters also trained as nurses and found work in general hospitals, but kept their identity as nuns a secret.

Thus, the Borromean nuns continued to be an active, if highly marginal, presence in the context of health care provision during the socialist period, which saw the state-led consolidation and control of the organisation, resourcing and purpose of health services. The universal right of free health care was of paramount ideological importance in socialist modernity, which aimed at the eradication of poverty and exploitation, and the creation of an equal and just society. Health care services were nationalised, and gradually expanded and consolidated in the years following 1948. From the early 1950s to the early 1990s, health care facilities were publicly owned, centrally managed and funded solely from taxation revenues. Official public health discourses championed the development of modern rational approaches to the understanding and treatment of ill health. Medical knowledge and expertise was objective and scientific, with a tendency to focus on the physical and biological aspects of health and illness (rather than social or environmental aspects). Health care personnel had a reputation for being distant with their patients. According to some accounts, doctors tended to display their medical authority, whilst nurses were preoccupied with the management of routine physical tasks on the wards and rarely communicated with patients (Heitlinger 1987, 1998; Read 2005, 2007).

Whilst it is certainly the case that Western ideals of 'holistic care' were not officially endorsed, it should also be recognised that health care practices were considerably more varied than dominant discourses or formal procedures might suggest. In many areas of social life in socialist societies, for instance, official procedures and forms of economic organisation were accompanied by informal economic arrangements (Lampland 1995; Gal and Kligman 2000: 49–50; Nash 2003), and Czechoslovak health care was no exception. A fairly common practice, and one to which I will return later in my argument, was the 'tipping' of health care staff in an effort to access preferential treatment. Individual patients or their relatives presented medical personnel with gifts of chocolate, alcohol or money in a bid to secure extra vigilance, attention or cooperation from doctors and nurses. Such activities were frequent and to a certain degree accepted (particularly in view of the low salaries for health care staff). They constituted an area in which formal professional identities and relationships between patients and staff became entangled with more personalised ties and obligations (Heitlinger 1987: 100; Read 2005, 2007).

The Borromean Sisters after Socialism

The political, social and economic transformations associated with the collapse of state socialism in 1989 ushered in a new era for churches and religious congregations. The lifting of various restrictions and prohibitions meant that religious orders were now officially permitted a visible role in public life. The property restitution programme also enabled churches and religious organisations to reclaim ownership of the land and buildings that had been confiscated from them under socialism. At the same time, major reform to the organisation of health care allowed for the reincorporation of religious organisations into public health frameworks as service providers.

Within this unfamiliar political space in the wake of socialism, the Borromean order envisaged new projects that would allow them to fulfil their vow to serve the 'most needy' and likewise reflect their presocialist endeavours. In Prague, the nuns sought to reclaim ownership of the Pod Petřínem hospital in the centre of the city, as well as a large building in the suburbs, where the order had managed a female prison up to the Second World War and now proposed to establish a nursing home for the elderly and long-term infirm. At the time the nuns were pursuing these claims through legal means, the reform of the Czechoslovak health care system was high on the agenda. Plans for a major liberal reform and modernisation of the health system were put in place as early as the end of 1990. A compulsory health insurance scheme comprising contributions from individuals and employers was to provide core funding for health care providers on a fee-for-service basis. This scheme would replace health care funding from central government tax revenues, but be complemented by financial support from local and central government, as well as individual or charitable contributions. At the same time, moves to radically decentralise the health system were introduced. These were intended to encourage competition between health service providers, and foster their organisational and financial autonomy (Raffell and Raffell 1992; Garcés et al. 2003: 355; Marrée and Groenewegen 1997: 60). In the context of these broad changes, the nuns' proposal to establish a nursing home run by the congregation was approved, and Domov sv. Karla Boromejského (the Home of St Charles Borromeo) opened in 1996. It provides residential nursing care for two main groups: the elderly infirm from several Prague districts, and patients in need of nursing care and convalescence following inpatient treatment at one of the major Prague hospitals. From its inception, the nursing home embodied post-1989 moves to create innovative forms of partnership and cooperation between religious organisations and state authorities in the arena of social security provision.

As I explore below, the tensions and difficulties associated with these alliances are also manifest in the social relations of the home itself. On the one hand, the nursing home might be considered as little different from any other public or 'state' care facility: it provides services to a wide range of Prague residents, for which it receives funds from the national insurance scheme, similar to other hospitals and clinics. The majority of medical, nursing and administrative personnel at the hospital and the nursing home are 'civil' employees, with no particular link to the congregation or strong religious faith. Moreover, civil staff predominates, as few nuns work on the wards or even live in the convent wing of the home itself. Nevertheless, the congregation owns and runs the home, the most senior manager being the mother superior (*představená Domova*). Furthermore, the services provided in the home are frequently advertised and represented in the light of the congregation's religious vows, beliefs and activities. This strategy can cause controversy. The question of how closely the care provided in the institution can be associated with the nuns (as opposed to the civil employees, or perhaps broader cultural idioms of state health care) is far from settled among the people who work in or who are in some way associated with the hospital and the nursing home.

Fundraising Practices

From the outset, the congregation and its supporters were required to develop skills in raising alternative sources of funding. In order to establish their new home, the nuns were obliged to raise funds to convert a dilapidated building into a modern residential nursing facility, for which there was no automatic prospect of state funding. Costs were partly covered by grants and sponsorship from various central and local government departments, but also through the congregation's own sources and networks of support. In 1993, the nuns established the charitable foundation Nadace Dobré Dílo (Foundation for Good Works), the aim of which was to generate funds for the work of the congregation. During my fieldwork in the nursing home from 1998 to 1999, several benefit events (such as concerts and summer fairs) were held and appeals for donations made in promotional literature about the congregation and/or the nursing home. The managers of the nursing home also applied for government, charitable and European funding for specific projects.

When I returned to visit in the summer of 2004 and spring of 2005, fundraising activities had intensified. Two full-time professional fundraisers were responsible for the development and coordination of a series of strategies for income generation. These included company sponsorship, individual donations, public collections and cultural events (*kulturní akce*) such as summer fairs, children's fairs, regular benefit concerts and charitable auctions. The nursing home is far from unique in seeking to generate funding through private donations, and is but one example of a rapidly growing number of organisations in the Czech Republic that use diverse and sophisticated fundraising strategies. The growth of the charitable, voluntary and not-for-profit sector in the Czech context has been accompanied by the expanded practice and public recognition of philanthropic giving. I will highlight how fundraising strategies in the nursing home constitute notions of 'standard' care, loosely associated with public services in the 'state sector', and 'above-standard care', which is both the goal and the outcome of private fundraising and philanthropic donation.

In talking to me about their strategies for communicating with commercial and corporate donors, fundraisers in the nursing home stressed the importance of being specific about what was needed and how sponsors or donors could meet that need. Lenka, a woman in her early thirties and one of the fundraisers, described her experience of seeking charitable donations or sponsorship from firms:

> They want to know precisely what we [the nursing home] do, some contact details, and then they want to know exactly what we want. In my previous experience, the worst you can do is say, 'Oh, we'd like something to improve our home'. We must be direct and concrete, and say, 'We want beds', or 'We want mirrors for the showers'. Last year was a really hot summer and we discovered we needed window blinds, so we called a firm that makes blinds and said our 'old ladies were terribly hot last year and we need shade'. Then it's concrete, and they can come and have a look around. Usually it's not a problem and they help us. So it's important to say what we want.

Martina, a woman in her fifties who had also worked at the nursing home as a fundraiser before moving to do similar work in the Borromean hospital, described the work of fundraising in terms of cultivating good relationships with donors and sponsors:

> It's work that takes a number of years. It's not instant, but very demanding because sponsors require personal contact, they need looking after, they want to be invited [to events], they need the interest of the fundraiser.... Only by doing this can you create a database of sponsors you can turn to.... Then there is the other aspect, when you have to collect money at a concert and coax it out of people. This means that [the audience] must be told in the promotional material *exactly* what they are contributing to, and given a way of finding out how their donation will be used. There are many ways of doing this.... If it's done, then of course sponsors remain loyal. Everyone in my experience likes giving ... but it must be the right thing and they have to know it's doing some good. Everyone likes being a sponsor, they like being treated as such by the organisation they are sponsoring.

Hence, fundraising requires a particular set of skills and detailed knowledge about potential and current donors. Fundraisers particularly stressed the immense significance of developing and nurturing a network of supporters who are encouraged to feel an ongoing sense of involvement in the nursing home, and who will be rewarded for their donations with a constant reminder that their contribution has had a positive effect. A key method of achieving this was to demonstrate the 'above-standard' care (*nadstandardní péče*) provided by the nursing home, which was felt by fundraisers to have a strong impression on donors:

We stress that we are above standard. In state (*státní*) nursing homes there are two nurses per thirty patients and here there are four, which means the care is better.... It's really important to invite [sponsors] here. Although they often have no time, they must always be invited. 'Come and have a look, it's worth it, you will see how pleasant it is here' [we say].... Once I was negotiating with a Volkswagen marketing executive, who was very aloof to begin with, somewhat cold and professional. Then we started talking about the nursing home, and she spoke of how her parents had been hit by a car the previous year ... [which meant that] she had personal experience of what state nursing homes are like. When she visited here, she couldn't believe her eyes.... Compared with standard care, she obviously thought this was really something exceptional and was very interested.

Lenka's account illustrates the emphasis fundraisers place on demonstrating that care in the nursing home is 'above standard'. 'Standard' care links the 'state sector' (here via a reference to 'state' nursing homes) with the idea of a norm, or 'typical' care practices. It is vital to highlight the distinction between standard and above-standard to potential donors, who want to reward themselves and identify with what is 'above standard'. Similar strategies were used in appeals to individual donors. Ivana, a fundraiser in her thirties who worked with Lenka in the nursing home, said of individual donors:

If, when a patient leaves [the home], his or her family are satisfied with the care, they are sometimes happy to give a gift, [or] to sponsor us. But this is only when the patient leaves, so it isn't that they are buying care.... It is something they do voluntarily, because they are satisfied and they want to do it.

There are clearly many similarities between donations of this kind and the older practices of 'tipping' health care staff discussed earlier. Nevertheless, Ivana's description recasts the practice of voluntary donation as an index of patient satisfaction and a matter of personal satisfaction and choice (as opposed to an underhand attempt to actively negotiate the standard of care to personal advantage). Ivana maintained that patients and their families were glad to make a donation for extra services received. These included rehabilitation, ergotherapy, a church with regular services in the grounds of the home, a hairdresser, a small shop, a smoking room, and the freedom to receive visitors twenty-four hours a day, unlike hospitals with strict visiting hours.

Ivana also pointed out that here, contrary to 'state' (*státní*) hospitals, there is 'an obvious spirit of compassion and Christianity'. The nuns are positively associated with 'above-standard' care; they not only symbolise it but provide the guarantee for its continuation. Ivana recognised that the home's fundraising efforts were greatly helped by the fact that 'the public have a strong impression that because it is a church organisation, it is good, the care is good'. Lenka had frequently found corporate sponsors and donors more inclined to believe their donations would be put to better use in a 'church institution managed by nuns' than in other charitable organisations.

The Borromean nuns and their fundraising staff have been remarkably successful in generating funds from non-state sources. They have appropriated and transformed practices of gifting in health care that extend back to the socialist era. The gifting of money and goods for the improvement of health care is dissociated from narrow self-interested behaviour and reconstructed into a language of charity, donation, sponsorship and good will. Donation retains a key quality of the gift, that is, the 'deep interconnection between the gift and the donor's personal identity' (Silber 1998: 139). Hence, corporate donors are approached to make gifts of their specialist products; individual patients and relatives are asked for donations on the basis of their personal experience of treatment in the home; and sponsors' logos are published in marketing materials, websites and newsletters. Importantly, the identity of the nuns as trustworthy recipients of donated funds is also stressed. Fundraising activities distinguish nursing-home care from 'standard' or 'state-sector' care. Simultaneously, it conceals the nursing home's dependence on state funding. According to its financial report for 2004, for instance, individual and corporate donation accounted for slightly less than 11 per cent of the nursing home's income. At the same time, income from national health insurance constituted 66 per cent while state subsidies from government ministries (the Ministry of Health, Work and Social Affairs and the Prague city authority) amounted to 23 per cent. In the report for 2003, accounts indicated that the total figure for 'gifts and contributions' (KCS 2,342,000) was more than a third of the amount supplied 'from state budgets' (KCS 7,207,000). However, the latter merely represents grants from three government ministries and does not include funding from national health insurance payments (KCS 20,683,000).[2] In short, the activities surrounding processes of philanthropic donation eclipse the nursing home's own location within the so-called state sector.

Volunteers

Like charitable donation, the practice of volunteering in the nursing home has become more visible and more organised over the last five years. In February 2005, twenty-nine volunteers worked in the nursing home. Jana, who has been the nursing home's volunteer coordinator for the past four years, informed me that about fourteen volunteers were 'regular' (*pravidelní*), that is, volunteered in some form in the home once a week. The remaining fifteen volunteered on an irregular basis. Only five volunteers were under the age of fifty, and tended to be among those who were less regular. Thus the majority of volunteers, including all who were committed and came regularly, were of retirement age.

Class and educational backgrounds varied. All the volunteers were Christians (*věřící*); two were members of a Protestant congregation, and the remainder were Catholics. Only four volunteers were men.

The Borromean nuns know many of the volunteers personally. Several regular volunteers I spoke to, for example, lived locally and attended church services at the nursing home. Another two had worked in the central Prague hospital run by the congregation. Others had been involved in supporting the Borromean sisters' charitable work in various ways. The congregation also advertised for volunteers in a number of churches in Prague. Those who had no prior contact to or knowledge of the nuns had discovered the possibility of volunteering in this way.

Volunteers could offer their services and become involved in a range of activities in the nursing home as often as they wished. Many of them worked directly with patients, either on one of the three wards that provided residential patient care, or at the day-care centre (*denní stationař*). Although owned and run by the nursing home, the day-care centre is a separate service offering day care for the elderly, infirm or disabled from anywhere in Prague for a fee of 125 KCS (about £3) per day.[3] Day-care centre clients tend to consist of elderly people with physical or mental disabilities, whose families are unable to look after them during the day. Clients are brought to the day-care centre in the morning (from 7 AM) and collected around 5 PM. Several ward patients also attend the day-care centre. Many of the volunteers choose to sit and talk to patients or day-care centre clients and keep them company. This can take the form of visiting and befriending particular patients who welcome their company. As part of these activities, volunteers might read to patients or clients, accompany them to the nursing home shop to buy something they need or take them to the gardens or to some of the daytime fundraising events, such as benefit concerts. Other volunteers prefer the more formal role of helping the nursing staff with their daily tasks. On the wards this includes washing, dressing and feeding patients; in the day-care centre it involves daily exercises, board games, cards, various forms of art work (drawing, painting, ceramics, knitting and sewing), singing, reading, etc.

In their work with patients, volunteers are also welcome to use any specialist skills they might have. One volunteer turned out to be a retired psychiatrist, for example, while another was trained in designing exercises to stimulate memory and the mental activities of people with dementia. Both activated these skills in their interaction with clients in the day-care centre. Some volunteers take patients to church services. One female volunteer made a point of finding out from patients and clients whether they were Catholic and whether they would like to be taken to church services or visited by a priest. Direct evangelising was not tolerated by the volunteer coordinator, however. Although herself a Catholic, Jana asserted her right to exclude volunteers whose primary purpose in volunteering was to engage patients or clients in discussions on religious beliefs, and viewed such behaviour as inappropriate and unwelcome. On these grounds she had asked volunteers on several occasions not to return, although she also admitted that the nursing home 'attracts this type of person'. Jana's position on this issue illustrates the negotiated, sometimes contested, place of religious expression within the nursing home, and the difficulty in resolving the extent to which the nursing home's activities were to be defined in terms of religious faith or ideals. Apart from the presence of a large number of agnostic or atheistic staff members, who would have objected to taking part in activities with an overtly religious agenda, the core function of the home was to provide nursing care to the public, a primary duty to which any additional religious services were officially subordinated. The volunteers I spoke to did not frame their motivation directly in religious terms. Instead, they spoke of wanting to help patients, of taking pleasure in lending a hand and feeling that their support made a qualitative difference to patients' lives. In what follows I will explore how volunteers' understanding of their action as a form of gift facilitates a further series of distinctions between 'standard' forms of care in health care institutions and care that is gifted.

Volunteering as a Gift of Care

In various ways, volunteers shared a certain understanding of what patients experienced as elderly people gradually approaching the end of their lives. Although conscious of the patients' physical suffering, the focus of their concern was the latter's mental and emotional state. Numerous patients and clients had more or less severe forms of dementia, a condition that was frequently the principle reason for their placement in the home or the day-care centre. Some of them rarely spoke, whilst others lived in a state of perpetual confusion about what was happening around them. Volunteers were acutely sensitive to what they saw as mental distress. They were equally keen to help patients who had no specific mental disability but simply felt lonely, isolated or depressed during their stay in the home or at the day-care centre:

> My motivation is simply to help. These patients have nothing before them except 'the end' (*ten konec*). So I like helping them, and see the good the help does.... This makes a volunteer very happy. (Sixty-six-year-old woman, retired teacher)

> I like people, and I like helping. The best thing for these people is to have contact with others. (Eighty-two-year-old woman, retired psychiatrist)

> I like working with old people. I looked after my father in his old age, so I have a feeling for them. (Seventy-four-year-old woman, retired accountant)

> I can't define it exactly – you simply have it in your heart to want to help someone.... I always visit the same people ... the ones who are the most abandoned or isolated. (Sixty-eight-year-old man, former factory worker)

In short, volunteers saw themselves as responding to a specific need of the elderly and infirm – not a material need for food, clothing or shelter (which were already provided), but a social or emotional need for company, friendship, social interaction and human warmth. While they did not describe their volunteering in terms of their religious beliefs (several denied a relationship between their faith and the motivation for becoming a volunteer), the above statements by volunteers are clearly shaped by the Christian (and particularly Catholic) duties of charity, good works and the requirement to help one's neighbour and those less fortunate than oneself (Kahl 2005; Allahyari 2000). The volunteers' own accounts of their actions also resonated with the descriptions of the mother superior in a pamphlet on the nursing home:

> The dedicated work of employees is very highly praised. But no less worthy of respect is every hour that a volunteer gives to the needy.... Everyone needs affection and human warmth. Especially those who because of illness or disability find themselves, temporarily or permanently, in a care institution. They can receive excellent care, but ... if they are isolated, left to their memories, homesick for close friends and family ... when the attention of the staff turns to the needs of others, they remain alone. There are people who find the time to come and listen, to fulfil some small wish.... It is a strong motivation when we find what we can do for another person, even some small act of charity that costs us nothing. (*Informační Listy*, 8–9)

If there was a clearly Christian moral subtext to their activities, the personal experience volunteers had with illness – particularly caring for sick relatives – also shaped their concern to help not just any 'needy', but the elderly and infirm. Several female volunteers spoke of their lifelong involvement in taking care of close members of their families and their need, even after their children had grown up and moved away and their husbands and parents had died, to continue to feel useful and active by caring for dependent people. One volunteer claimed to have a special bond with elderly people because she had looked after her own father during ill health. Her adult son had married and left, and she wanted 'to be useful to someone other than myself'. A male volunteer attributed his initial desire to work with the sick to a cancer scare he had experienced earlier in his life. The experience had made him sensitive to the feelings of the infirm and promoted the desire to help them. Another volunteer claimed she felt indebted to her mother, and that she wanted to 'give something back' to elderly people who suffered the same bad health her own mother had experienced prior to her death. Yet another female volunteer said that the circumstances of her husband's death had acted as a catalyst for her subsequent choice to become a volunteer:

> It's now over three years since my husband died from cancer. I looked after him at home, but we went to (a local hospital) regularly so he could get treatment. That's

where I saw how sick people are treated. I saw what they needed; they needed to be lifted out of the stressful situation they were in.... There were no volunteers there at the time.... When my husband died, it took me a long time to get over it. But all the time I was thinking that I would like to do some volunteering. Then I saw a leaflet in the church here and decided to come and do it.

Other volunteers spoke of how their experiences of ill health (their own or that of close relatives) had exposed some of the failings of health care systems and health care personnel: 'I have another friend in (a Prague hospital) and I visit her often. The nurses there are so rude, they just throw plates of food down in front of patients without a word.' The volunteer who was a former psychiatrist and had worked much of her life in clinical settings told me that she had experienced some 'very impatient nurses' in some of the larger Prague hospitals. I asked her why she thought they were impatient: 'Because they have no relationship to people. It is just work for them. They have no love for people. When someone only works because they have to, they become hard bitten.' This distinction between people who are only interested in material gain or work there 'because they have to' and those who care for no other apparent reason than a selfless desire to help others was often invoked by volunteers. It provided them with a clear moral framework within which to think about their own caring practices. Interestingly, if volunteers saw their work as countering the anonymity and coldness of institutionalised care, they also associated these failures with *both* the socialist past *and* the capitalist present.

Some volunteers, for example, attributed what they perceived as a lack of understanding and compassion for the infirm and disabled to the legacy of socialist health care. One volunteer stated that she had not been aware of voluntary work of the kind she was currently involved in during the socialist period. When I asked why she thought this was so, she replied: 'I guess because voluntary workers might have noticed that the staff did not behave well towards their patients. Chronically ill patients were in institutions (*ústavy*), hidden away, and sometimes mistreated.' Another volunteer claimed it was a good thing that more and more young people were volunteering to look after the disabled and the sick, since it allowed them to grasp that good health is not a given and should not be taken for granted. She added that, in the socialist period, 'the disabled were locked up in institutions and no one knew of their existence.... Politicians and the state didn't want anyone to know that disabled people existed in this country (*u nás*). Now ... there is more openness.'

These volunteers associated socialist health care policies and practices with lack of compassion and overmedicalisation of the disabled and infirm, and their consequent exclusion from mainstream society. Yet volunteers also pointed to contemporary problems they felt had emerged from consumerist and materialist values associated with the new liberal economy. As one female volunteer put it: 'Voluntary work is about making people happy. It's not about money. Why don't more people do it? Because they are too concerned with money. Especially now – this is particularly evident now.' A male volunteer said:

> Capitalism seems to mean that people are becoming more individualistic and more isolated. People don't want to go out and be with others. Under communism – although [communists] didn't practice what they preached of course – at least we were always being told that everyone mattered, everyone was of value. Now, under capitalism, it's apparently the survival of the strongest, and the most successful are the most valuable. And when people hear this message all their lives, it has an effect on them, just as the communist message had an effect. Competition between people means they are cut off from each other.

According to these statements, contemporary Czech capitalism supports and sustains the values of competition and individualism, and makes economic success the key marker of social value, which in turn creates new forms of exclusion for those unable to compete, such as the disabled and infirm. This volunteer and others felt that volunteering was a means of countering the situation, bringing people together and fostering a sense of social connectedness and shared responsibility.

These testimonies work to morally situate volunteers' own philanthropic practices, as well as the broader contribution of the nuns. Albeit in rather different ways, capitalism and communism are charged with creating anonymous, impersonal staff-patient relations in health care and an uncaring, atomised and overly self-interested society, which is a marked contrast to the selfless, compassionate care that volunteers give freely to patients. Volunteers' discourse thus invokes two linked oppositions: giving freely versus acting in self-interest, and intimate or compassionate versus anonymous and impersonal relations of care. Yet as anthropologists have long recognised, oppositions such as those between the notion of the pure or free gift and the equally pure or free commodity are cultural constructs that historically emerge in the context of capitalist socio-economic relations (Parry 1985; Carrier 1995; Zelizer 1994; Osteen 2002). Philanthropic practice and the idea of the free gift have developed extensively where the ideological valorisation of the market and self-interest has a strong hold (Silber 1998). The apparent antagonism between these spheres of activity masks their interdependence. According to Parry, 'a universalistic ethic of disinterested giving can surely only encourage the creation of a separate sphere which is immune from the requirements of such a demanding precept. The ideology of the pure gift may thus itself promote and entrench the ideological elaboration of a domain in which self-interest rules supreme' (Parry 1985: 468–69). This is not to suggest that volunteers were in fact providing a 'free gift' through volunteering. Leaving aside the long-established intellectual scepticism about the existence of such a thing (Osteen

2002; Parry 1985), volunteers' actions clearly create obligations and relationships. We have seen how volunteers speak openly about the pleasure and enjoyment they derive from their labours with patients, particularly when the latter express their gratitude and return volunteers' affections. Nevertheless, volunteers use the conceptual apparatus of the free gift to make their action meaningful to themselves and others. In elaborating a vision of contemporary social life as increasingly anonymous, uncaring, atomised and materialistic, volunteers create a social need and a morally sanctioned space for their own volunteered practice.

Volunteers' discourse had a further set of consequences for social relations within the home. Their framing of care as a matter of love and not money places the payment staff members receive for their work in a light that is both symbolically and morally questionable. Volunteers were careful not to criticise the staff directly or accuse individual employees of not caring adequately for patients. Indeed, some volunteers were keen to point out the dedication of the nursing staff to their profession, compared to their experience of employees in other health care facilities. At the same time, however, the commitment of paid staff to provide high-quality care was attributed to the presence of the nuns in the nursing home. In the eyes of the volunteers, the nuns were a model of selfless devotion to patients. As one volunteer expressed it: 'The nurses here are polite, helpful and caring to patients as a result of the nuns' example (*vzor*). The nuns create an atmosphere of kindness and compassion, which has a good influence on the paid nursing staff (*civilní*). This is what makes this place so different to other hospitals.'

As in the case of fundraising, the altruistic compassion of the nuns for the needy and infirm is represented as a safeguard for high standards of care. Their work and their supporters are portrayed in such a way as to eclipse the location of the nursing home in the state-regulated system of social security, and its dependence on that system. On a more practical level, these depictions also mask the daily reliance of volunteers on paid staff to inform them how best to serve the patients. Questions of who to visit and what activities to engage in, as well as generally making the inclusion of volunteers into daily routines possible all generated extra work for those concerned. Moreover, the fact that hardly any of the nuns worked in a nursing capacity in the home, as mentioned earlier, was also obscured through these descriptions. Most of the nursing staff were paid civil staff. Thus volunteers' accounts of their own practices were not widely shared by the staff of the nursing home. Some nurses vigorously disagreed with the idea of linking the ability to care with religious faith, or the example of those who had it with those who did not:

There are plenty of evil (*zlý*) people among the Christians (*věřící*) and plenty of good people among those with no faith (*nevěřící*). I do this work because I enjoy it and because *I want to help people* [her emphasis]. Either someone has a talent for this work or they don't – that's what is important. One so-called volunteer who used to come here said that she prayed she wouldn't have to wipe the patients' bottoms!

Other employees indicated their awareness that the public image of nuns and volunteers as motivated purely by altruistic compassion for the elderly and infirm was merely one element of a more complicated reality. As one employee stated: 'The congregation operates with two faces (*dvou tváří*). One is image, and the other is how it really is. The nuns are shut off from reality to a large extent, they don't have to deal with the same problems as everyone else.'

Concluding Remarks

In her essay on Maussian gift theory and modern American philanthropy, Illana Silber asks what impact the increasing interpenetration of state, market and nonprofit sectors will have on notions of donation and philanthropy, and how resilient 'dichotomic conceptions of the relation between gift and market, or interest and disinterestedness' will prove to be in this context (1998: 146). These questions were taken up in this chapter in relation to the social security provided by a Czech nursing home, which relies on both state and private forms of funding and on the work of employees and volunteers. My findings suggest that the interpenetration to which Silber refers does not necessarily bring about the collapse of cultural and cognitive boundaries that equate quite different meanings to state funding, on the one hand, and private donation, on the other.

In examining two particular areas of philanthropic activity I have shown how the notion of the free gift (and in some cases its dichotomic opposition to that of the state, as well as to the market) is actively used to promote and morally endorse donation and volunteering, and that in these contexts the nursing home's dependence on and location within state institutions, structures, regulations and forms of funding is eclipsed. Yet these practices of eclipsing are temporary and contextual; representations of the nursing home that seek to closely interlink philanthropic activity, the nuns and high-quality care are clearly open to challenge. The interpenetration of the state and charitable sectors enables actors in the nursing home to make varied and context-specific use of values associated with both sectors. It also makes for the fragility and vulnerability of any singular interpretation that would seek to associate care, and what makes good care, with either 'the gift' or 'the state'.

Notes

1. In what follows I draw on ethnographic material gathered at the nursing home for the long-term elderly infirm in the course of fieldwork from 1998 to 1999, and in 2004 and 2005. I am grateful to the Economic and Social Research Council (UK) and the British Academy for funding this research.
2. See also Read (2005: 158), where the reference to the nursing home's 'total funding' for the year 2003 indicates the total funding from state sources.
3. Figures correct at time of fieldwork in January 2005.

References

Allahyari, R. A. 2000. *Visions of Charity: Volunteer Workers and Moral Community*. Berkeley: University of California Press.

Benda-Beckmann, F. von, K. von Benda-Beckmann and H. Marks, eds. 2000. 'Coping with Insecurity: An "Underall" Perspective on Social Security in the Third World'. *Focaal* 22/23: 7–35.

Carrier, J. G. 1995. *Gifts and Commodities: Exchange and Western Capitalism Since 1700*. London: Routledge.

Feder, E. K. and E. Feder Kittay. 2003. 'Introduction', in *The Subject of Care: Feminist Perspectives on Dependency*. Oxford: Rowman and Littlefield, 1–12.

Ferguson, J. and A. Gupta. 2002. 'Spatializing States: Toward an Ethnography of Neoliberal Governmentality'. *American Ethnologist* 29(4): 981–1002.

Frič, P., R. Goulli and O. Vyskočilová. n.d. 'Small Development within the Bureaucracy Interests: The Non-Profit Sector in the Czech Republic', in *Future of Civil Society* (DVD), Wissenschaftszentrum Berlin für Sozialforschung.

Gal, S. and G. Kligman. 2000. *The Politics of Gender After Socialism*. Princeton, NJ: Princeton University Press.

Garcés, J., F. Ródenas and S. Carretero. 2003. 'Observations on the Progress of Welfare-State Construction in Hungary, Poland and the Czech Republic'. *Post-Soviet Affairs* 19(4): 337–71.

Heitlinger, A. 1987. *Reproduction, Medicine and the Socialist State*. London: Macmillan Press.

Herzfeld, M. 1997. *Cultural Intimacy: Social Poetics and the Nation State*. London: Routledge.

Hochschild, A. R. 2003 [1983]. *The Managed Heart: Commercialisation of Human Feeling*. Berkeley: University of California Press.

Kahl, S. 2005. 'The Religious Roots of Modern Poverty Policy: Catholic, Lutheran, and Reformed Protestant Traditions Compared'. *European Journal of Sociology* 46(1): 91–126.

Lampland, M. 1995. *The Object of Labour: Commodification in Socialist Hungary*. Chicago: University of Chicago Press.

Marrée, J. and P. P. Groenewegen. 1997. *Back to Bismarck: Eastern European Health Care in Transition*. Aldershot: Avebury.

Mitchell, T. 1991. 'The Limits of the State: Beyond Statist Approaches and Their Critics'. *American Political Science Review* 85(1): 77–96.

Nash, R. 2003. 'Re-stating the Family: Kinship and Care in the Czech Republic'. PhD diss., University of Virginia.

Osteen, M. 2002. 'Introduction: Questions of the Gift', in *The Question of the Gift: Essays Across Disciplines*, ed. M. Osteen. London: Routledge.

Parry, J. 1985. 'The Gift, the Indian Gift and the 'Indian Gift'. *Man* (N.S.) 21: 453–73.

Raffell, M. W. and N. Raffell. 1992. 'Czechoslovakia's Changing Health Care System'. *Public Health Reports* 107(6): 636–45.

Read, R. 2005. 'Altering Care: Gifts and Emotion in Nursing Practice within a Czech Nursing Home', in *Generations, Kinship and Care: Gendered Provisions of Social Security in Central Eastern Europe*, vol. 17, ed. H. Haukanes and F. Pine. Bergen: University of Bergen, Centre for Women's and Gender Research, 137–62.

———. 2007. 'Labour and Love: Competing Constructions of "Care" in a Czech Nursing Home'. *Critique of Anthropology* 27: 203–22.

Russ, A. J. 2005. 'Love's Labor Paid For: Gift and Commodity and the Threshold of Death'. *Cultural Anthropology* 20(1): 125–55.

Scott, J. C. 1998. *Seeing Like a State: How Certain Schemes to Improve the Human Condition Have Failed.* New Haven, CT: Yale University Press.

Silber, I. 1998. 'Modern Philanthropy: Reassessing the Viability of a Maussian Perspective', in *Marcel Mauss: A Centenary Tribute*, ed. W. James and N. J. Allen. Oxford: Berghahn, 134–50.

Zelizer, V. A. 1997. *The Social Meaning of Money: Pin Money, Paychecks, Poor Relief and Other Currencies.* Princeton, NJ: Princeton University Press.

Chapter 8

'Church Shopping' in Malawi

Acquiring Multiple Resources in Urban Christian Networks

Barbara Rohregger

Introduction

Multiple religious affiliations are a widespread reality in Malawi.[1] People can belong simultaneously to the charismatic Pentecostal churches, the Roman Catholic Church or the Church of Central African Presbyterian, the largest established churches in Malawi. Others are loosely affiliated to some of the numerous religious groups. This is all the more true in the urban context, where people from different regions and denominations live and pray side by side, and where innumerable churches and religious groupings co-exist.

Taking this reality as a starting point, the present chapter will explore how urban migrants in Lilongwe City, Malawi, mobilise multiple religious affiliations to secure their lives and those of their families, and in this context are active in creating complex, multilayered religious networks. I argue that these dynamic and frequently overlapping networks play a vital role in securing the material, emotional and spiritual well-being of migrants. I also maintain that actors partake of individual resources offered by the various churches in what could be called 'church-shopping', thereby contradicting a straightforward distinction between material and nonmaterial support.

Individuals create overlapping religious networks that serve different social security purposes. On the one hand, there is the vertical support, that is, support given by the churches themselves, and on the other, the horizontal network relations that emerge between members of a congregation. The latter have proved to be the most vibrant social support networks within the churches.

Notes for this chapter begin on page 161.

Migration, Social Security and Religious Networks

The crucial role of religion in the migrant context – both within national boundaries and transnationally – has received considerable attention from anthropologists working in Africa in recent decades (see, e.g., van Dijk 1999, 2001; de Bruijn et al. 2001). The importance of religious institutions for the social, spiritual and material well-being of those far from home has been the subject of heated debate in relation to the charismatic Pentecostal movements. In recent decades, these movements have proliferated in many parts of the world, and are particularly attractive to migrant communities, both in the urban centres of numerous African countries and in African transnational communities in the US and Europe.[2]

The popularity of these churches is primarily due to their strong emphasis on material values as the key element to individual salvation. The Pentecostal doctrine embodied in the so-called prosperity gospel perceives personal well-being in physical and material terms as the sign of God's blessing, and the result of a good Christian life. Consequently, those who fail to achieve prosperity and a more sophisticated lifestyle, including expensive clothes and cars, are not merely looked on as poor – their indigence is further regarded as the sign of a life led in sin (Meyer 1999; see also van Dijk 1999).

This focus on consumption and the material is seen as a recent development in Christian doctrine. Contrary to the notion of the material in traditional Christian churches, whose gospel preaches modesty and a sense of humility towards material possessions and is intricately linked to the idea of redistribution, the prosperity gospel introduces a materialistic slant to religious belief and practice, shifting it to the very core of its doctrine. This in turn impacts on social relations, accelerating processes of individualisation and leading to a further breakdown of mutual support networks and a general reinterpretation of the notion of reciprocity and solidarity (for a critical discussion, see Meyer 1999). Central to this argument is the redefinition of personal exchange relations and gift exchange, originally based on moral obligations of reciprocity and solidarity largely free of commitment or fears and ambiguities (Comaroff and Comaroff 1993; van Dijk 1999).

The material, spiritual and social process of individualisation visible in the credo of the Pentecostal movement is interpreted for the most part as a spiritual reflection of the processes of modernisation and globalisation[3] that have left their imprint on African societies over the last three decades. The social, economic and political decay numerous African countries have experienced, combined with vast migration flows, have affected religious practices and considerations (Hackett 1995; de Bruijn et al. 2001). This new independence from social links and relations implies a complete break with the past, that is, with the family or the village community (Meyer 1999; van Dijk 1999). Many authors see this break with the past – often marked by a ritual rebirth – as a major difference to conventional Christian churches. The goal of the latter was to reconstruct the migrant's sense of belonging and identity, and by the same token, to satisfy the yearning for support in a hostile and anonymous urban environment (van Dijk 1998).[4]

In the following I will look into both established and new charismatic Pentecostal churches on an urban fringe of Lilongwe City, Malawi. I will demonstrate that the religious networks of poor migrants not only overlap, but evolve in highly complex, dynamic and somewhat contradictory ways. Rather than approaching religious networks from an ideological or material point of view, I focus on a perspective that considers the social (in)securities experienced by the social actors involved. Apart from the material support religion provides, which goes well beyond the urban context, it is also a valuable identity resource for the making of an integrative social space. Bound by religious practices and commonly shared values and norms, this space becomes a vital source of spiritual support, functioning at the same time as a form of symbolic, emotional and social security in an increasingly insecure and socially fragmented urban environment, marked by high levels of in- and out-migration. Religion is likewise an important breeding ground for the creation of new social networks characterised by friendship or kinship outside the church context (Rohregger 2006). Moreover, we will see that the materialistic dimension of religion is not confined to Pentecostal churches, but that worldly matters are central to all religious networks in the area (Meyer 1999). In fact, I will argue that both aspects are of crucial relevance to urban migrants, and that spiritual and material aspects of religion are not mutually exclusive, nor do they follow a different rationale, but frequently go hand in hand. This also holds true for Pentecostalism. We will observe that the poor migrants in my research site were particularly drawn by the strong spiritual element of the Pentecostal churches.

Against the backdrop of migration and the overall economic and social transformation as a result of Structural Adjustment[5] and HIV/AIDS, spiritual and material support provided by religious organisations has gathered momentum. This is particularly evident in the poorest segments of the population, who live under extremely harsh social and economic conditions, who shift between churches to satisfy needs that can no longer be met by the state, the family or other security providers such as friends or the workplace. I will call this practice 'church shopping', borrowing an expression from Keebet von Benda-Beckmann (1984), who speaks of 'legal forum shopping' in analysing dispute settlement in Indonesia and the practice of social actors choosing between different legal systems – religious, state, customary law – in order to influence disputes over land, water or inheritance.[6] This forum shopping process relates to heightened competition for increasingly scarce resources and a growing sense of insecurity. I will show that the practice of church shopping has become highly relevant as a result of the spread of HIV/AIDS, which has led to enormous psychological and material pressure on network relations and support capacities, profoundly changing needs and insecurities.

Religious Organisation in Sector 7

My fieldwork took place in Sector 7/Area 25A, an urban fringe area hidden behind the international airport road northwest of Lilongwe City. The area emerged at the beginning of the 1990s in the process of illegal land invasion and was subsequently upgraded by the city council; confronted with lack of resources to develop new settlement areas and the growing expansion of the city, this policy has enjoyed popularity since the democratic transition in 1994. The absence of infrastructure was the major concern of the several thousand mostly very poor migrants who lived in the area in 1998, when I carried out my research. Three years later the situation had changed utterly. Supported by an urban community project funded by GTZ,[7] the inhabitants had gained access to funding for water, electricity and a primary school from a number of international donors. However, these urbanisation attempts brought about a change in the social structure of the area. While the poor continued to form the majority of those living in the area in 2001, higher-income civil servants had slowly begun to trickle into Sector 7. Ousted by major social reforms, such as the public housing system and Structural Adjustment policies, the latter had become attracted to the area because it had affordable plots and rents, and basic infrastructure. As a consequence of continued gentrification, the number of inhabitants had almost tripled to approximately 8,000 by 2001. Many of the poorer inhabitants sold their plots to wealthier civil servants and moved to the edges of town and beyond, where they suffered further marginalisation (Rohregger 2006).

In Malawian society in general and Sector 7 in particular, religion plays a key role in people's lives. Every person I met during my fieldwork belonged to one or more religious associations and considered religion an integral part of their lives. In Malawi on the whole as in many other African countries, this also applied to the Pentecostal churches whose popularity had mounted in the area over the previous decade (see Gifford 1994; van Dijk 2001).[8]

Apart from a small Muslim minority, most people in Sector 7 are Christians, belonging to a broad spectrum of churches and denominations, the largest of which are the Church of Central African Presbyterian (CCAP), the Roman Catholic Church (RCC) and the Seventh-Day Adventist Church. Other smaller churches include the Lutheran Church and a series of Pentecostal congregations, such as the Church of Christ, Assemblies of God and the Industrial Mission.

The significance of religion in the daily lives of the local people is evident in the architectural landscape of the area. While schools, hospitals and other public buildings are still largely absent, religious communities were the first to colonise the area with the construction of prayer houses and mosques. Apart from the Catholic and the Presbyterian Churches, which have their own mission stations, the Lutheran Church and two Pentecostal churches – The Living Waters and the Church of Christ – have also established their own religious centres in the area. Most of the prayer houses of other churches are within walking distance, such as the Seventh-Day Adventist parish attended by many Sector 7 inhabitants.[9]

Viewing religious associations in the context of social security reveals them to be an important element in the creation of dense network relations, which in turn fulfil multiple social security functions. These relations have either emerged individually in a religious context or are highly institutionalised within the church hierarchy, as church support relations typically occur either on the vertical or horizontal level.

Social Security Service Offered by the Churches

Vertical support relations – direct support provided by Christian organisations to their individual members – are principally confined to the provision of support for funerals. On these occasions, a fixed amount of money is given to the bereaved family to purchase a coffin or food for the mourners. The money is taken from a special fund, financed by the community itself. Apart from the large mainline churches, which are in part supported by their sister churches at national or overseas levels, most churches are self-sufficient. As a rule this works through the 'tithing' scheme, that is, monthly contributions based on individual income.[10] In addition, most religious associations ask for contributions from the congregation for members in trouble, such as long periods of illness, victims of crime or lack of shelter because rents have not been paid or houses are crumbling due to heavy rains. The money is collected during Sunday services.

Apart from this direct support, most churches are major providers of social services and infrastructure. Here, the paramount role of Christian churches as providers of health and educational services in Malawi has changed little since colonial times.[11] Dzenza mission from the CCAP runs a hospital and a large secondary school. The Kagwa parish of the RCC in Area 49, attended by most Catholics from Sector 7, runs a primary school. The Roman Catholic church and the Kingdom of God church, which are not yet complete, plan to establish full-scale mission stations in Sector 7 that will comprise a preschool, primary and secondary schools, and a hospital. It is worth noting that the latter was built on land originally planned for the public health care centre, which was sold to the congregation when a shortage of public funds prevented its construction. The Lutheran Church runs a preschool that is to be extended to include a primary school. Apart from a few exceptions – for example, the Catholic parish does not charge school fees for orphans – all of these services have to be paid for. In addition to extra contributions from the congregation, the proceeds from these services have to cover maintenance costs of mission stations and parishes. Everyone has access to health and educational services.

Another important aspect of vertical support is religious entrepreneurship. Many of the NGOs operating in Malawi are of Christian origin. Hence religious affiliation is highly significant for support and care. For example, those who apply for a loan to Habitat for Humanity (the Christian NGO that provides loans for housing construction and operates in Sector 7) are asked to produce a letter from the church confirming their active membership. This letter is just as important as the pay slip that serves as collateral. The same holds true for some of the new microcredit loan organisations, many of which are financed and managed by Christian NGOs such as Opportunity International (OI).[12]

Horizontal Support in Religious Networks

While vertical support relations are limited and confined to specific occasions and key religious ceremonies, most support from religious organisations takes place at the horizontal level, that is, between the members of the congregations. Support on this level tends to be more crucial and creates effective, highly organised networks that act as a framework underlying the overall church hierarchy. The congregation is usually divided into different groups according to age and gender; this would include a women's group, a youth and men's group and finally, the group of the church elders, who carry moral and religious authority. Each of these groups has their own funds to which they contribute separately on a monthly basis. The money is used for group purposes, such as missionary work, festivities or as support for widows and orphans. The women's group in the CCAP, for example, owns four acres of land, on which they cultivate maize and store it until it is required for funerals and larger regional or national CCAP women's meetings. Funds are also used to provide for members who are ill or have a death in the family.

Numerous churches are organised on a geographical basis. They are made up of small groups of believers who live close to each other, and are usually led by a church elder. The purpose of these 'area groups', 'cell groups' or 'praying circles' is first and foremost religious. People meet for additional prayers during the week, so-called mid-week prayers, in order to foster their faith, discuss theological questions and gather spiritual and emotional strength. The microcongregations form the core of every religious support structure. They have their own funds, which are predominantly used for funerals or in the case of illness. Members of praying circles take over visits to hospitals or members' homes; provide money for medicine, food or soft drinks; and look after children or carry out household chores should the need arise. They collect firewood, *ufa*[13] and money to cater for funerals in the neighbourhood, if the chief has not already recruited young people to do this. Along with members of the women's group, they stay with the bereaved to pray and sing for the deceased. They wash the body and prepare it for the funeral, and on the day itself organise the cooking for the mourners. Being free of household chores during the mourning period allows the bereaved to mourn and regain their strength.

While the praying circle is thus a vital support element in religious networks, it also demonstrates a blurring of the boundaries of different religious networks. Firstly, people are frequently anchored in local praying circles as well as in other church groups, such as the women's guild or the youth group, thereby fostering their social security potential. Secondly, the fact that praying circles are highly localised makes them an invaluable point of departure for the weaving of network relations beyond the immediate religious realm. Members become friends and begin supporting each other outside the institutional framework of everyday life, and exchange information on topics other than religious issues, such as public affairs, work opportunities or housing.

Whereas the religious sphere penetrates into the wider secular world of daily insecurities and needs, paving the way for network relations, the religious background remains an important parenthesis of shared values, norms and social cohesion. The strong economic and symbolic dimension takes on greater significance against the backdrop of increased polarisation, both in Sector 7 in particular, and Malawian society in general. While social support between rich and poor is rare in the reality of daily life, and dominated by a sense of shame on the part of the poor, and the suspicion and fear of exploitation felt by the rich, personal acquaintance through church activities makes crossing social barriers easier for both sides – or as some people expressed it, they would 'feel more free to ask' for support. In this regard, there is no difference between the various denominations. As far as the poor are concerned, there is a clear entitlement embodied in the notion of charity and solidarity. For the rich, on the other hand, the religious context provides a regulatory framework that prevents possible abuse of their benevolence by the poorer brothers and sisters in Christ, and at the same time upgrades their own spiritual and social status within the church and the community as a whole.

The use of religion as a tool to access a broader social support network that would otherwise remain impenetrable is particularly obvious in the case of ethnic and regional differences, which in Malawi are key when it comes to social differentiation and in- or exclusion with regard to social support networks. In the domain of religious networks, these boundary lines become more permeable, allowing for a broadening of potential support relations: 'The church is important because it improves the social relationships with the people living in the area. We're all Christians, no matter how rich or poor you are and no matter what tribe you belong to' (Mr Mbela, Interview 58, CCAP). The social role of the church to which Mr Mbela refers in his statement is perceived as its major function in town. Both in the immediate church context and the wider social environment, it is this dense fabric of overlapping multilayered relations and networks that people refer to when they talk about 'the church':

> The church is very important in town. In the village there's a network of uncles and cousins, and the level of assistance is very high. You're cut off from them in town and it's essential to get support from the church, especially for funerals. The church replaces village support in town. Going to church in town gives you consolation for the difficulties in life. In town there's a lot of violence so more people go to church; they resort to the church when they're in trouble. (Member of the Seventh-Day Adventist Women's Guild, Interview 41)

Although the spiritual dimension, to which I will return later, is significant, the 'social factor' appears to be the driving force behind most people's immense religious activity in town. Those who did not regularly attend a church or a mosque in the village now did so in town. New social relations are more easily established in the social realm of religious associations. The social cohesion of the associations and the high moral values of Christian doctrines guarantee that networks stay resilient and rarely fail. Emerging networks in the religious sphere equate these aspects with kinship relations: 'When you come to town you have to look for new relatives. You find them in church and at your workplace. If you want to get support, you've got to be a member of the church. That's why so many people in town are church members. If you don't pray or work, you can't expect to get any help' (Seventh-Day Adventist female activist, Interview 67).

I was to hear this statement again and again in numerous interviews and discussions. At first sight it seems to confirm the notion of a break with the past, as practised in Pentecostal rites. Yet looking at social security practices, this is not necessarily the case. People tend to hold on to their kinship relations over distance, even after many years in town, although obligations are rarely met in reality and are confined to times of crisis, such as hunger, illness or death. The comparison of religious networks to kinship is merely the result of a sober and practical perception of how things are from the wider, translocal perspective of the migrants in town. Surviving in town means organising support without the assistance of kin; an effective method is to engage in religious activities. The following statement from a female migrant on the definition of distant and close kin also applies to the brothers and sisters in the church: 'Close relatives in town are not those from the same mother, but those who live close together. Distant relatives are those in the village because they are far away. But if I were in the village, the situation would be the other way around' (Mrs Tall, Interview 83). This proximity of religious networks contains a strong emotional aspect, creating in town a kind of substitute for home (*Ersatzheimat*). Numerous migrants perceive their new urban environment as dangerous and inimical. Attending church services and participating in religious activities produces a strong sense of belonging and identity. In the context of an otherwise anonymous neighbourhood characterised by a high turnover rate, the church community provides for a stable point of reference.

Translocal Religious Networks

The notion of religious networks as a solid framework within which people live and support each other also has a translocal dimension. Although this may appear insignificant from the urban migrant perspective, where 'village' is primarily related to the presence of kin and 'town' is not, religious networks also play a decisive role in the village context.[14] Membership in a religious association is an important translocal network within which migrants move, and an invaluable point of entry for newly arrived migrants. Similar to kinship and ethnic or local identity, religious belonging presents opportunities for identification and can provide all-important access to social, symbolic and material resources in town:

> The people from the church are your best friends, relatives, everything. They are the first people who will help with problems or celebrations.... Most of my friends are from church. It's much easier when you come to a new area if you have church friends. Wherever I went with my husband, we always found the church was the best community to belong to. (Mrs Mangani, rich Roman Catholic woman, Interview 120)

This translocal religious identity is particularly evident in the traditional mainline churches that still have a stronghold in the countryside, and is also becoming gradually more common in Pentecostal communities. The general practice is for members of the local praying circles to introduce and welcome newcomers in the area to the local congregation. This paves the way for initial neighbourhood contacts, which may in turn become close friendship or kinship relations. The significance of a mobile religious identity is underlined by so-called transfer letters. While different languages and specific expressions make ethnic identities easy to identify, religious identities are subject to extensive scrutiny.

Generally, conversion to a new denomination requires a certain evangelisation period. Newcomers to the congregation must at least undergo a period of grace before being accepted as full members. This is the main reason for the existence of transfer letters, issued as a rule by local village priests to members who intend to migrate, referring to both long-term migration or short absences, for example, when villagers visit their kin in town for a few weeks or months. This enables people to practise their religion in a more extensive spatial radius, since access to religious associations would otherwise be difficult.

A transfer letter allows them to attend church immediately and be accepted as fully fledged church members:

> When people come to town, they usually bring a transfer letter from the church they come from. It's a Christian custom to bring a transfer letter. The pastor writes in the letter whether the person in question has made contributions to the church and partaken of the Lord's Supper. If church members don't bring transfer letters, it's difficult for the pastor to believe they belong to the church. Then he has to examine them. They're asked about their former parish and the name of their old pastor or questioned on Lutheran doctrine. If members arrive and don't report to the church immediately, they are not recognised as members of the church when they die. The letter helps you to know if a person is a genuinely confirmed member and knows his or her strength. It also tells you if they've been excommunicated from their previous church. (Pastor of the Lutheran Church, Interview 98)

This statement highlights the function and spiritual dimension of the letter, and its significance for numerous migrants, who are devastated by the idea they could die in town and be unable to prove their membership of a church, and as devout Christians their entitlement to a decent funeral. In a secular sense the letter is a statement confirming membership of an exclusive network that furnishes people with social and material advantages.[15]

Hence religion has a multiple function in town. While religious organisations support members via a set of partly overlapping networks, religion itself constitutes a symbolic and social space where relationships can be created outside the immediate realm of religious networks. This overlapping multiple function of religion is a vital asset when it comes to accessing resources. The role of religion as an access criterion for support extends into the public domain of social support, as seen in applications for loans or housing to NGOs and other donors. Furthermore, the translocal dimension of religion contradicts the notion that relations other than those of kinship are mere substitutes, a belief that still lingers in some of the urban migration literature, and specifically in the Pentecostal idea that religious membership implies a complete break with the past and previous support relations. Instead, we have seen that translocal religiousness facilitates material and spiritual adjustment in town, providing a form of communal bond, similar to ethnic, regional or kinship ties.

The Church as a Spiritual Network

Unlike the material dimensions of religious networks, scholars have given little prominence to their spiritual features, unless in the context of the witchcraft debate (see, e.g., Moore and Sanders 2001; van Dijk 2001). Yet the spiritual dimension of religious communities, here understood as a set of spiritual, emotional and psychological support measures, is crucial to count-less migrants. Town life engenders specific needs and insecurities that lead to psychological and emotional pressures or crisis situations. Unfamiliar living conditions, the anonymity in comparison to village structures, and the lack of kin and family are all factors perceived by migrants as the downside of town life. The social and economic consequences of HIV/AIDS and its disastrous psychological effects, coupled with overall economic decline and permanent food shortage have aggravated an already tense situation. When I returned to Sector 7 in 2001, I was struck by the atmosphere of depression and sense of apathy among the people. Although originally considered a quiet place, petty crime, violence and alcohol and drug abuse had soared in Sector 7 within the space of only three years.

This scenario allowed religious associations to gain enormous influence as a source of spiritual, moral and psychological support. Several churches institutionalised this counselling aspect with the group of church elders. They decided on excommunication or reintegration of members involved in adul-tery or drug abuse, but also intervened in family disputes, domestic violence and relationship problems. Counselling on HIV/AIDS had become pivotal. Here, the Pentecostal doctrine gained enormous ground with its healing ideol-ogy: 'The people from church come when you're sick. They pray for you and you get healed. Mostly they don't give you money though. Relatives might say this isn't great support because they don't give you money. But for me it is, because I get well' (Mr Kagoma, Church of Christ, Interview 56). This state-ment uncovers a strong ambiguity in religious network relations and how they are perceived by competing network partners, such as relatives. At the same time, it points to the enormous value attached to spiritual support in times of difficulty and characterises the quality of support relations. Religious associa-tions and support relations are often rightfully criticised as cleverly disguised exploitative relations, whereby the poor tend to give more than they receive in material terms (see van Dijk 1999). This applies to churches of all kinds. I argue, however, that from the perspective of networks in the making, spiritual and emotional support should not be reduced to a by-product of religious membership, but as a consciously chosen and equally important asset to which religious associations provide access.

The Changing Role of Religious Networks and Practice

Thus far we have seen religious networks in town play a major role in provid-ing migrants with social support in the urban context. The meaning and func-tion of these networks encompasses a wide range of aspects, among which the material is just one. At the same time, circumstances have changed radically and now challenge the role of religious networks. While religious organisations have always been a key source of support when other networks have failed, the overall strain on more intimate network relations appears to have led to an increased 'outsourcing' of support to institutions beyond the household and wider kinship relations. The virtual collapse of networks due to the death of countless providers of material support has created new groups of people in need, that is, widows and the orphaned, including young people and frequently elderly parents. Faced with disintegrating family and household arrangements, it is they who are obliged to turn to more institutionalised support structures. Their basic needs, such as food, clothing, health and education, would previously have been provided by family networks. Various church communities report that the number of individuals, especially women, who look for support in periods of crisis has soared in recent years.

Religious organisations are likewise faced with severe financial constraints, making it increasingly difficult to realise even the most basic services. As members become poorer, they contribute less to collective funds. At the same time, lack of income-generating activities, the growing number of orphans and, last but not least, the indefinite number of funerals are stretching the already dwindling funds to the limit. As a result, some churches have introduced Sunday collections designated for specific purposes. The Roman Catholic parish, for example, keeps an emergency fund for people in critical circumstances, and throughout the rainy season runs a support programme for orphans in Sector 7. The orphans receive a monthly ration of maize flour and are given clothes and a blanket. Other churches have also begun to collect money in the community for orphans and widows in need. Among them are the Pentecostal churches: Zachifundo,[16] a fund introduced by the women's group of the Nazarene Church in Area 25C, provides basic necessities such as salt, sugar or clothes for poor orphans and widows in the area. However, most of these funds do not constitute a reliable support structure; for their beneficiaries the items distributed are just a welcome token, randomly received.

Although most programmes are dedicated to the whole of Sector 7, and not to members of the congregation alone, they seem to be the driving force behind the involvement of countless young orphans in church activities. This applies explicitly to the major churches, some of which run programmes for orphans. The orphans, on the other hand, combine church membership with the hope of greater support and access to its educational infrastructure. The following statement referring to the Roman Catholic parish in Sector 7 indicates as much:

> I used to go to the African Church in the village, but I couldn't find it in town. Now I want to change my denomination to the Roman Catholic Church. At the moment I'm attending classes to be confirmed. The church gave me jelly and soap, because

I am an orphan. I do not expect the church to give me more because I believe that the church is also not able to provide more. But if it provided more, then I would expect the church to support me with education and clothes. I hope that they will support me with education, because other orphans are also helped with education. (William, age seventeen, Roman Catholic, Interview 143)

Apart from the fact that the type of assistance offered has made people change their church affiliation, in addition I found that people went through a 'spiritual adjustment' (Hackett 1995: 205). Changing congregations or shifting between them is not a new phenomenon. In contrast to the European context, people in Malawi are as a rule loosely affiliated to religious associations. Changing religions can be the consequence of a process of spiritual development or be simply based on profane, practical reasons, such as marriage. Shifting religious affiliation is not uncommon, especially among migrants, since their religious community at home may not exist in the locality they migrate to, as seen in the statement by William, the young orphan.

The overall grim situation has, however, led to an upsurge of this phenomenon in recent years, reshaping religious practices and behaviour over time. For many, the promise of a better life in town did not work out in reality. On the contrary, the situation deteriorated, giving way to growing feelings of powerlessness and resignation. In this situation people have begun to 'shop' around for support at different churches, using multiple religious identities as a tool to simultaneously access different types of security.

The spiritual aspect is explicit in the new charismatic movement of the evangelical churches. The powerful salvation and healing aspect of the Pentecostal doctrine is particularly attractive for those in dire circumstances, as evidenced among the inhabitants of Sector 7. While the prosperity gospel of the evangelical and charismatic churches is perceived as more supportive in spiritual and emotional terms, material support is looked for in other churches. The separation of material and nonmaterial support constitutes a dilemma for many people, who are forced to reconsider their religious affiliations according to their contingent needs.[17] Mrs Chiumbudzo, a woman who takes care of six orphaned grandchildren and who was a Catholic before converting to the Assemblies of God Church after the death of three of her children and two of her grandchildren from HIV/AIDS, stated in this context:

They provide you with emotional strength at daily prayers and when you are sick they come to pray with you. The supply *ufa* and firewood for funerals and come to pray and chat. But the Assemblies of God don't give any other assistance, not even the women's guild. If I'm in trouble, they come and pray with me, and give me strength. If you've no food, you go to the people of your church and they'll pray with you and tell you God will provide. I should just believe and pray, and bread will fall from the sky. But it never happens. Then I start thinking about going back to the Catholics. The Catholics and the other churches help people, especially the orphans. They give them food and sometimes even pay their school fees. I saw it with my brother's child who lives with me. They came last month to write her name down. She'll get a bucket of maize per month, blankets, and some money at the end of each month during the rainy season. (Mrs Chiumbudzo, elderly woman, low income, Assemblies of God, Interview 137)

This statement reveals that most people are aware of the opportunities and resources available to family members through church membership. However, Mrs Chiumbudzo's story also points out the spiritual considerations people have to weigh up. Despite the somewhat ironic tone she uses in speaking of the prosperity gospel failing to materialise, its significance in terms of spiritual and emotional support does emerge. Pentecostalism seems to provide the spiritual and psychological power that other churches lack.

Conclusions

In this chapter I have attempted to unravel the multiple dimensions and dynamics of religious networks in the urban context of Malawi. Religion is the key element of social security in town. This concerns the role of religious associations as direct providers of support, on the one hand, and their role as a community or social space within which a dense network of mutual support relations evolves, on the other; these networks partly extend beyond the religious context, acquiring even kinship quality. Looking at religious networks through the prism of social security reveals that religion acquires a multitude of functions and meanings in town and provides a complex blend of social, material, symbolic and spiritual practices, among which communication with God is merely one aspect. The various meanings and functions of support do not stand in isolation but instead form a dense, overlapping network of often competing support circles, both among each other and in relation to other network relations in which people are engaged, such as those of kin.

Most religious network support takes place outside the institutional framework, which is typically confined to support in the form of rituals, such as funerals. In reality, religion reveals its power as a social network within which people live, work, practice their beliefs and support each other even at a distance.

A common religious identity is therefore an indispensable framework of shared values and norms that makes it easier to deal with life in the urban context; it is a key factor in social cohesion, and, similar to kinship, allows the personal dyadic network relations emerging from this context to function. The cohesive power of religion in social networks transcends hitherto insurmountable social boundaries between network partners, to a certain extent permitting the otherwise inconceivable redistribution of resources, for example, between the rich and the poor.

At the same time, economic circumstances are changing and modify religious support circles, compartmentalising their functions, religious practices and behaviour in the process. Because spiritual and material needs multiply as social and economic pressure mounts, religious organisations are gaining more importance as direct providers of support. Religious practices seem to be increasingly dominated by different, partly contradictory considerations that make people shift between churches in an effort to satisfy their material and spiritual needs. It seems that the function of religion as a social identity factor, considered crucial to making friends and establishing the semblance of community or home in an otherwise anonymous environment, has gradually been superseded by the support function as the key element of religiousness and spirituality.

These findings give important insights into the current religious movement debate in Africa, which centres on the materialistic aspect of the new charismatic churches. The everyday perspective reveals that the topic of spiritual adjustment (Hackett 1995: 205), which takes up so much room in the ethnographic debate on new charismatic movements, is not confined to Pentecostalism alone (for a historical analysis of the Protestant mission in Ghana, see, e.g., Meyer 1999).

The Pentecostal discourse undoubtedly has a strong appeal for the poor and the very poor, instilling people with hope of material well-being and healing in a situation of growing pauperisation and psychological pressure due to HIV/AIDS. From the 'underall' perspective of religious networks, however, the Pentecostal practice and its debate are not that straightforward when analysed from a socio-economic point of view, embedded in everyday practice and insecurities. Even Pentecostal churches have begun to engage in some kind of charity, albeit at random. In the light of the church shopping incidence in this chapter, it appears that the prosperity gospel is a highly stratified theological concept that largely works with people who are better off, where promises of prosperity and wealth can be realised to a certain extent. The poor, on the other hand, seem trapped in a moral dilemma when it comes to their spiritual and material needs. In order to satisfy both, they gradually begin shifting from one church to another, shopping for material and spiritual support. While aiming for salvation via the prosperity gospel, they continue to attend the more generous mainline churches in their attempt to cope with insecurities and the worldly matters of everyday life.

Notes

1. The research was funded by the Austrian Science Fund (FWF), the Austrian National Bank and the Max Planck Institute for Social Anthropology, Project Group Legal Pluralism in Halle/Germany. I would like to thank Tatjana Thelen, Anja Peleikis and Carolin Leutloff-Grandits for their much-appreciated comments on previous versions of the chapter.

   This chapter is based on fourteen months of fieldwork in an urban fringe area of Lilongwe City, Malawi, which took place between May 1998 and December 2001. The research explored the social security networks of urban migrants in the key religious associations. While examining migrant efforts to create networks in town, I came into contact with a multitude of Christian and Muslim religious organisations. Most of those in which my informants were involved became the focus of my research effort on religious networks. This explains why my information is primarily based on Christian churches and to a much lesser extent on the very small Muslim community in Sector 7. Most of the material I collected was on the large mainline churches, that is, the Presbyterian Church and the Catholic Church, which many of my informants attended for different reasons.

   The Pentecostal churches that became so popular with migrants over the years were a further focus of my research. I concentrated on the largest of these groupings in the area, that is, the Assemblies of God and the Seventh-Day Adventist Church. In the chapter I mention a series of other Pentecostal groupings, whose social security activities are of vital importance to migrants and the survival of their families. The information collected consists of individual interviews with migrants on their religious network activities, as well as interviews with representatives of the different churches on their functions and social security services.

2. See Paul Gifford (1994) for a brief history of the rise of Pentecostal movements on the African continent since the late 1980s. For a history of Pentecostalism in Malawi, see van Dijk (2001).

3. As various authors have shown for nineteenth-century proselytising or twentieth-century Pentecostal movements (e.g. de Bruijn et al. 2001; Meyer 1999), religious conversion is always related to notions of civilisation, progress and modernity, including access to education, health care or Western consumer goods. In her article on the pietist mission, 'Nineteenth-Century Gold Coast', Meyer (1999) discusses the double meaning of clothing as a sign of Christian belief and sense of shame and as a desirable Western commodity reflecting the latest fashion.

4. See also van Dijk (1998) and his discussion on nostalgia as a dominating element in the anthropological debate on African migration and belonging.

5. Structural adjustment seeks to enhance the role of markets so as to enhance development. The main characteristics of this neoliberal development strategy which formed the core of World Bank und the IMF (International Monetary Fund) policy since the 1980s include measures to produce a more stable economy (higher interest rates, fiscal constraints, etc.) followed by policies to alter the structure of the economy (privatisation, trade liberalisation, etc.) in order to make it better suited to the global market. Loans from these institutions were almost invariably made conditional on the implementation of such policies (Führmann 2003).

6. See also the normative order created by development organisations, the so-called project or development law that adds yet another legal sphere to the existing legal pluralism of society (von Benda-Beckmann 2001; Weilenmann 2005).

7. The federally owned Deutsche Gesellschaft für Technische Zusammenarbeit GmbH is the technical arm of German development cooperation.

8. Today, 57 per cent of the population belong to Christian communities; 16 per cent are Muslims, most of them Yao from the South; while 11 per cent practise 'natural religions' (*Naturreligionen*) (Bouzek 1992: 29). Recent statistical data indicates that approximately 7.9 million or 80 per cent of Malawians are Christians and 1.3 million or 13 per cent are Muslims (NSO 2000). The majority of Christians, amounting to 96 per cent of the population, live in the north compared to 84 per cent in the central region and 73 per cent in the south. The distribution of the Muslim population is the other way around, with the majority or 21 per cent living in the south, 7 per cent in the centre and 1 per cent in the north (NSO 2000). The Roman Catholic Church, the Church of Central African Presbyterian, the Anglican Church, the Seventh-Day Adventist Society and the Watchtower Society are the largest communities in the Christian churches. Malawi has experienced a new wave of charismatic evangelical churches in recent years, such as the Assemblies of God, the Living Waters or Born Again (see van Dijk 2001). In this context, Gifford (1994) states that the number of full-time American missionaries in Pentecostal churches at the beginning of the 1990s rose steadily. Between 1989 and 1993 in Malawi alone the number increased from 155 to 199 (Gifford 1994).

9. Most of these small churches, such as the Zambezi Evangelical Church, the Industrial Mission, the Nazarene Church, the United Methodist Church or the Anglican Church, have congregations in neighbouring areas. Membership varies substantially. The newly established parishes in the area, such as those of the Assemblies of God, frequently have no more than eighty to one hundred permanent paying members.

10. Most churches place a lower limit on contributions. In the Presbyterian Church, for example, the minimum lies at MK5 per month. The money is used to maintain the church, pay the priests, and cover expenses for funerals, illness and other contingencies.

11. For a discussion on the impact of mission educational services on the structure of the Malawian economy, above all in the farming sector, see McCracken (1977).

12. See R. Hackett (1995) for the role of religion as a source of income and specifically in the formation of national and global economic activities and networks.

13. ChiChewa for 'maize flower', which is used to cook Nsima – the staple food of Malawi – a thick, rather tasteless porridge made of boiled Ufa. It is accompanied with relish, that is, all kinds of vegetables or meat.

14. The role of religious organisations in the rural areas has grown in significance in recent years as a result of the overall tightening of social and economic conditions. At least this was the impression I got from accounts of newly arrived migrants in Sector 7, and of those who returned to their home villages on a regular basis. All of them reported that religious organisations had a growing influence in the villages.

15. Whereas the understanding of religious networks in translocal contexts is usually discussed in relation to out-migration, it is important to note here that religious identities seem to be gaining importance in the area of remigration. In his research in Zambia, Ferguson (1999) mentions religion as a vital asset for reintegration in the village context with regard to access to land, housing and the community as a whole.

16. ChiChewa for 'mercy'.

17. Van Dijk (2001) comments that membership in a new charismatic movement does not suggest having to leave the old mainline churches, since the former are less interested in recruiting members than in convincing people to change their religious behaviour and consequently, their lives. Notwithstanding, for the migrants in my fieldwork area, the issue of conversion was not that simple. It was first of all a spiritual dilemma of enormous difficulty to solve. Secondly, the strong social cohesion of the religious communities meant that membership of two churches would lead to consequences such as the exclusion from material favours.

References

Benda-Beckmann, K. von. 1984. 'Forum Shopping and Shopping Forums: Dispute Settlement in a Minankabau Village in West Sumatra, Indonesia', in *Anthropology of Law in the Netherlands. Verhandelingen von het KITLV 116*, ed. K. von Benda-Beckmann and F. Strihbosch. Dordrecht: Foris Publications, 77–95.

———. 2001. 'Transnational Dimensions of Legal Pluralism', in *Begegnung und Konflikt – Kulturanthropologische Bestandsaufnahme*, ed. W. Fikentscher. Munich: Bayerische Akademie der Wissenschaften, 33–48.

Bouzek, W. 1992. 'Die Entwicklungspolitik der Republik Malawi'. Master's thesis, University of Vienna. Unpublished.

Bruijn, M. de, H. van Dijk and R. van Dijk. 2001. 'Cultures of Travel: Fulbe Pastoralists in Central Mali and Pentecostalism in Ghana', in *Mobile Africa: Changing Patterns of Movement*, ed. M. de Bruijn, R. van Dijk and D. Foeken. Brill: Leiden, 63–88.

Comaroff, J. and J. Comaroff, eds. 1993. *Modernity and its Malcontents: Ritual and Power in Postcolonial Africa*. Chicago: University of Chicago Press.

Dijk, R. van. 1998. 'Pentecostalism, Cultural Memory and the State: Contested Representations of Time in Postcolonial Malawi', in *Memory and the Postcolony: African Anthropology and the Critique of Power*, ed. R. Werbner. London: Zed Books, 155–81.

———. 1999. 'The Pentecostal Gift: Ghanaian Charismatic Churches and the Moral Innocence of the Global Economy', in *Modernity on a Shoestring: Dimensions of Globalization, Consumption and Development in Africa and Beyond*, ed. W. van Binsbergen, R. Fardon and R. van Dijk. London: SOAS/Leiden: ASC, 71–89.

———. 2001. 'Witchcraft and Skepticism by Proxy: Pentecostalism and Laughter in Urban Malawi', in *Magical Interpretations, Material Realities: Modernity, Witchcraft and the Occult in Postcolonial Africa*, ed. H. L. Moore and T. Sanders. London: Routledge, 97–117.

Ferguson, J. 1999. *Expectations of Modernity: Myth and Reality on the Zambian Copperbelt*. Berkeley: University of California Press.

Führmann, B. 2003. 'Abkehr vom Washington Consensus? Die wirtschaftspolitische Strategie der Weltbank zur Armutsbekämpfung'. *INEF Report 71*. Duisburg: Institut für Entwicklung und Frieden.

Gifford, P. 1994. 'Some Recent Developments in African Christianity'. *African Affairs* 93(373): 513–34.

Hackett, R. I. J. 1995. 'The Gospel of Prosperity in West Africa', in *Religion and the Transformations of Capitalism: Comparative Approaches*, ed. R. H. Roberts. London: Routledge, 199–214.

McCracken, J. 1977. 'Underdevelopment in Malawi: The Missionary Contribution'. *African Affairs* 76(303): 195–209.

Meyer, B. 1999. 'Christian Mind and Worldly Matters: Religion and Materiality in the Nineteenth-Century Gold Coast', in *Modernity on a Shoestring: Dimensions of Globalization, Consumption and Development in Africa and Beyond*, ed. W. van Binsbergen, R. Fardon and R. van Dijk. London: SOAS/Leiden: ASC, 155–77.

Moore, H. L. and T. Sanders. 2001. 'Magical Interpretations and Material Realities: An Introduction', in *Magical Interpretations, Material Realities: Modernity, Witchcraft and the Occult in Postcolonial Africa*, ed. H. L. Moore and T. Sanders. London: Routledge, 1–27.

Rohregger, B. 2006. *Shifting Boundaries: Social Security in the Urban Fringe of Lilongwe City, Malawi*. Shaker Verlag: Aachen.

Weilenmann, M. 2005. 'Project Law – Normative Orders of Bilateral Development Cooperation and Social Change: A Case Study from the German Agency for Technical Cooperation', in *Mobile People, Mobile Law: Expanding Legal Relations in a Contracting World*, ed. F. von Benda-Beckmann, K. von Benda-Beckmann and A. Griffiths. Aldershot: Ashgate 233–55.

PART III

Transnational Networking

Chapter 9

The (Re-)Making of Translocal Networks through Social Security Practices

The Case of German and Lithuanian Lutherans in the Curonian Spit

Anja Peleikis

Introduction

On my way I see loads of people walking towards the church. When I get to there it's already packed. There is no room left in the gallery either. Even the extra chairs were not enough for the waiting crowds. People were pressed close together at the entrance and in the forecourt of the church, waiting. A loud buzz of 'Hello, are you here too, how are you?' fills the church. Suddenly there's a hush and the pastors enter....

The holiday service ends with a short prayer. The organ begins to play and the congregation sings the hymn 'Almighty God, We Praise You' in gratitude. I get so emotional that I cannot go on singing and start thinking about my youth, when sturdy fishermen, including my father, used to stand in the gallery in their dark clothes, their hands folded, and sing that very same hymn as loud as they could. And it used to ring out through the windows and the doors into the open like the boom of the waves in the sea. (Nida, Lithuania, Sunday, 10 August 1997)[1]

This is how Johann Pippis, a German Second World War refugee from former East Prussia, describes his impressions of the memorial service held in 1997 at the Protestant church in Nida (German: Nidden), Lithuania, fifty years after he had fled his native village, which at that time belonged to Nazi Germany.[2] More than one hundred former German inhabitants followed the invitation of Lotte Sakuth, an old Niddener herself, who not only organised the commemoration service but mobilised the network of former inhabitants to collect

---

Notes for this chapter begin on page 183.

money and support for the reconstruction of 'their' local Protestant church. Health and age permitting, they assembled in Nida in 1992, 1997 and 2002 to celebrate the reopening of 'their church', the inauguration of a memorial chapel in the church and the reconstruction of the gate to the cemetery.

During the fifty years of the Cold War, Nida and the Curonian Spit, a narrow, elongated peninsula on the Baltic Sea, were locked behind the Iron Curtain and closed to their one-time inhabitants. When the opportunity to travel arose after Lithuania's independence from the Soviet Union in 1990, many former German inhabitants revisited the sites of their childhood and youth. The re-inauguration of the old local church was a suitable occasion to travel back 'home' and symbolically re-appropriate local and religious spaces. Coming home after fifty years was a highly emotional event, and many of the visitors – like Johann Pippis – were deeply moved by the sound of the organ and the singing of the old hymns in the church. It mobilised memories of the past and a sense of grief and of loss. There was, however, also a sense of happiness and gratitude at having been able to return at last.

Since their forced displacement at the end of the Second World War in 1945, the inhabitants, now refugees, were scattered all over eastern and western Germany.[3] Over the years they succeeded in integrating into their new places of residence.[4] Many remained in contact with relatives, friends and former neighbours from their locality, and built up what I will call translocal networks of relations.

Taking the case study of the village of Nidden, in the following I will describe and analyse the making of this particular translocal network over time and its changing dynamics. I argue that the network is still of vital significance to the members involved, since it provided them with various forms of social security for more than sixty years. Apart from official state and church support, for example, the network provided these people with access to basic material needs in the postwar period, such as food, shelter or job opportunities. At the same time, creating and maintaining connections gave them emotional and spiritual security.

Further, I will describe how this translocal network constituted a crucial element of people's social security mix, which was based on a multiplicity of social relationships (von Benda-Beckmann 2000: 20). Hence people draw on family relatives, friends, patrons, religious institutions or governmental agencies in mobilising the resources to secure their lives (von Benda-Beckmann 2000: 20). They show different patterns of insecurity and need in different life-cycle phases and under changing circumstances, all of which demand diverse forms of support. In this context people not only act as providers or recipients of social security, but these roles can also change over time (von Benda-Beckmann 2000: 20).

Refugee and migrant studies have indicated that transnational and translocal networks based on shared local, religious and family background can make a strong contribution to people's sense of belonging and identification, and provide a sense of stability and security in exile or migration (Glick Schiller et al. 1992; Al-Ali 2002: 95; Peleikis 2003). My case study will illustrate how people become involved over time in imagining, remembering and discursively (re)producing deterritorialised places, thereby creating social, emotional and spiritual security. The dynamics of this phenomenon will be historicised and analysed against the background of changing political, economic and social conditions.

Up to this point the network under review appears as predominantly 'local' and 'translocal', as it consists of people who belonged to one particular village community. Following their displacement they began to create deterritorialised networks based on a shared local identity.[5] However, it should be kept in mind that local, religious and family networks overlapped in the village of origin. The population of the Curonian Spit prior to the Second World War was one of pious Protestant convictions, which provided them with spiritual security and confidence in the face of the hardships of fishery and of a life under environmental conditions that were extreme. Local and family identities were frequently reproduced through religious practices. Sunday was the only day of the week that local fishermen did not go out fishing. Similar to the rest of the villagers, they attended religious services at the local church. This coming together to pray and to worship contributed to the making of local identities. Weddings and burials were likewise highly significant social and religious events that reinforced local identities. While the majority of the local population was officially organised in the Protestant (Lutheran) Church, services and Bible readings in parishioners' homes in the company of neighbours and relatives were common as well.[6] It can therefore be said that religious identities were expressed and lived through local and family relations independent of official church organisation. I will illustrate that these prewar informal religious networks were vital during the postwar era, when they functioned as religious organisations for those who remained in the region. Faced with the destruction of former church structures and church persecution by the Soviet state, Lutherans were able to rely on their old informal religious networks (see Hermann 2001: 357).

Generally speaking, I will demonstrate that the merging of religious, family and local networks continued to be of valuable assistance in the postwar era, when the local population was spread between the home locality in Soviet Lithuania, in eastern and western Germany and places of deportation in Siberia. By connecting with others from their native village, the old Niddener were able to create a new deterritorialised network through which they could not only express their religious beliefs and practices and their faith in God, but also provide and receive social, emotional and spiritual support. In the process their local church – far away and unattainable for many during the Cold War – became a forceful and cohesive symbol of the evolving translocal community.

State policies can either restrict or support transnational and/or translocal networks. In the context of shifting political situations, new networks evolve, old connections are revitalised and as a result of political restrictions existing links may even collapse. Thus, translocal networking not only depends on the particular interests and strategies of the actors involved but also on the overall social, political and economical structures at a given time. Both the Soviet and East German states made connections between refugees from former East Prussia who lived in both parts of Germany and those who stayed behind extremely difficult. Nevertheless, families managed to connect during the first postwar years despite the Cold War and other political constraints. When most of the ethnic Germans left the Soviet Union in the late 1950s, translocal networks were reconfigured to span the new places of residence of the former inhabitants of Nidden.

This situation changed with the collapse of the Soviet state and led to an entirely new configuration of the existing network, integrating more actively the few people of German origin who had remained in Soviet Lithuania as well as the Lithuanian Protestants. Hence, in the second part of this chapter I will describe how translocal connections between German and Lithuanian Lutherans and between former and current inhabitants of Nida were revitalised and remade on the occasion of Lithuania's independence. A powerful religious symbol of the past and the present, the local church once again became the focal point of interest, drawing German and Lithuanian actors closer together.

I will argue that this new network developed as a result of the social security interests involved. There was in fact an obvious exchange of social security between the Germans and Lithuanians involved. The Lithuanian Lutherans received substantial donations in kind and money from the Germans, which were more than welcome. This new source of social security provision for local Lithuanians became highly appreciated in the course of transformation.[7] When the old Soviet state welfare arrangements ceased to exist, basic needs were only partially met by the new official social security system. People made huge efforts to mobilise other security providers. The former German inhabitants of the region and members of the Protestant Church, who were persecuted and repressed during the Soviet era, were able to fill this gap to a certain extent. The local Lithuanians, on the other hand, apart from having become social security recipients, were now able to provide German returnees with emotional security by giving them access to their former local places, such as the church and the cemetery. These places have a profound emotional value for the Germans, inasmuch as they trigger memories and emotions. I argue that the opportunity to revisit these places and confront emotions and memories related to their old lives in the locality, to war, flight and displacement, has allowed these former inhabitants at the end of their lives to readapt to their past and come to terms – at least partially – with their own personal history. This process frequently provides them with new forms of security in the present.

Receiving and Providing Social Security through Translocal Networking

In late 1944, the German inhabitants of Nidden fled the region of the so-called Memelland (Memel Territory), to which the Curonian Spit belonged. Fearing the Red Army, they joined about 12 million others who fled Central and Eastern Europe. Most of them came to either the western or eastern part of Germany, where they had to cope with the experience of displacement, loss of their home localities, poverty, discrimination and general insecurity in a foreign environment. Unlike the long-established population, which was somewhat hostile to the newcomers, politicians in both parts of Germany recognised the national sense of belonging of the refugees and introduced new legislation. On the basis of these laws and with the explicit aim of fostering integration, the two newly established German states developed a series of social and material aid programmes. Refugees in West Germany were officially, symbolically and legally recognised, for example, via the Emergency Aid Law (1949) (*Soforthilfegesetz*), the Federal Displaced Persons Law (*Bundesvertriebenengesetz*) (1953) and in the laws on equalisation of burdens (*Lastenausgleich*) (1952). These laws formed the basis of state social security programmes directed at refugees. The *Lastenausgleich* meant that refugees in West Germany were able to apply for compensation for the property they were forced to leave behind (Nahm 1974). Apart from the laws and programmes that made the fate of the refugees visible in the West German public sphere, expellee organisations (*Heimatverbände*) became powerful political actors that addressed and represented the interests of refugees.

Unlike West Germany, the German Democratic Republic (GDR) pursued a repressive policy of integration and assimilation (Schwartz 2006). Refugees were not addressed as such or as expellees but simply referred to as the 'repatriated' (*Umsiedler*), and forbidden to publicly organise themselves. Hence it became the explicit policy of the state to work against any form of translocal networking or revival of former local and regional identities. The 'repatriated' were to become GDR citizens as soon as possible. To achieve this aim, the state likewise introduced laws on which social security programmes were based. Despite restrictive East German assimilation policies, the refugees themselves made efforts to contact each other, and in the 1950s organised homeland meetings (*Heimattreffen*) in East Germany (Schwartz 2006: 99). Before the Berlin Wall was erected in 1961, many of the refugees had participated illegally in *Heimattreffen* in West Germany. Information in the form of expellee journals and books also found their way into East Germany. After 1961, it was more difficult for East German citizens and refugees to participate in the translocal refugee networks that had meanwhile been established. However, many of them kept in touch via letters and parcels despite official restrictions and control. Since the overall economic situation was more prosperous in West Germany, refugee families living in the West frequently sent parcels to relatives in East Germany, thereby contributing to their material security. At the same time, provision of social security fostered the making of networks among those who came from the same families, villages and regions in the East. Taking the case study of one specific family from the Curonian Spit, the Kubillus family, I will portray in the following the efforts of this family to stay in touch with each other in spite of the distance between them. They did their utmost to help each other, redistributing means to the poorest of the family, and became involved in the making of translocal social security networks in the process.

Immediately after the war, people endeavoured to find out what had happened to their relatives, kin, friends and former neighbours. In fact, every fourth German was looking for a relative in the initial years after 1945 (von Hehl 2006: 137). In West Germany they received help from the Red Cross and from church organisations, both of which established official tracing services (*Suchdienste*) (von Hehl 2006: 137). The disruption of extended family relations constituted the most obvious break with prewar local family structures. The Kubillus family from Nidden is a typical case in point. Some members of the family had managed to flee and came to an area close to Kiel in the northern part of Germany in 1945, while others were overrun by the Red Army and had to return to Nidden. The name Nidden had become Nida after the war and now belonged to the Lithuanian Soviet Socialist Republic. In July 1947, Elisabeth Kubillus, who was fifty-three years old at the time, wrote a letter to her son Paul and daughter-in-law Elfriede, who made it to West Germany:

Nidden, 1.7.1946

Dear all,

We received your letter of 8.05.46 on 28.06. We are so glad that you are all together and still in good health. But we are very sorry to hear that our cheerful Elsa is seriously ill or maybe even dead by now. But we pray to almighty God that he might let us all live and meet again. The four of us are still together and healthy too. We have been together since the end of July 45: both go fishing with Hans. We're living in the Dullies' house in Nidden, the new one. There's no one left in Preil. Else Kairies wants to know where Fritz Pietsch is. There are only a few Niddeners left at home. Balschick, Pinkis Johann, Else, the wife, is dead, the children are still alive, auntie is dead too. Mrs Wilhelm Pietsch also died.

Nidden, Preil, completely empty....

So look after Elsa well, God will reward you a hundredfold. If she dies, decorate her grave for us. And may God provide that this letter finds you all in the best of health. Especially our beloved Elsa. All of you are in our thoughts day and night.

And now 100 greetings and kisses from Papa, Mama, Hilda and Hans. Bye-bye!

The letter shows how people tried to discover what happened to family relatives and other members of the village, to exchange information and give themselves and the recipients spiritual support. Being able to send and receive such letters, and thus slowly create family networks beyond borders and despite Soviet persecution, constituted a vital source of hope, confidence and partial security in times of postwar chaos and overall insecurity.

About three hundred people of German origin were still living in the Curonian Spit in the late 1940s and early 1950s. Nevertheless, most villages were almost empty of inhabitants. The Soviet state began to request people from all over the Soviet Union, predominantly from different regions in Lithuania, to settle in the Curonian Spit. Fishermen in particular were recruited to move there, as the interest of the state was to increase fish production (Arbušauskaitė 1997: 186). The long-time residents of the area endeavoured to adapt to the new socialist structures and took up work in the local fish kolkhoz, where they taught the Lithuanian newcomers how to fish properly.

Although local Germans in Nida were faced with anti-religious propaganda and all-encompassing changes to their village, they managed to keep their church alive during the postwar era.[8] Used to religious home services before the war, the Lutherans in the region began to organise; they repaired the church and appointed a male Niddener as deacon. He conducted the Sunday sermons, and baptised, married and buried the local Germans. In this sense the Lutheran church remained the sole place where ethnic Germans were among themselves. It was here that they were able to symbolically reconnect with prewar times through prayers and hymns. The local church thus became a crucial meeting place, a 'real' and symbolic convergence of local, religious and family networks. When most of the 'last Germans' left the region in the late 1950s, following new laws on family reunions in the West, Protestant church life came to an end. The few who stayed behind were unable to pay the exorbitant rent and taxes imposed on churches by the Soviet state. The interior of the church in Nida was later destroyed and the building converted into a museum in the 1960s. By then Protestant life had been banished to the private realm of the few remaining Lutheran Germans and Lithuanians.[9]

The late 1940s saw massive deportation of Lithuanians to Siberia. Between 1944 and 1953 approximately 128,000 people were deported, or about 5 per cent of the overall population (Kiaupa 2002: 413). Among the deportees were ethnic Germans and other families from the Curonian Spit. In this context, Elisabeth and Richard Kubillus and their two children, Hilda and Hans, were deported in 1947 to the Krasnojarsk region of southern Siberia, where they were forced to live and work in a labour camp for more than ten years in conditions of deprivation and extreme poverty. The Kubillus family exemplifies a translocal family scattered by war, forced migration and deportation over several continents. Despite such harrowing conditions, however, the family managed to remain in touch between Siberia, Soviet Lithuania and postwar West Germany, supplying each other with material, emotional and spiritual support. The term *translocal* refers here to the fact that refugees living in different places continued nonetheless to build up deterritorialised networks on the basis of local kin and religious identity. These family networks could be also defined as transnational families following the definition of Bryceson and Vuorela (2002: 3): "'Transnational families' are defined here as families that live some or most of the time separated from each other, yet hold together and create something that can be seen as a feeling of collective welfare and unity, namely "familyhood", even across national borders.'

Members of translocal network families succeeded in providing themselves with social security resources despite the vast spatial differences between them. The Niddener who came to the western part of Germany were given the official status of 'refugee' and hence access to state social security programmes, which for the most part were developed to integrate refugees both socially and economically (Beer 2006). This in turn allowed refugees to redistribute their means and take care of their destitute relatives in the labour camps of Siberia. Although it was by no means easy to send parcels from West Germany to Siberia, it did happen, often via circuitous routes over Switzerland and through the Red Cross. It was less difficult for the Niddener who remained in Soviet Lithuania to send parcels to Siberia, as the following letter demonstrates. Sent by Elisabeth Kubillus to her daughter-in-law in West Germany, the letter reflects the tremendous significance these letters and parcels had for the spiritual and emotional security of family members obliged to live in a Soviet labour camp:

Pokateewa, Siberia, 1 January 1957

My dear Elfriede,

You made us so happy again with your lovely letter. Thank you with all my heart for your very dear Christmas and new year greetings. Yes, my dears, we have now spent the eighth Christmas up here in the north. Please God it will be the last. We want, again with God's help, to come into the new year and all its trials and tribulations. You guided me this past year like a father. And when I was overcome with worry, You gave me help and consolation. I praise You with all my soul and entrust myself once again, God, to your wise guidance.

We got over the Christmas celebrations more or less alright. We had a little tree and lit two small lights on it, which we had received from Uncle Martin the year before. You, my dears, were all under that little tree, and in our thoughts we were with you far afield. Dear Uncle Martin sent us a sumptuous parcel with wonderful presents for everyone. It's incredible how much he has given us over the last eight years. It obviously was supposed to be that he would remain in our home place so he could help us. Isn't that amazing!...

Everything is as usual here. Nothing seems to be happening as far as our release is concerned. Haven't heard a thing. The Siberian earth will probably cover us all. God's earth is everywhere. It seems to be our fate. Anyway, very best wishes Elfriede from Papa, Mama, Hilda, Hans and family. May God protect you.

Their Protestant faith and translocal family connections gave Elisabeth Kubillus and the rest of her family the physical and spiritual strength to survive the years in Siberia. Similar to events in postwar Lithuania, the German Protestant families who were deported to Siberia built up religious networks, with a 'lay responsible' who carried out prayers, married people, and buried them. Since Richard Kubillus had been a church elder in Nidden, he now took charge of several German and Lithuanian Protestant families from the Curonian Spit and the Memelland, all of whom lived in the same labour camp in Pokateeva, in the region of Krasnojarsk in Siberia. Through this informally organised religious network, people gained spiritual, material and emotional security in a foreign and anti-religious world.

In 1959, Elisabeth and Richard Kubillus and their two children, along with many other ethnic Germans who had either been deported to Siberia or remained in Lithuania, received the opportunity to leave the Soviet Union. This was made possible by new agreements between the Soviet Union and the two German states on family reunions (see Kibelka 2002: 85–123). The Kubillus family came to a town in northern Germany where the rest of the family had found refuge after the war. Those in the family who had remained in Nidden were also allowed to emigrate to Germany. Thus, the entire family was finally reunited in West Germany in 1959, thousands of miles from their native village but together in one place after fifteen years of separation.[10] The Cold War had prevented them from revisiting their birthplace, but many of their children and grandchildren travelled as roots tourists to Nida after Lithuanian independence in 1989.

To sum up, in this section of the chapter I demonstrated the power of translocal family networks to provide social security under the punishing conditions of forced migration, war and deportation. While the refugees in West Germany were recipients of social security provided by the church and the state, they mobilised their family networks for emotional and spiritual security, and at the same time became providers of social security for family members who had no access to such resources but suffered dire poverty in Soviet Lithuania and Siberia. Furthermore, I have shown that these deterritorialised networks simultaneously constituted informal religious networks enabling people to live and practise their local religious traditions far from 'home'. Thus, as overlapping family, local and religious networks, these translocal connections contributed to the provision of social security across borders and boundaries in the face of heavy constraints, and above all across the Iron Curtain.

Creating Security through the Remaking of Place

With the emigration of the majority of ethnic Germans from the Soviet Union at the end of the 1950s to East and West Germany, translocal networks were redefined according to the new spatial and social positions of the actors involved. Since hardly any of the old Niddeners remained in their home village, information on the situation back 'home' was scant and rarely spread within the network. However, Nidden continued to play a significant role in the lives of its former inhabitants. Re-imagining the homeland (*Heimat*) from a distance had become a key social event in West Germany during the 1950s, uniting the former inhabitants albeit dispersed throughout the country (see Svašek 2000, 2002).

People came together for family meetings, village gatherings and in post-expulsion associations (*Heimatvertriebenenorganisationen*). These organisations connected people who had once lived in the same villages, towns and districts of the Memelland. The Working Committee of the People of the Memel Territory (Arbeitsgemeinschaft der Memelländer, AdM), for example, had local groups from the Territory in many German cities. People could meet there, exchange important news about the *Heimat*, discuss West German refugee policies, and create a secure and familiar home from home. These associations were vital nodes for refugees, a place where informal social security could be received and provided. The AdM organised two-day meetings every two years. These were ritual events that included cultural, political and religious ceremonies and brought Memelländer together who now lived all over West Germany. Most people were drawn to these meetings because it meant contact with former relatives, kin and neighbours and an opportunity for common remembrance of the past, of local and regional traditions, of language and of history. In fact, these post-expulsion associations resembled the present-day 'ethnic clubs' of minorities, who remake their cultural traditions in migration.

The remaking of their native villages in these associations or in the course of village or family meetings was dominated by a highly nostalgic mode of presentation. During displacement the village of origin gradually developed into a distant, unattainable and idealised place, an emotional landscape and a projection site for the need to feel at home and be rooted. Hence, the making of 'nostalgic places of memory' provided refugees with a sense of security and mitigated the emotional pain of homesickness, loss and displacement. 'Place' and the possibility of (re)imagining, (re)telling and remembering the native village in a situation of displacement can therefore become a vital resource in creating a subjective sense of security and confidence. Notwithstanding fundamental ruptures in their lives, the refugees managed to create a sense of order and continuity with regard to their personal biographies through place-making and thus reassure ontological security (Giddens 1991: 53).[11] Following this argumentation, 'places' should not be understood as areas with surrounding boundaries but rather as articulated moments in networks of social relations (Massey 1994: 154). These articulated moments have the power to create feelings of security and continuity in migrants and refugees, despite the uncertainty of their lives.

At the same time, it is essential to note here that the predominant mode of nostalgia contributed to the fact that refugees and a broad spectrum of the West German population constructed themselves exclusively as victims, that is, as victims of the Nazi regime, of the Red Army and of the Soviet state. This focus on self-construction and experience as victims often superposed and ignored a potential memory of the Holocaust and German war crimes. While politics and the public focus in West Germany during the 1960s turned to the role and responsibility of Germans as perpetrators of the Nazi regime and to accepting the new borders in Eastern Europe, the West German *Heimatvertriebenen* organisations remained a place of politicised longing for the past. By ignoring the new borders and continuing their claims of the 'right to residence in their homeland' (*Heimatrecht*) and the 'right to return', expellee organisations generally pushed themselves to the margins of society (Kossert 2005: 376).

Against this backdrop, many of the younger refugees distanced themselves from the expellee identity and convictions of their parents, and from the nostalgic relation to 'places of origin'. Instead, many of them concentrated on building their own lives and socially, economically and politically integrating into the West German state – putting aside their own traumatic childhood emotions and memories of war, flight and the postwar era. They found a new 'place' and a sense of security in the economic miracle of German postwar society, where they were gradually accepted over the years and not excluded. Thus, in comparison to other refugee or migrants networks,[12] those of German Second World War refugees from Eastern Europe to the western part of Germany did not succeed in integrating the second or third generation. This was furthermore due to the fact that these networks did not represent a key source of security or identity for second-generation refugees. They integrated economically and politically into the West German state, married local women and men in their places of residence, and gradually became less interested in the re-imagined places of origin. This had consequences for the translocal networks of the old Niddener, Memelländer and East Prussians. Lack of new recruits who could develop into active, dedicated members prevented expansion of the networks. In fact, their networks have grown 'old' over the years, and membership continues to dwindle as the old people die.

Thus, when the old Niddener celebrated the centenary of their local church in 1988, those who came together as relatives, friends or former neighbours were to a large extent elderly people, all of whom were born in Nidden or the surrounding villages. They stayed in touch over the years, discursively remaking Nidden in the process, albeit from a distance. Since Nida was still behind the Iron Curtain in 1988, the former inhabitants celebrated the church centenary in the West German city of Hamburg. Religious and cultural ceremonies were at the centre of this two-day meeting, where the old Niddener church once again symbolised the extensive network of those who had once belonged to the same local parish in the Curonian Spit.

The example of the old Niddeners' attachment to their place of origin over a period of sixty years has shown that images, narratives and memories of place can become a key source of emotional, spiritual and ontological security. By discursively remaking their memories and images of Nidden for over sixty years, they managed to maintain a certain continuity with their prewar lives and identities despite having become economically and politically integrated in their new homeland. I have also shown that this translocal network constituted a form of security to a specific generation with specific needs. The refugees who came as children to Germany rarely became active in these religious social security networks.

The Remaking of Translocal Networks through Social Security Provision

State policies on travel, for example, have the potential to restrict translocal and transnational networking. At the same time, shifting political situations such as the fall of the Berlin Wall and the collapse of the Soviet Union and the emergence of successor states can lead to the remaking of networks and establishing of new forms of translocal social security arrangements. Focusing on the evolving network between the former German inhabitants and present-day Lithuanian Lutheran population of Nida, I will demonstrate in the following the importance of social security interests and strategies in the making of these connections.

When Lithuania became independent and introduced opportunities for travel, the first Westerners to arrive in Lithuania were the former German inhabitants – roots tourists, often referred as 'homesick tourists'.[13] Since 1989, many of the old Niddener have travelled to the present-day locality of Nida, carrying with them their memories and images of place. In many cases entire families of three generations journey together to places of family memory. Even the children who previously showed little interest in the nostalgic links of their parents to the past started to visit the places of memory.

Coming to present-day Lithuania and recognising the fundamental changes that had taken place over a period of almost fifty years has forced many to face the traumatic events of their own fractured lives. Thus, the return visit has frequently come to symbolise a pilgrimage to their personal past, an undertaking that is both joyful and distressing. Places have the ability to trigger emotions and memories. The physical impressions, views, flavours, smells, textures and sounds of a place can conjure up specific feelings related to the past. The local church, the cemetery and private houses are the places in Nida that particularly evoke memories and emotions. They are the most forceful symbols of their local prewar history and expose the ruptures and fragmentation they experienced in the context of war and displacement. By revisiting these places, caring for the graves of relatives, and engaging in the reconstruction of the church and the cemetery gate, these former inhabitants actively create an opportunity to reconnect symbolically to their ancestors and to their own local past. In the process they have become involved in re-appropriating these places of history.

In fact, all over former East Prussia, that is, Poland, Kaliningrad Oblast and Lithuania, former inhabitants were active in restoring churches and graveyards and/or assisting the present population after 1989 (see, e.g., Mai 1997, 2005; Svašek 2002; Peleikis 2006). The small Lutheran parish in Nida, comprising about forty people, addressed the former inhabitants, who were themselves Lutherans, for support in their efforts to reconstruct the old church. Since the church is a powerful symbol of their local and religious past, several old Niddener became active. During the Soviet era, the church was used as a museum and a concert hall. In 1988, local Catholics had reclaimed the church from the Soviet state. Most of the inhabitants who settled in Nida in the 1950s were actually Catholic Lithuanians who were forbidden to practise their religion in public. In the course of the struggle for Lithuanian independence, however, religion was mobilised and played a significant role in opposing the Soviet state. The nationalist opposition identified strongly with the Catholic Church. It was in this context that the Catholics of Nida were mobilised and successfully went on to reclaim the local church, where they were also permitted to hold services. As they constitute the majority in the village, they were in no doubt that the church belonged to them. During the fifty years of Soviet rule these people had appropriated the locality and made it 'their' Lithuanian village. A Catholic church was precisely what they needed in their opinion. After Lithuanian independence, state legislation on the restitution of church property was passed, and many Lithuanian parishes began to reclaim their property. The local Nida church was officially recognised as a Catholic church. At the same time the small number Protestants in Nida, made up of the few remaining ethnic Germans who stayed there throughout the Soviet era and several Protestant Lithuanians who had come to the Spit in the 1950s,[14] also attempted to hold services in 'their' church.

Maria Pinkis, the head of the Protestant parish, explained: 'It was in the early 1990s. We asked the Protestant priest to come to Nida to give a sermon. But the Catholics wouldn't let us put a foot inside the church. We were forced to hold our sermon outside!' In the years that followed, the Protestant inhabitants of Nida made huge efforts to regain their church, seeking the support of former village inhabitants in the process. As the church was the most vital symbol of their local Lutheran and German past, they promised to help. One elderly woman in particular, Lotte Sakuth, took an active part. She wrote to the German Protestant Church with a request for old documents, established contact with the great-grandson of the German pastor who had initiated the

construction of the church in 1888, and together with the local Protestants visited the Lutheran and Catholic bishops. Their attempts were successful and the
Nida church was officially returned to the Protestant parish, which is now the
legitimate owner of the church and the Lutheran parish hall. In addition, the
Catholic population was granted the right to use the church for their services.
However, this was not without conflict. The Catholics urged local politicians
and Catholic representatives to build a new Catholic church in Nida. A new,
eye-catching Catholic church was finally completed in 2003 and marked the
Catholic presence in the village and the Catholic Lithuanianness of the place
and the region.

Lotte Sakuth organised support among the former inhabitants in the form
of donations for the reconstruction of the church, which was then carried out
according to original plans and photographs. The benches and the pulpit were
made of oak, and the lectern painted 'Nidden blue', a strong aquamarine. The
words 'Blessed are the pure of heart, for they shall see God' (Selig sind, die
reinen Herzens sind; denn sie werden Gott schauen)[15] were written in German
on the arch above the choir, just as they were before the war.

In 1992, the re-inauguration of the church was celebrated with a festive
commemoration service carried out by German and Lithuanian priests, and
attended by many of the old Niddener. For a short time, by singing 'their'
church hymns, by chatting and remembering, the old Niddener re-appropriated 'their church' and filled it with memories and emotions, and their local
past, a past that was almost palpable in the present.

Unlike many other places, where Germans had become involved in recon-
structing their local churches, investing considerable money and effort only to
realise that the local parishes were unable to cover the running costs or that not
enough people wanted to use them, Nida is a different case. Despite the fact that
the Nida Protestant parish is very small, the church has turned into a renowned
'place of memory', attracting not only former inhabitants but also Germans
from other areas of former East Prussia or tourists who simply come to visit the
Curonian Spit. The church, which is open daily, has become a place of silence
where people can remember their personal lives and those of their relatives, as
well as a place of discussion on the course of German-Lithuanian history. For
some years the German Protestant Church (Evangelische Kirche in Deutschland, EKD) has been sending German holiday pastors to Nida during the summer months. They stay for periods of three weeks and are responsible for the
Sunday sermons in German in cooperation with their Lithuanian colleague. In
addition, they conduct guided tours of the church in the mornings. The Sunday services are well attended by the German (roots) tourists and the church
is frequently transformed into an emotional place of memory. The Germans
are extremely moved when they sing old German hymns in this erstwhile East
Prussian church. They are grateful for this experience and are prepared to give

generously in return. The money is in turn a key source of income for the local Lutheran parish, with which the Lithuanian priest is paid and church or parish hall repairs financed. The donations given by the former inhabitants constitute a valuable source of material security for the small Lutheran Lithuanian parish.

Furthermore, contacts established between the former German inhabitants and Lutheran Lithuanians (including Lithuanians of ethnic German origin) after 1989 not only led to the reconstruction of the old church but also to continued translocal social security provision. In the initial difficult years of transformation, when dire poverty prevailed in Lithuania and material goods were scarce, many former inhabitants collected donations in Germany and organised relief transport to the Lutheran parishes. Maria Pinkis, the head of the Lithuanian Lutheran parish, is the central figure in the re-emerging translocal religious network between German and Lithuanian Lutherans. She has become a key contact person for the old Niddener who come to visit their childhood places, as well as for German tourists in general. She can recount the Soviet history of the place and is familiar with the Germans who lived and died there. An indispensable figure in the translocal network, she became an intermediary between German and Lithuanian Lutherans. During the poverty-stricken years after independence, she collected donations from Germany, that is, clothes and other items, and distributed them among the Lutheran community of Nida. She also helped many other poor families in Nida.

In the early 1990s it was a common practice for the Lutheran parish to give loans to other Lutherans from donations received by the church. In this way Lutherans were able to invest in renovating their homes so as to rent them out to tourists, which in turn meant they were able to pay back the loans within a short space of time. These examples show how the mobilisation of translocal contacts provided the Lutherans of Nida with new opportunities for social security. They received donations in money and kind, as well as loans to invest in new lucrative businesses. Thus, while the Lutherans of the Memelland (Lithuania Minor) were forced to conceal their German-Lutheran background during the Soviet era and suffered persecution, translocal and transnational connections introduced new sources of social security after Lithuanian independence. Yet local Lutherans are not only dependent on social security via this network. They are in a position to provide former inhabitants and roots tourists with 'places of memory' that have the potential to create partial and temporal spaces of emotional and ontological security. Re-appropriating the local church and the cemetery allows former inhabitants to develop a sense of continuity in relation to events in their own lives, in other words, a sense of ontological security. Hence, becoming involved in the making of a translocal Lutheran network provided both sides, the German and the Lithuanian Lutherans, with new forms of social security. This circumstance proved to be a key motivation to engage in the network.

Conclusion

This chapter analysed the emergence of a translocal religious network over time. Prior to the Second World War, the members of this network belonged to the same parish in the Curonian Spit. After the forced displacement that led them to Germany as refugees, or to Siberia as deportees, people tried to remain in touch with each other including those who stayed behind in their native village despite Soviet restrictions. They communicated translocally and exchanged news, prayers and material goods. Resources were redistributed first and foremost to the poorest within the network. Since the refugees in West Germany received social security from the state and the church and soon found jobs, they were able to send money and other items to those who had been deported to Siberia. In fact, the need for emotional, spiritual, material and local security in times of forced displacement, deportation and grave insecurity motivated people to establish contacts and thereby create overlapping social security networks beyond boundaries. Reconnecting translocally and being in touch with family, kin, former neighbours and members of the congregation provided them with a feeling of being at home far from their native land. While to a certain extent refugees in the West found a religious home in the Protestant churches of their new places of residence, keeping in touch with members of their old parish meant sharing and practising local religious traditions that were familiar to them and slightly different to those of the West German parishes. Faced with religious restrictions and bans on religious activism, the privately organised religious meetings and prayers were of crucial significance to those who had remained in the Curonian Spit or were deported to Siberia. Contact to kin from the same village and parish of origin gave people in exile strength, faith and hope, a general sense of spiritual and ontological security in the face of harsh living conditions.

I illustrated that the meaning and function of translocal social security networks can change when people's needs or positions change. Material provision in this context became less decisive when members of the network were finally able to leave the Soviet Union and come to West Germany. Here they were supported by the state and church agencies, and could also earn their living with wage labour. On the other hand, the network maintained its significance, since it gave the German resettlers from Siberia and Soviet Lithuania the assistance required to adapt to life in West Germany. While the material aspect dominated translocal social security networks in the aftermath of the Second World War, it was the making of 'places of memory' that contributed to people's ontological and emotional security from the 1960s on, and motivated them to engage in and rely on the network.

After the fall of the Iron Curtain, revisiting places of origin, which had turned into 'nostalgic places of memory' was yet another turning point in network arrangements. By that time many of the former inhabitants had died and the number of people involved in the network had radically declined, not least because the network provision of social security was not pertinent to the second and third generation. Thus, while the network continued to be an important provider of social security for the elderly, the younger generation had no reason to rely on networks of this kind, securing their lives by means of other social arrangements.

For the old people, the strongest symbol of their religious connections beyond borders remained the church of origin. As soon as travel restrictions were lifted, they returned to their place of origin and engaged in the reconstruction of the church and the cemetery, symbolically re-appropriating these religious spaces in the process. At the same time, the network expanded to incorporate the Lithuanian Lutherans of the village of origin. In this context very different social actors with different life trajectories were drawn into the network through the exchange of social security means.

By analysing people's changing social security needs over a period of sixty years, I wanted to draw attention to the dynamics and flexible changes involved in the process of (re)making translocal religious and social security networks. Social actors are producers of networks. If their needs, interests and strategies change, the characteristic of the network also changes. People were integrated in this network for over sixty years, which provided them with various forms of social security. Similarly, the role of 'provider' or 'receiver' of social support also changed. Finally, I wanted to indicate a twofold process: translocal networking can, on the one hand, produce social security for its members, while, on the other hand, social security interests and provision lead to the making of translocal networks.

Notes

1. This is quoted from a letter written by Johann Pippis in 1997 to other former inhabitants of the village. Johann Pippis and many of the inhabitants were my informants in the research project on 'Who owns the village? Legal Pluralism, Cultural Property and Social Security in a Baltic Tourist Centre: The Case of the Curonian Spit/Lithuania', which I carried out between 2003 and 2007 at the Max Planck Institute for Social Anthropology, Halle/Saale. I visited them in their homes all over Germany and accompanied them on trips to their native village. (All names in the text are pseudonyms.)
2. The northern part of the Curonian Spit, which belongs at present to the area of Lithuania Minor (referred to historically as Memelland or the Memel Territory), was characterised in the course of the twentieth century by inconsistent national affiliation and the attendant change in population. Part of East Prussia for many centuries, it was integrated into the German Reich in 1871. The First World War brought deep changes to the Curonian

Spit. The northern Spit was cut off from the rest of East Prussia and came under a League of Nations mandate. Annexed by Lithuania in 1923, Memelland was granted autonomy status in the newly created Lithuanian state. Nonetheless, the inhabitants of the northern Spit continued to identify with Germany, and German nationalist ideology spread rapidly in subsequent years. In 1939, following the Hitler-Stalin Pact, the Nazis re-appropriated Memelland, incorporating it into the Third Reich. After the Second World War, local life in the Curonian Spit came to an abrupt end. Most of the inhabitants fled to the West, and the area itself became part of the Lithuanian Soviet Socialist Republic. In 1990, Lithuania reclaimed its independence.

3. The majority of the approximately 12 million refugees, that is, 8.1 million, came to the Allied Occupation Zones (American, British and French) in the western part of Germany, while 4.1 million came to the Soviet Occupation Zone in the eastern part of the country (Schwartz 2006: 91). As the majority of the old Niddener came to West Germany, I focus on their situation in this chapter.

4. On the integration of refugees in both parts of Germany after the Second World War, see, for example, Bauer (1987); Benz (1995); Donth (2000); Hoffmann et al. (2000); Kossert (2008); Rock and Wolff (2002) and Schwartz (2004).

5. On the making of translocal villages, see Peleikis (2003), and Levitt on transnational villagers (2001). On the concept of translocality in general, see Appadurai (1995) and Freitag/von Oppen (2005).

6. The practices of the local population were influenced by 'community movements', that is, the pious lay movements that spread in the middle of the nineteenth century in East Prussia (Hermann 2001).

7. On transformation and state social security systems in Eastern Europe, see, for example, Aidukaitė (2003), Lehtonen (1996) and Wagener (2002).

8. On the situation of the Lutherans in the Memelland in Soviet Lithuania, see especially Hermann (2001: 356–65) and Kibelka (2000, 2002).

9. Tamara Dragadze has shown similar processes for Georgia and Aserbaidjan, where religious practices and rituals shifted to the private space in the face of antireligious Soviet campaigns (Dragadze 1993).

10. Richard Kubillus died in West Germany in 1969 at the age of eighty-five. Elisabeth Kubillus died in 1993, having lived to the age of ninety-nine.

11. See also Thelen (this volume) on ontological security in the case of East Germany.

12. Many transnational migrant, diaspora and refugee networks integrated different generations and were thus reproduced and developed over time and space. The Armenian, Palestinian and Jewish diasporas and networks are some examples in this context.

13. On roots tourism, see especially Hirsch and Spitzer (2003); Basu (2004, 2007); and Peleikis (2009).

14. The history of Protestantism in Lithuania is closely linked to Prussia's presence in the region. In fact, the Protestant faith was a crucial factor in integrating people of ethnic German, Curonian and Lithuanian background in the Memelland (Lithuania Minor) prior to the Second World War (Počyte 1998: 86–87). Hence, while the majority of people in the territory were of the Protestant faith, the majority of those who lived in 'Lithuania Major' were Catholic. Today, approx. 0.56 per cent of the Lithuanian population, that is, 19,673 from an overall population of 3.68 million, belong to the Lutheran church. In contrast, the majority of the Lithuanian population or 79 per cent belong to the Roman Catholic Church (Statistikos Departamentos 2001).

15. *New Testament*, Matthew 5: 8 (from the 'Sermon on the Mount').

References

Aidukaitė, J. 2003. 'From Universal System of Social Policy to Particularistic? The Case of the Baltic States'. *Communist and Post-communist Studies* 36: 405–26.

Al-Ali, N. 2002. 'Loss of Status or New Opportunities? Gender Relations and Transnational Ties among Bosnian Refugees', in *Transnational Families in the Twenty-first Century*, ed. D. Bryceson and U. Vuorela. Oxford, New York: Berg, 83–102.

Appadurai, A. 1995. 'The Production of Locality', in *Counterworks: Managing the Diversity of Knowledge*, ed. R. Fardon. London, New York: Routledge, 204–25.

Arbušauskaitė, A. 1997. 'Sociological Analysis of Family Cards of Neringa Residents in 1956', in *Everyday Life in the Baltic States*, ed. M. Taljunaite. Vilnius: Lithuanian Institute of Philosophy and Sociology, 185–93.

Basu, P. 2004. 'Route Metaphors of "Roots-Tourism" in the Scottish Highland Diaspora', in *Reframing Pilgrimage: Cultures in Motion*, ed. S. Coleman and J. Eade. London and New York: Routledge, 150–74.

_____. 2007. *Highland Homecomings: Genealogy and Heritage Tourism in the Scottish Diaspora*. London and New York: Routledge.

Bauer, F. J. 1987. 'Zwischen "Wunder" und Strukturzwang. Zur Integration der Flüchtlinge und Vertriebenen in der Bundesrepublik Deutschland'. *Aus Politik und Zeitgeschichte* 32: 21–33.

Beer, M. 2006. 'Flüchtlinge und Vertriebene in den Westzonen und der Bundesrepublik Deutschland', in *Flucht, Vertreibung, Integration*, ed. Stiftung Haus der Geschichte der Bundesrepublik Deutschland. Bielefeld: Kerber Verlag, 109–23.

Benda-Beckmann, F. von and K. von Benda-Beckmann. 2000. 'Coping with Insecurity', in *Coping with Insecurity: An 'Underall' Perspective on Social Security in the Third World*, ed. F. von Benda-Beckmann, K. von Benda-Beckmann and H. Marks. *Focaal* 22/23: 7–31.

Benz, W. 1995. *Die Vertreibung der Deutschen aus dem Osten. Ursachen, Ereignisse, Folgen*. Frankfurt am Main: Fischer Taschenbuch Verlag.

Bryceson, D. and U. Vuorela. 2002. 'Transnational Families in the Twenty-first Century', in *The Transnational Family New European Frontiers and Global Networks*, ed. D. Bryceson and U. Vuorela. Oxford and New York: Berg, 3–30.

Dragadze, T. 1993. 'The Domestication of Religion under Soviet Communism', in *Socialism: Ideals, Ideologies, and Local Practice*, ed. C. Hann. London: Routledge, 148–56.

Donth, S. 2000. *Vertriebene und Flüchtlinge in Sachsen 1945 bis 1952. Die Politik der Sowjetischen Militäradministration und der SED*. Cologne, Weimar, Vienna: Böhlau Verlag.

Freitag, U. and A. von Oppen. 2005. 'Translokalität als ein Zugang zur Geschichte Globaler Verflechtungen'. *Beitrag im Fachforum geschichte.transnational*, http://hsozkult.geschichte. hu–berlin.de/-forum/type=artikel&id=632 (10.06.05).

Giddens, A. 1991. *Modernity and Self-Identity: Self and Society in Late Modern Age*. Stanford: Stanford University Press.

Glick Schiller, N., L. Basch and C. Blanc-Szanton. 1992. 'Transnationalism: A New Analytic Framework for Understanding Migration', in *Towards a Transnational Perspective on Migration: Race, Class, Ethnicity, and Nationalism Reconsidered*, ed. N. Glick Schiller, L. Basch and C. Blanc-Szanton. New York: The New York Academy of Science, 1–24.

Hehl, U. von. 2006. 'Flüchtlinge, Vertriebene und die Kirchen', in *Flucht Vertreibung Integration*, ed. Stiftung Haus der Geschichte der Bundesrepublik Deutschland. Bielefeld: Kerber Verlag, 133–43.

Hermann, A. 2001. 'Die Evangelische Kirche im Memelland des 20. Jahrhunderts'. *Nordost-Archiv* 10: 337–67.

Hirsch, M. and L. Spitzer. 2003. '"We would not have come without you": Generations of Nostalgia', in *Contested Pasts: The Politics of Memory*, ed. K. Hodgkin and S. Radstone. London and New York: Routledge, 79–95.

Hoffmann, D., M. Krauss and M. Schwartz. 2000. *Vertriebene in Deutschland. Interdisziplinäre Ergebnisse und Forschungsperspektiven*. Munich: Oldenbourg Wissenschaftsverlag.

Kiaupa, Z. 2002. *The History of Lithuania*. Vilnius: Baltos Lankos.

Kibelka, R. 2000. *Ostpreußens Schicksalsjahre. 1944–1948*. Berlin: Aufbau-Verlag.

_____. 2002. *Memelland. Fünf Jahrzehnte Nachkriegsgeschichte*. Berlin: BasisDruck Verlag.

Kossert, A. 2005. *Ostpreussen. Geschichte und Mythos*. Munich: Siedler Verlag.

_____. 2008. *Kalte Heimat. Die Geschichte der Deutschen Vertriebenen nach 1945*. Munich: Siedler Verlag.

Lehtonen, P. 1996. 'The Social Security System in the Baltic Countries', in *Regulation and Institutionalisation in the Baltic States*, ed. R. Blom. Tampere: University of Tampere, 51–65.

Levitt, P. 2001. *The Transnational Villagers*. Berkeley: University of California Press.

Mai, U. 1997. 'Deutsche Eichen und polnische Linden: Ethnische Symbole in Masuren'. *Forschung an der Universität Bielefeld* 16: 18–24.

_____, ed. 2005. *Masuren: Trauma, Sehnsucht, leichtes Leben. Zur Gefühlswelt einer Landschaft*. Münster: Lit Verlag.

Massey, D. 1994. *Place, Space and Gender*. Minneapolis: University of Minnesota Press.

Nahm, P. P. 1974. 'Lastenausgleich und Integration der Vertriebenen und Geflüchteten', in *Die zweite Republik. 25 Jahre Bundesrepublik Deutschland – eine Bilanz*, ed. R. Löwenthal and H.-P. Schwarz. Stuttgart: Seewald.

Peleikis, A. 2003. *Lebanese in Motion: Gender and the Making of a Translocal Village*. Bielefeld: transcript Verlag.

_____. 2006. 'Whose Heritage? Legal Pluralism and the Politics of the Past: A Case Study from the Curonian Spit (Lithuania)'. *Journal of Legal Pluralism and Unofficial Law* 53/54: 209–37.

_____. 2009. 'Reisen in die Vergangenheit. Deutsche Heimwehtouristen auf der Kurischen Nehrung/ Litauen'. *Voyage. Jahrbuch für Reise- und Tourismusforschung*, No. 8, Tourismusgeschichte.

Počyte, S. 1998. 'Die Sozialen Strukturen im Memelland zwischen 1918 und 1940', in *Die Deutsche Volksgruppe in Litauen und Memelland während der Zwischenkriegszeit und aktuelle Fragen des deutsch-litauischen Verhältnisses*, ed. B. Meissner, S. Bamberger-Stemann and D. Henning. Hamburg: Bibliotheca Baltica, 85–98.

Rock, D. and S. Wolff. 2002. *Coming Home to Germany? The Integration of Ethnic Germans from Central and Eastern Europe in the Federal Republic*. New York: Berghahn.

Schwartz, M. 2004. *Vertriebene und Umsiedlerpolitik. Integrationskonflikte in den neuen Nachkriegs-Gesellschaften und die Assimilationsstrategien in der SBZ/DDR. 1945–1961*. Munich: R. Oldenbourg Verlag.

_____. 2006. '"Umsiedler" – Flüchtlinge und Vertriebene in der SBZ und DDR', in *Flucht, Vertreibung, Integration*, ed. Stiftung Haus der Geschichte der Bundesrepublik Deutschland. Bielefeld: Kerber Verlag, 91–101.

Statistikos Departamentos. 2001. *Statistical Yearbook of Lithuania 2001*. Vilnius: Metodinis-leidybinis centras.

Svašek, M. 2000. 'Borders and Emotions: Hope and Fear in the Bohemian-Bavarian Frontier Zone'. *Ethnologia Europaea* 30(2): 111–26.

_____. 2002. 'Narratives of "Home" and "Homeland": The Symbolic Construction and Appropriation of the Sudeten German *Heimat*'. *Identities: Global Studies in Culture and Power* 9: 495–518.

Wagener, H.-J. 2002. 'The Welfare State in Transition Economies and Accession to the EU'. *West European Politics* 25(2): 152–74.

Chapter 10

Women's Congregations as Transnational Social Security Networks

Gertrud Hüwelmeier

Introduction

Women's congregations provide both members and non-members with different forms of social security. However, the charity extended to non-members and the social security arrangements for Catholic sisters are always closely interlinked with and embedded in changing political and historical circumstances. Many women's congregations were founded in the nineteenth century in Europe. Due to political conflicts, a number of Catholic sisters left their home countries and settled in the US and elsewhere, maintaining social and religious ties with their respective motherhouses in Europe. Although they had been engaging in cross-border activities since the end of the nineteenth century, the sisters only became fully aware of being transnational at the end of the twentieth century. Because of the decline of new sisters in Europe and as a result of the Second Vatican Council (1962–1965), many Catholic women's congregations opened their doors to women from India and other 'nondeveloped' countries. I will argue that these processes, alongside with rapid globalisation, shaped the concepts of social security within women's congregations as well as their ministries. On the one hand, sisters in Western countries have become more dependent on the welfare system of their respective states since the 1970s, in contrast to previous decades when their communities had provided for them. In addition, transnational care chains have been established to provide for elder sisters in the West. On the other hand, since numerous sisters from Asia and Africa began entering Western women's congregations from the 1960s onwards, they have needed material and spiritual

---

support from their co-sisters in Europe. The sisters required such support in order to make their own living and found new branches in India, Kenya and other places, and to provide education and health care for poor people in their countries of origin. The provision and receipt of social security is a fundamental pillar of global Catholic networks, within which women's congregations form the most effective groups aiding those who are in need.[1]

In the nineteenth and first half of the twentieth centuries, social security for Catholic sisters was organised in the congregation along the lines of the family model, that is, it functioned as a unit for the provision of emotional and material care for its members. Until the 1960s, membership in a female religious order required that women break almost all ties with their families of origin. Some of the sisters even migrated to countries far from home. The congregations also provided for non-members who were needy, and engaged in a variety of social and community services, such as the building and maintaining of schools and hospitals. These services and the material needs of the sisters themselves were primarily covered by donations from the larger Catholic community.

The Second Vatican Council (1962–1965) constituted a historical break that gave women's congregations an opportunity to extend their engagement and charitable activities even further, that is, abroad, implying the provision of social security to the 'world'. At the same time, the restrictions on contact to their families of origin were relaxed. Face-to-face relations with their kin and the possibility of visiting them for a holiday altered the sisters' personal social security arrangements, for example, outside the religious community, and their ability to engage in transnational charity activities as a result of possible financial support from relatives and the respective parish of origin.

Today, women's congregations are NGOs, whose members act beyond the borders of their own communities and cooperate with lay people as well as women religious from other congregations. Contrary to former times, when membership was exclusive and sisters did not even talk to nuns from different congregations, Catholic sisters now maintain networks all over the world, even living and working with sisters from other religious orders, as well as with associates or lay people. In addition, they forge and maintain social relations with all branches of their congregations throughout the world. As women's congregations are vital actors in the process of globalisation, particularly in the struggle against poverty and the dialogues on human rights and global justice, analysing them will provide specific insights into the practices of transnational social security.

Since the 1960s, demographic changes and the decline in membership in most congregations in Western countries have caused severe problems in the care of elderly sisters. After the Second Vatican Council, aspirants from non-Western countries entered Western women's congregations. African, Indian and Latin American women left their countries of origin and became novices in Europe and the US. They were trained as nurses, midwives or doctors, and after many years eventually returned to their home countries to serve their own people. Meanwhile, a number of younger sisters from India have come to live and work in hospitals and homes for elderly people in European countries, caring for their older co-sisters and thus creating global care chains (Hochschild 2000). Reaching beyond the confines of the congregation, transnational networks also strengthen the sending of remittances to provide for the poor and the sick, in particular children and the elderly, as well as those suffering from diseases such as malaria, AIDS or leprosy. The contact between the Catholic sisters and their families, villages and parishes of origin in Europe plays a key role here. Donations are given by lay people via the European motherhouses of the women's congregations to support housing and health care projects in Asia and Africa.

In attempting to grasp the two kinds of social security offered by the congregation and its members, the use of the term *religious networks* seems appropriate, as it enables us to analyse the social security practices within the congregation, as well as the changing nature of the welfare provided by the sisterhood to outsiders. In addition, contrary to the term *community*, conceptualised as a bounded entity, the notion of a religious network suggests the changing character of women's congregations, and reflects the new ethnic and cultural diversity in women's congregations of the last few decades. Moreover, the term *religious network* refers to the interconnectedness and cooperation between different congregations, a collaboration that did not exist before the Second Vatican Council.

My chapter draws on a historical and anthropological perspective. In the historical perspective, I will focus on the founding process of hundreds of women's congregations in the mid-nineteenth century, arguing that membership of these groups was the sole option for women who desired to live a religious way of life within a community, to work outside the home and to act in public without the control and protection of husbands or fathers. A hundred years ago, social security was not provided by the state or the family of origin but by the religious congregation: the sisters practiced mutual assistance in the case of emotional distress or illness. From the anthropological perspective, I would like to emphasise contemporary perceptions of social security in women's congregations and point out the processes of transformation following the Second Vatican Council, when ethnic diversity and transnational social security ties came into play in religious congregations. The sisters in Latin America, India and Africa are highly dependent on remittances from their co-sisters in Europe and the US. Taking the tsunami of December 2004 as an example of ecological disaster, I would like to demonstrate how Western and non-Western branches of a transnational women's congregation supported each other in their efforts to help the people of Tamil Nadu/South India.

Based on my fieldwork with the Poor Handmaids of Jesus Christ, a Catholic women's congregation with branches throughout Africa, Latin America, the US, Europe and Asia, I will outline their 'transnational connections' (Hannerz

1996)[2] and the global flow of money as one of the many cultural flows recently discussed in anthropology (Appadurai 1991; Glick Schiller et al. 1992, 1995; Glick Schiller 1999; Vertovec 1999; Portes 2003). In their attempt to understand and explain the changing nature of contemporary migration flows and how global identities are constructed 'from below' and 'on the move' (Vertovec and Cohen 1999: xiii), scholars have brought fresh ideas to the social sciences. Although the celebration of the 'newness' of these ideas on transnationalism was criticised (Foner 1997), very little work has been done on historicising transnational connections. This chapter intends to contribute to the debate, pointing to the continuities and transformations of past and present cross-border relations. A further aspect seems significant. The above-mentioned flows have attracted surprisingly little attention in the context of religious networks. Social security, a vital factor in connecting people across borders, is as important in maintaining transnational religious ties as it is in creating transnational family ties (Bryceson and Vuorela 2002) or other cross-border activities based primarily on international migration and therefore merits further study.

Religious Congregations in the Nineteenth Century

In response to secularisation, industrialisation and increasing poverty, hundreds of Catholic women's congregations were founded in Europe in the initial decades of the nineteenth century (Ewens 1978; Hüwelmeier 2000c). This wave of new congregations was part of a process that Claude Langlois has called the 'silent revolution' (1984). Catholic sisters were active in the establishment of schools and hospitals, in educating children and in taking care of the sick and the poor both within and outside their countries of origin (Hüwelmeier 1999, 2000a, 2000b, 2004a, 2005a, 2005b, 2006a, 2006b). Due to political conflicts in Europe and mass migration to the US, many of the European sisters left their home countries, settled in new places and moved once again in order to meet people's needs. The reasons for creating translocal and transnational networks were quite different in various countries, and were for the most part linked to social, economic and political circumstances in the sisters' home societies. In the case of Germany, two major facts encouraged these women to leave their convents and settle elsewhere. The first concerned the political situation in Germany, where conflicts between the Roman Catholic Church and Protestant-dominated Prussia led them to leave their home country. Secondly, women religious[3] were generally part of the 'great migration' in the second half of the nineteenth century.

The founding of numerous women's congregations was part of the religious revival in Europe. The revitalising processes of public religious life, devotion, piety and pilgrimage were an inspiration to Catholic women, one of whom was Katherine Kasper, the founder of the Poor Handmaids of Jesus Christ (PHJC).

Born in a small village in the western part of Germany in 1820, she attended school for only two years. Later she worked as a day labourer in the fields of more wealthy peasants. On Sundays she would join other young women from her village in order to pray, read the Bible and look after the poor and the sick. Many years later, Katherine Kasper had a vision, but it was not until 1851 that the local bishop of Limburg, finally convinced by her persistence and humility, confirmed the group as a religious congregation.[4] She and her companions, who were predominantly from the lower classes and members of the 'pious association', lived together in a small house. Almost all of them had worked as domestic servants before entering the community. It was common at that time for young girls to leave their homes at the age of fourteen to work in the houses of more prosperous peasants, usually as maids. These households looked after the young women, gave them food and shelter, and occasionally some money for their hard work as farm hands in the fields. After joining the pious association, the young women worked as day labourers when they were not taking care of the sick in the region. They received food from those they served, to a certain extent an act of reciprocity for the services provided by the sisters. Even in the 1950s and 1960s, according to stories I was told by people in the villages and anecdotes recounted by Catholic sisters, it was by no means easy to obtain meat, eggs or vegetables from villagers or townspeople. Most of the Catholic laity were as poor as the sisters themselves. Nuns were perceived as 'beggars', since collecting food and money was characterised as 'begging' (Hüwelmeier 1999: 40).

Although the Poor Handmaids worked primarily among the poor, they were asked to act in a nursing and healing capacity in the neighbouring villages and small towns of the surrounding area. Upper-class women, in particular Catholic noblewomen, also had a demand for the nursing services of the sisters. Through Catholic networks of baronesses, priests and bishops of other dioceses, the Poor Handmaids were invited by the local gentry of various localities to come and live in their domains, where they took up social work and teaching. In exchange for their services, the gentry provided the sisters with clothes, accommodation and food. Supported by noblewomen in non-Prussian regions and their transnational kinship and marriage relations, the Poor Handmaids founded houses in the Netherlands, Bohemia, Belgium and Luxembourg (Hüwelmeier 2005a: 95). These convents were significant for the German *Kulturkampf*, a political contest between the newly formed Protestant-dominated German nation state and the Catholic Church.[5] In the 1870s, the government passed several laws to curtail the influence of the Catholic Church. Priests were imprisoned, bishops forced to leave the country and the sisters no longer permitted to teach in schools (Blackbourn 1993; Hüwelmeier 2004a). After some had been compelled to wear ordinary clothes while teaching instead of the traditional habit, those who worked in schools left Germany and emigrated to England, the Netherlands and the US.

The 'Great Migration'

Apart from political conflicts between the state and the Catholic Church in Germany, there was a second reason why the sisters left their home country and joined in the 'great migration' of millions of people from Europe to the United States. American bishops of German origin requested German superiors to send nuns to assist with the integration of immigrants in their American dioceses. Qualified sisters were needed to build schools, kindergartens and hospitals in remote areas as well as in big cities like Chicago. Churches and parishes were vital places of support for the millions of European immigrants to the US (Gillis 2003), and were frequently the only ones that existed for 'gatherings in diaspora' (Warner and Wittner 1998).

French, Polish, German and Irish women religious in the US founded convents and established special spheres of work in the final decades of the nineteenth century, in particular teaching in parochial schools.[6] With almost no knowledge of English, countless sisters began a new life under completely different climatic, social, political and cultural circumstances than those they had previously known. They lived communally in small groups in various houses, organising their work and daily lives unaided, without male protection. The priests and bishops were often a great distance away. The sisters forged a way of life quite different than the middle-class ideals of womanhood and motherhood, one that was characterised by adherence to religious rule and by hierarchies of local, regional and transnational power relations among women. Each convent in the US had a local superior who acted as the female head of the household. At the level above, the regional superior lived in the provincial house, where the administration was accommodated and novices trained. She and her assistants paid regular visits to the convents and made decisions on financial and political matters, such as the closing down of convents, the moving of sisters to other places or the founding of new houses. The sisters in the US province were responsible for their own funding, and collected money and food from the rich and the poor. They were occasionally given quite large sums of money, as well as houses or plots of land. In some cases the German motherhouse sent money to the US province to build a hospital, which was eventually paid back after a number of years.

Transnational Spiritual Security

Although the German motherhouse provided only a small amount of financial support to the American province in the nineteenth century, the mother general gave constant spiritual support to her sisters abroad. Due to health problems and excessive travel costs, as well as to the arduous transatlantic journey, the mother general was unable to visit her 'daughters' on the far side of the ocean. Apart from letters back and forth, prayer was the sole means of daily communication. The mother general maintained contact through written correspondence, thereby creating a sense of collectivity or 'common consciousness' (Vertovec 1999: 450) and shared imagination. The community was 're-created through the mind' (Cohen 1996: 516) by recalling the common 'origin' and pointing to the same religious 'roots'. I quote from a letter written by the mother superior to her sisters in America in 1886, almost twenty years after the first Poor Handmaids had settled in the US:

> If only I could once be in that America, God willing. But it seems it is not to be in my case. I am so often in America, even several times a day. In all my poor prayers, I especially bring the beloved sisters together.... We live and work in one religious community. We all have the spirit of a Poor Handmaid of Jesus Christ; we all have one rule. The more we live and work in this one spirit, the closer we are to one another....

In another letter she wrote: 'I travel to my beloved sisters in America several times a day in my mind.'[7] Katherine Kasper regretted not having personal contact with her daughters on the other side of the ocean, but: 'Although I never met our American sisters face to face, they are very close to me. I have a great desire to get to know them in person. But if this is not the holy will of the Lord, we will accept it. I visit you every day in my mind and even more often in prayer.'[8]

Writing letters, sending prayers across the ocean and participating in the lives of others across international borders can be best interpreted within the framework of a 'transnational social field' (Glick Schiller and Fouron 1999: 344). This concept focuses on the personal social relationships immigrants entertain, by means of which they continue to be part of the social fabric of their home countries, while simultaneously remaining incorporated in the activities of their new surroundings. These relationships frequently encompass immigrants as well as those who have never left their native country. Transmigrants are people 'who migrate and yet maintain or establish familial, economic, religious, political or social relations in the state from which they moved, even as they also forge such relationships in the new state or states in which they settle' (Glick Schiller and Fouron 1999: 344; Fouron and Glick Schiller 2001). Although these theoretical concepts focus on contemporary societies, similar to most debates on transnationalism and migration, they can also be applied to the situation in the nineteenth century. As Donna R. Gabaccia has lucidly shown in her historical work, thousands of Italian migrants commuted between the US and Italy in the late nineteenth century (Gabaccia 2000). Even more than a hundred years ago, not unlike family members who lived dispersed around the globe, members of religious communities participated in the daily lives of their co-sisters in Europe, and vice versa. They felt both emotionally and religiously connected, although physically separated by the ocean.

As the state did not offer financial support for the sisters in the nineteenth century, they created translocal and transnational social networks to provide specific services for themselves and for the people they served. In the US, 'the Catholic sub-culture managed to provide for the new immigrants.... The schools, run by religious sisters, served as major agents of socialization and were entirely financed by the Catholics themselves' (Adloff 2006: 8). Obliged to support itself, the sisterhood was dependent on donations from local people. The condition for this way of life, particularly with regard to emotional and material social security, was mutual assistance in daily life, at work and in the case of illness or death. Foundations, gifts and donations, as well as the transfer of houses, land and shares to the sisters enabled them to look after others in hospitals, schools and orphanages. The dowry each sister brought into the religious congregation formed part of the latter's property. In the case of the Poor Handmaids of Jesus Christ (PHJC), however, this was only a small sum of money, since most of the sisters came from lower-class families. By carrying out social work and performing charity, the sisters anticipated the state-based system of nursing and social welfare. The general superior was regarded as the 'mother' who visited her 'daughters' regularly in the German and Dutch branches, wrote letters and sent prayers across the ocean to England and America. Social security was provided in the same way as families and kin groups organise their daily lives. Kinship terms (mother, child, daughter, sister) were adapted from the secular family system, but given additional religious meaning. Highly respected local superiors took over the responsibilities of the female head of the convent, taking care of the emotional, physical and spiritual well-being of their 'daughters'.

After the Second Vatican Council

The Second Vatican Council (1962–1965) in Rome, a meeting of world bishops, had vast consequences for Catholicism as a global church, particularly since it 'now expected Catholics to devote themselves publicly to social justice issues' (Adloff 2006: 14). It renewed its liturgy, strengthened the influence of the laity, and opened the door to dialogue with other religions. It put an end to Catholic sisters 'being treated like children' by the male Catholic hierarchy, as one bishop explained. Debates emerged in women's congregations at the end of the 1960s on questions of dress and democracy, and of emotions and the body. As the sisters explained during my fieldwork, some co-sisters decided to live their lives 'in the world' and took leave of their communities. Even during and after the Second Vatican Council, those who left were treated as 'black sheep', meaning that further contact with their former co-sisters was forbidden, and all ties were cut from one day to the next. Only since the 1980s have the sisters begun to re-establish social relations with their one-time co-sisters. At the end of the 1990s, the US leadership team of the PHJC organised special events, and invited those who had left the order a long time ago. Both parties, the sisters who stayed and those who went to live 'in the world', enjoyed the meetings and spoke of their innermost feelings and the hurt they had experienced at the time. Some of the former US sisters even became members of lay groups of more than two hundred people closely associated with the charism of the Poor Handmaids of Jesus Christ. This is one way of maintaining emotional and spiritual security among women, who once lived together but separated from each other for different reasons. Reconciliation renewed and strengthened former ties, simultaneously creating new bonds of affinity through the possibility of becoming a member in one of the congregations' lay groups.

Several sisters who had remained in their congregations during the troubled 1960s and 1970s experienced deep personal crises. Many of the sisters suffered due to strictly interpreted religious rules and rituals of subordination. In addition, they were not permitted to have close friends within the congregation with whom they could share their doubts. It took several years for the US leadership team to respond to these problems. In the end, the provincialate decided to provide professional help for all who were willing to take part in psychotherapeutic programmes. I talked to some of the sisters who had taken a sabbatical to reflect on their emotional distress and grief. Those who went through these healing processes returned to become creative and active sisters again. They are grateful to their congregation for giving them the opportunity of participating in these programmes so generously.

At the institutional level, severe conflicts emerged between the German and the American branch of the PHJC after the Second Vatican Council, leading the American sisters to speak of separation from the German motherhouse. US sisters and those from Holland wanted to wear ordinary clothes instead of the traditional habit, but were not permitted to do so by the general superior. The American and Dutch sisters finally made their own decisions. To fully understand the range of conflict in the late 1960s, we must contextualise the debates of the sisters – mainly focused on the habit and bodily practices – within the framework of a changing Catholic Church and its de-privatisation (Casanova 1994), and within a changing world shaped by the student movement, the women's movement and the anti–Vietnam War movement, all of which had emerged in the countries of the West.

In addition to the issues mentioned above, the sisters began to realise the existence of a generation gap. Very few novices entered the congregations in the 1960s and 1970s. Aspirants to work in the kitchens, the gardens, the fields, the cowsheds, the sewing room or the laundry were no longer available. Questions arose about who would take care of the older nuns. Until to this time, Catholic sisters in Europe and the US still worked without a salary, and they had no health insurance or pension scheme. The superiors of many women's congregations saw no necessity for state social security systems. When the sisters were ill, they were treated by doctors who worked in hospitals owned by the congregations. Since there was an ample number of young sisters to take care of those who were elderly, a pension scheme was not considered essential. In the 1970s, however, the leadership teams became aware that the decline in the number of novices entering the order meant that only a few sisters would be left to nurse the older nuns. Many congregations, including the PHJC, were forced to hire people from outside to do the work. More and more women's congregations and their institutions were transformed into modern enterprises. Their hospitals, schools, nursing homes and centres for the handicapped were looked at from an economically efficient point of view. As the sisters were not trained in hospital administration, people with professional skills were hired as managers. Nuns thus became the employers of well-educated men. In the meantime several sisters had begun to improve their professional skills and eventually became management experts themselves.

During the 1990s, German social welfare legislation (*Sozialgesetzgebung*) became more and more complicated with the introduction of compulsory long-term nursing care insurance (*Pflegeversicherung*). This had vast consequences for women's congregations. The care of countless elderly nuns in nursing homes had to be financed by the community. As there were no young novices in Germany and only few sisters who earned salaries as teachers or nurses, the PHJC decided to sell some of their property, including houses and land.

In the US, on the other hand, where the PHJC had several branches with a total of about four hundred sisters, the leadership team opted for a different solution to the question of looking after elderly nuns. Their plan corresponded to the American health insurance and pension scheme systems, both of which are organised on a more private level. When the sisters sold a hospital in Chicago, they invested the proceeds in stocks and mutual funds. Dividends from these investments now cover the cost of the required care of the sisters. Other bonds bring enough interest to finance various social projects. For example, the PHJC bought a house in Gary, Indiana, a town near Chicago – the American city known as 'murder capital number one' – where they carry out social work among black American female drug addicts and their children. Like many other women's congregations, the American branch of the PHJC was transformed into an enterprise. In the southeast of Chicago, a region with no industry, the PHJC – including its motherhouse and a college belonging to the community – became the largest employer in the county. More than 250 people from outside found jobs in individual sections of the PHJC corporation.

Ethnic Diversity

Due to the process of globalisation and the response to the Second Vatican Council, the PHJC founded new branches in India. As early as 1963, the first young

Indian women travelled to the German motherhouse requesting admission to become Poor Handmaids. There they took up their postulancy, the first stage to becoming a sister. The arrival of new members with a different ethnic background had several consequences for the power relations between Western and non-Western religious women as well as for the negotiation of cultural conflict within the order. When their novitiate ended, the Indian nuns were trained as nurses, midwives and doctors in Germany, and eventually returned to India to found hospitals, boarding schools and leprosy treatment centres. Indian sisters were also engaged in the fields of girls' and women's education. Long after they had entered the community, they demanded more 'independence' from the generalate based in Germany. They wanted to establish their own novitiate in India, to have their own 'government', that is, their own provincialate and leadership team, and their own candidates and elections in India. In 2001, thirty years after the Indian sisters had returned to their country of origin, the generalate in Germany agreed to grant them full autonomy. Financially, however, Indian sisters are still dependent on the generalate in Germany. Contrary to their co-sisters in the Netherlands, England, Germany and the US, they have no financial resources. Since India is an extremely poor country and Hinduism the dominant religion, the donor pool for the sisters remains meagre. However, unlike Western countries, the Indian branch of the PHJC is in the process of developing. While the Western provinces are dying or in decline, branches in non-Western countries are in the process of expanding. Up to now, Western influence in the Indian province has been visible to a certain extent. This will change in the coming years, and Indian sisters will most likely take over the leadership of the PHJC. Moreover, the transnationalisation of the community is intensifying rapidly. At the end of the 1990s, the PHJC founded new branches in Mexico and Brazil, and at the beginning of the new millennium introduced novitiates in Kenya and Nigeria.

Social Security in a Globalising World

In the last section I would like to illustrate the extent to which social security is created and maintained across borders. On the one hand, transnational social security networks exist among the sisters *within* the religious congregation. On the other hand, these networks go *beyond* the boundaries of the religious congregation, with the sisters providing social security to others, particularly in countries where the state cannot guarantee the well-being of its people with regard to body and soul.

All PHJC provinces are politically independent of the motherhouse in Germany. Although the constitution is binding for all members, the individual provinces in each country have their own particularities, and manage their property and leadership teams. However, the final say lies with the general superior, her assistants and the general chapter, who have the power to decide on the status of the PHJC in specific countries. The Dutch province, for example, was degraded to a region, since only a small number of elderly sisters remained. The status of region means dependency on the generalate in financial and political affairs. When Indian sisters wanted to establish their own province, the issue first had to be discussed in the general chapter, a long process accompanied by tensions that had arisen during the founding of the Indian branch. Indian sisters trained in Germany returned to their home country in the 1970s. A German superior was sent to India to support the Indian sisters in their mission work. As a regional superior, she had contact via fax and phone with the generalate in Germany, which was exclusively German at the time. In the eyes of some of the Indian sisters, the German sister, who was much older than her Indian co-sisters, was regarded as the 'mother' who looked after them and provided social security. For more than twenty years she maintained contact with local bishops, made arrangements to buy land, talked to architects and collected money to build a provincial house in Bangalore. She was later responsible for the founding of new branches of the PHJC all over India. In addition she made arrangements for the young aspirants and postulants trained in India by Western sisters in the initial years. Even today this German sister, who lives in India, is highly respected, albeit no longer in office. She still exerts considerable influence on financial affairs, and occasionally on the work of the new provincial team, making it a difficult situation for the Indian sisters. Questions of seniority and generation come into play, as well as issues of power and ethnicity.

In the course of debates on whether the Indian province should become politically independent of the motherhouse, financial problems had to be solved. The generalate was convinced, and still is, that the Indian province should not rely solely on money donated by lay people and the motherhouse in Germany. Meanwhile a combination of 'income-generating' and 'non-income-generating' projects has emerged in the Indian province. Schools and boarding schools are considered income-generating projects. The convents concerned can survive without the financial support of the generalate, although money to buy land and build schools did come from the German motherhouse. Teaching sisters have some income, as parents of school children pay small fees. Children with a 'tribal' background receive financial support from the Indian government. Apart from income-generating projects, numerous others have to be supported by the congregation itself. Sisters live with and look after leprosy patients, that is, people who were forced to leave their villages as a result of their disease and who can never return to their relatives. Some sisters perform social work among the men, women and children who live and work in quarries, others are engaged in AIDS awareness programmes.[9]

The Indian sisters are well aware of the issue of reciprocity towards their co-sisters in the West. The first Indian sisters who arrived in Europe in 1963 were trained in Germany and lived in their host country for almost ten years. During my fieldwork they talked about the emotional constraints involved in taking care of their older German co-sisters, in a situation where only a small number of young German sisters performed work of this kind. As in transnational families (Bryceson and Vuorela 2002; Levitt 2001) where reciprocity circulates across territorial and national borders, Catholic sisters take care of each other in different parts of the world. Indian sisters are aware of the generation gap between the 'old' German and American sisters, on the one hand, and the 'young' Indian sisters, on the other. In kinship terms and according to generation, many German, American, Dutch and English sisters are the 'mothers', 'grandmothers' or 'great-grandmothers' of the Indian sisters. In a secular sense, as sisters they have the same rights and duties towards each other. In a religious sense, being a sister means obeying the rules, that is, accepting the congregations' hierarchical structure. Dealing with these issues and negotiating questions of ethnicity, race and generation represents a major challenge in women's congregations in the future, not merely among the PHJC.

Beyond the level of transnational social security networks maintained *within* the congregation, we must consider a second level: the social work with local people, which is almost exclusively financed by the religious congregation itself, and partly based on travelling. German and American sisters travelled to India in the 1970s, working as novice mistresses and regional superiors. American sisters worked in Indian leprosy centres and lived in refugee camps in Thailand in the 1980s, German sisters left for Rumania to run orphanages after 1989, while today Indian sisters work with Sri Lankan refugees in the Netherlands, as well as in hospitals and homes for the elderly in Germany. Travel expenses are provided by the congregation (Hüwelmeier 2006a: 70). For many of its social activities the congregation is dependent on external financial resources. Hence the 'global flow of money' (Appadurai 1991) is a central aspect in the creation and maintenance of transnational connections and cross-border social projects. Based on my fieldwork with the PHJC in India at the time of the tsunami, I will now discuss issues of social security and the sending of remittances by various people and institutions from the West to the Indian branch.

After the Tsunami

The transnationalisation of numerous women's congregations after the Second Vatican Council transformed financial support from non-Western Catholic communities, particularly in the case of natural disasters. In December 2005, the houses and fishing boats of thousands of people in Tamil Nadu, South India, where a branch of the PHJC is based, were destroyed by the tsunami.

Local people, village inhabitants and Catholic nuns and priests, all of them eye-witnesses or victims of the tsunami, criticised the Indian government for their delayed reaction, as well as on the count of corruption. According to one eye-witness I met, a Catholic priest, and to the narratives of the Indian PHJC, whose school building and convent was partly destroyed, state bureaucracy failed to help the local people in the initial weeks after the disaster. In contrast, Catholic orders, with their well-organised structures, were seen to be quick in providing nonbureaucratic relief. Catholic sisters were the first to organise food and shelter for those whose homes had been devastated.

As a result of personal contacts in her home country, the above-mentioned German sister and former superior in Bangalore was one of the main 'managers' to provide international support in the aftermath of the tsunami. Over the years she maintained transnational connections with her kin and former classmates in her native German village. Her German relatives and numerous other people in her village collected huge sums of money for the victims of the tsunami within the space of a few days. This was partly due to the fact that local German newspapers – having been informed by the German sister in Bangalore – reported on the situation in South India. The latest reports from India were received within hours. In addition, photographs taken by Indian sisters documenting the situation after the disaster reached the German villagers via email, while personal accounts recorded by Indian sisters who distributed food to tsunami victims on the south coast of India were sent to the German village by fax. The German sister personally sent letters to relatives and to the priest in her native village, as well as to the mayors of surrounding villages.

The intensity of transnational connections between home and host country results, among other factors, from new communication technologies. There is, however, another important aspect, closely connected with fax, email and phone. The changes introduced by the Second Vatican Council in the 1960s, in particular with regard to the reinterpretation of the vows of poverty, chastity and obedience within women's congregations (Hüwelmeier 2004a), have strengthened the ties between Catholic sisters and their families of origin in recent decades. These renewed bonds between sisters and their kin, as well as their home communities, are one of the reasons why transnational financial support worked so well between several German parishes and the Indian branch of the PHJC following the tsunami. As shown in the example, relatives, friends and former co-villagers of Western sisters collected vast amounts of money for the tsunami victims. Based on these ties, Indian sisters received donations of tens of thousands of euros within a few days.

Financial support from co-sisters in the Western provinces was also forthcoming. The American province of the PHJC and co-sisters in the Netherlands, England and Germany sent considerable sums of money. As soon as they had heard the news, they decided to send cheques to India via the generalate. Each branch of the PHJC knew that their co-sisters in India lived and worked among the poor in the south of the country, and were ready to help at once. Thanks to the immediate and nonbureaucratic financial and material aid via the transnational network of the PHJC, the Indian sisters were able to provide tsunami victims with food directly after the disaster when support from the Indian government had not yet materialised. They hired cars and assistants to organise the transport of rice and vegetables, and gave shelter to Hindus, Muslims and Christians. They also bought new boats for the fishing families in Tamil Nadu, and covered the costs for boat repairs and new nets. Furthermore, they purchased plots of land to build new houses for families who had been left homeless.

However, because the personal and financial capacities of the Indian sisters were limited, they were able to help only a certain number of people. Based on the sisters' experiences in their families of origin and their knowledge of women in Indian society, the nuns are involved in issues of caste, class and gender in the communities they serve. This led to their decision to direct their assistance primarily towards women and thus contribute to their empowerment in the local society. Prior to the tsunami, many of the women in poor fishing families were obliged to pay male boat owners when they needed to go fishing. The sisters initiated social projects for women, such as purchasing several boats and distributing them to individual groups of five women. Supported by the sisters, the women organised cooperatives, went out to sea every day and subsequently sold the fish at the market, making them independent of the male boat owners. Although this pattern of female cooperation was not invented by Catholic nuns, their knowledge of living and working communally helped the village women to bring about a change in the security arrangements of the Indian community by giving more power to women. Thus the PHJC in India encourage the most neglected groups in the Indian subcontinent.

Conclusion

The analysis of processes of transformation in a Catholic women's congregation provides ample evidence of the complex relations and historical embeddedness of transnational social security practices. As shown from a historical perspective, the congregation constantly provided social security for its members once they had left their families. In doing so, the sisters were free to perform social services not only for other sisters in the congregation, but for the needy population of the society they lived in, as well as those in other countries. In the nineteenth century, when many European sisters migrated to the US to help immigrants settle in new places, women's congregations provided health care, housing and food, as well as emotional and spiritual support for their co-sisters and other immigrants to the US. Additional financial and material support for the building of schools and hospitals was donated by members of the parish.

Nowadays social security for Catholic sisters in the West, in particular pension schemes and health care, is partly provided by the national social security system of the welfare state. As a result of declining membership rates, however, aging congregations are in need of care from non-members. This is provided to some extent by lay people, but also by the co-sisters from branches founded more recently in other parts of the globe, who migrate to Western countries to be trained as nurses. For this reason, such a transnational care system can be classified as a medicoscape (Hörbst and Wolf 2003: 4), a term developed by scholars from Appadurai's concept of global 'scapes' (1990) to describe networks of people and organisations active in a global medical health care system. Apart from the global flow of knowledge as an element of global cultural flows, the sisters constitute a specific transnational care chain. Additionally, while working as nurses in hospitals and nursing homes in the West, nuns from non-Western countries earn money to support their branches in India, Latin America and Africa financially. In this sense, Catholic sisters are female migrants who live abroad for a number of years and send remittances to their home communities, not unlike domestic servants from non-Western countries who work in Europe or elsewhere and transmit money to support their families at home (Willis and Yeoh 2000; Levitt 2001). Travelling between continents, maintaining mutual contact with co-sisters around the globe, and keeping in touch with families and villages of origin via budget travel, phone connections and new communication technologies have become more crucial than ever.

At the same time, the services of Catholic sisters in non-Western countries like India are heavily dependent on the financial contributions of their Western co-sisters. Other than their female predecessors, who were supported by the large Catholic population of the local parishes they worked in, today the sisters also live and work in regions without a Catholic (majority) population, serving people with different religious backgrounds. As shown in this chapter, without the sponsorship of their co-sisters and donations from Western parishes, institutions and individuals, the sisters in India would not be in a position to fulfil their ambitious mission, that is, to take care of lepers and those suffering from AIDS; to educate poor Hindu, Muslim and Christian children; or to buy land and build houses for the victims of the tsunami. The cross-border provision of social security by women's congregations works both ways – for the inner circle of sisters and members of the religious congregation as well as for the 'worldly' recipients. As this chapter illustrates, the rapid process of globalisation in many parts of the world has modified and improved the ability of transnationally organised Catholic sisters to perform charity and social work focused on coping with poverty, disease and natural disasters in the twenty-first century.

Notes

1. This chapter is based on a research project financed by the German Research Foundation (DFG). The 'Transnational Religion' project (Director: Prof. Dr Ute Luig) was affiliated with the Institute for Social Anthropology at the Free University Berlin. I conducted fieldwork in various convents of the Poor Handmaids of Jesus Christ (PHJC) in Germany, England, the Netherlands, the US and India. The empirical material in the chapter is drawn from archives, participant observation and the biographical narratives of sisters of different generations, as well as interviews with members of the generalate, the superiors of the different branches in various countries, lay people, priests and bishops.
2. Ulf Hannerz was among the first anthropologists in the 1990s to theorise cross-border relations and the interconnectedness of the global world. His books and articles inspired the succeeding generation of anthropologists, who then carried out 'multi-sited' fieldwork that focused on concepts such as mobility, locality and place-making.
3. The term *women religious* refers to the self-labelling of women in Catholic orders such as 'Leadership Conference of Women Religious' in the US.
4. For a detailed analysis of the life history of Katherine Kasper, see Hüwelmeier 2004a.
5. Blackbourn analyses the *Kulturkampf* in his book on the German 'Lourdes' (Blackbourn 1993).
6. The parochial school system relied 'solely on private money given by Catholics. This was possible because of the growing and cheap labour resources represented by the religious orders, most of them women' (Adloff 2006: 9n7).
7. Letter to America, 10 December 1888, Archives of the Generalate, translated by the author.
8. Letter to America, 17 July 1890, Archives of the Generalate, translated by the author.
9. Similar to Africa, AIDS is a major problem in India (Hüwelmeier 2006b).

References

Adloff, F. 2006. 'Religion and Social-Political Action: The Catholic Church, Catholic Charities, and the American Welfare State'. *International Review of Sociology* 16(1): 1–30.

Appadurai, A. 1990. 'Disjuncture and Difference in the Global Cultural Economy'. *Public Culture* 2(2): 1–24.

_____. 1991. 'Global Ethnoscapes: Notes and Queries for a Transnational Anthropology', in *Recapturing Anthropology: Working in the Present*, ed. R. G. Fox. Santa Fe, NM: School of American Research Press, 191–210.

Blackbourn, D. 1993. *Marpingen: Apparitions of the Virgin Mary in Bismarckian Germany.* Oxford: Oxford University Press.

Bryceson, D. and U. Vuorela, eds. 2002. *The Transnational Family.* Oxford, New York: Berg Publishers.

Casanova, J. 1994. *Public Religions in the Modern World.* Chicago, London: University of Chicago Press.

Cohen, R. 1996. 'Diasporas and the Nation State: From Victims to Challengers'. *International Affairs* 72: 507–20.

Ewens, M. 1978. *The Role of the Nun in Nineteenth Century America.* New York: Amo Press.

Foner, N. 1997. 'What's New About Transnationalism? New York Immigrants Today and at the Turn of the Century'. *Diaspora* 6(3): 355–75.

Fouron, G. and N. Glick Schiller. 2001. 'All in the Family: Gender, Transnational Migration, and the Nation-State'. *Identities* 7(4): 539–82.

Gabaccia, D. R. 2000. *Italy's Many Diasporas*. London: University College of London Press.

Gillis, C. 2003. 'American Catholics: Neither out Far nor in Deep', in *Religion and Immigration: Christian, Jewish, and Muslim Experiences in the United States*, ed. Y. Yazbeck Haddad, J. I. Smith and J. L. Esposito. Walnut Creek, CA: AltaMira Press, 33–60.

Glick Schiller, N. 1999. 'Transmigrants and Nation-States: Something Old and Something New in the U.S. Immigrant Experience', in *The Handbook of International Migration: The American Experience*, ed. C. Hirschmann, P. Kasinitz and J. DeWind. New York: Russell Sage Foundation, 94–119.

Glick Schiller, N., L. Basch and C. Blanc-Szanton, eds. 1992. *Towards a Transnational Perspective on Migration*. New York: Gordon and Breach Publications.

_____. 1995. 'From Immigrant to Transmigrant: Theorizing Transnational Migration'. *Anthropological Quarterly* 68: 48–63.

Glick Schiller, N. and G. E. Fouron. 1999. 'Terrains of Blood and Nation: Haitian Transnational Social Fields'. *Ethnic and Racial Studies* 22(2): 340–66.

Hannerz, U. 1996. *Transnational Connections: Culture, People, Places*. London: Routledge.

Hochschild, A. R. 2000. 'Global Care Chains and Emotional Surplus Value', in *On the Edge: Living with Global Capitalism*, ed. W. Hutton and A. Giddens. London: Jonathan Cape, 130–46.

Hörbst, V. and A. Wolf. 2003. 'Globalisierung der Heilkunde: Eine Einführung. Medizin und Globalisierung', in *Medizin und Globalisierung*, ed. A. Wolf and V. Hörbst. Münster, London: Lit Verlag, 3–30.

Hüwelmeier, G. 1999. 'Ordensschwestern und Jungfrauen', in *Religion und weibliche Identität*, ed. U. Krasberg. Marburg: Curupira, 35–51.

_____. 2000a. 'Vom Dienstmädchen zur Dienstmagd Christi', in *Religion und Geschlechterverhältnis*, ed. I. Lukatis, R. Sommer and C. Wolf. Opladen: Leske und Budrich, 215–23.

_____. 2000b. 'Gendered Houses: Kinship, Class and Identity in a German Village', in *Gender, Agency and Change: Anthropological Perspectives*, ed. V. A. Goddard. London: Routledge, 122–41.

_____. 2000c. 'Women's Congregations as Transnational Communities'. *ESRC Transnational Communities Programme Working Papers*, WPTC-2K-13, http://www.transcomm.ox.ac.uk.

_____. 2004a. *Närrinnen Gottes. Lebenswelten von Ordensfrauen*. Münster: Waxmann Verlag.

_____. 2005a. 'Ordensfrauen unterwegs: Gender, Transnationalismus und Religion'. *Historische Anthropologie* 13(1): 91–110.

_____. 2005b. '"Nach Amerika!" Schwestern ohne Grenzen'. *L'Homme. Zeitschrift für feministische Geschichtswissenschaft* 2: 97–115.

_____. 2006a. 'Ordensfrauen im JumboJet: Katholische Schwestern als Akteure im Prozess der Globalisierung', in *Transnationale Karrieren. Biografien, Lebensführung und Mobilität*, ed. F. Kreutzer and S. Roth. Wiesbaden: VS Verlag für Sozialwissenschaften, 64–82.

_____. 2006b. 'AIDS in Indien: Ein Sterbehaus für Frauen und Kinder'. *Curare: Zeitschrift für Ethnomedizin und transkulturelle Psychiatrie* 28: 201–11.

Langlois, C. 1984. *Le Catholicisme au féminin: Les congregations françaises à supérieure générale au XIXe siècle*. Paris: Éditions du Cerf. PUCHEU.

Levitt, P. 2001. *The Transnational Villagers*. Berkeley: University of California Press.

Portes, A. 2003. 'Theoretical Convergencies and Empirical Evidence in the Study of Immigrant Transnationalism'. *International Migration Review, Special Issue: Transnational Migration: International Perspectives*, ed. P. Levitt, J. De Wind and S. Vertovec, 37(3): 874–92.

Vertovec, S. 1999. 'Conceiving and Researching Transnationalism'. *Ethnic and Racial Studies* 22(2): 447–62.

Vertovec, S. and R. Cohen, eds. 1999. *Migration, Diasporas, and Transnationalism*. Cheltenham: Elgar.

Warner, R. S. and J. Wittner, eds. 1998. *Gatherings in Diaspora: Religious Communities and the New Immigration*. Philadelphia: Temple University Press.

Willis, K. and B. Yeoh, eds. 2000, *Gender and Migration*. Cheltenham: Edward Elgar.

Chapter 11

Negotiating Needs and Obligations in Haitian Transnational Religious and Family Networks

Heike Drotbohm

Introduction

In the course of my fieldwork in the Canadian city of Montréal, Florence, a vodou priestess[1] from Haiti, became my most important referee.[2] She had already been living in the city for some years, cultivating and broadening her knowledge of vodou, and was active at the centre of a vodou society, a so-called *sosjeté*. When I asked Florence about her role in this religious network, she explained: 'You see, these people here feel tremendously lost, they don't know what to do. Here in Canada there are no answers to these kinds of problems. Some people in Montréal, Boston or New York might have the necessary knowledge and can offer some help, but in severe cases most people are obliged to travel back to Haiti.'[3] In her description, Florence hints at two key aspects relevant to an understanding of the importance of the religious network and the activities involved. Firstly, she mentions the 'necessary knowledge'. This refers to the spiritual consultation, the triangular conversation between one or more clients, the priest or priestess, and the vodou spirits. Consultations are the mainstay of vodou practice in Montréal and the primary source of Florence's income as a priestess. They are availed of by Haitians as well as people from other ethnic backgrounds, all of whom wish to discuss their personal sorrows or, depending on the severity of their problems, need mental or physical healing.[4] Secondly, Florence reminds us that vodou networks are not

---

confined to a specific locality but connect people living in Montréal, in other Canadian cities, all over North America and in Haiti. Given the popularity and translocal connectedness of the services offered, I wondered what type of social security circulated within these translocal religious networks and was particularly interested in the particular kinds of collaboration and support offered among migrants, whose basic material needs are normally met by the services of the Canadian welfare state.[5]

My argument centres on the role of vodou priests and priestesses, who take on the crucial position of intermediaries in vodou societies. Of particular interest here is the fact that frequently consultations are necessary for reconciling the clients' personal conflicts, and these do not only deal with conflicts in the own spiritual group, but also with those that arise within the migrant community and between the Haitian diaspora and Haiti itself, the home country. The position of the priests, who contribute significantly to the reproduction of personal relations among the members of vodou societies scattered in many different places, constitutes a nodal point of religious connectedness.

While my chapter deals with the transnational dimensions of these networks, it cannot be denied that parallel to this translocal and transnational interconnectedness, network members live in different local and national contexts, where their needs are met in a variety of ways. Thus I will follow up on the question of how transnational religious and kin networks complement, substitute or overlap, and how network members living in one place have to deal with needs that are quite different to those of members living somewhere else. With these ideas, my chapter contributes to an area of research that has stressed the meaning of religious practice and religious networks for post-migration communities and their communities of origin (Levitt 1998, 2001; Baumann 1999; Warner and Wittner 1998; Orsi 1999; Vertovec 2000; Veer 2001). Although there is a growing body of work on immigrant incorporation, the relation between religious affiliation and the globalisation of everyday practices seems nonetheless to have remained less explored, particularly in terms of the cohesive forces contained in these networks and their strategies of coping with risk and vulnerability in both places of living.

My contribution is structured as follows: I will first describe the particularities of Haitian religiosity in the 'transnational social space' (Pries 1999) that creates the link between Haiti and the Haitian diaspora. Taking Florence's vodou network, her *sosjeté*, as an example, I will describe her position and role within the group. Two pillars of religious practice seem to attract network members most: the collective performance of religious ceremonies and the consultation with the priest or priestess mentioned above. These two elements will be described and interpreted for their influence on and function in the transnational space that connects Haiti with Montréal and other places in the Haitian diaspora.

Haitian Religiosity in Transnational Social Fields

Haitian vodou as practised in Canada today is a transformation of West African vodou, which was transported to the New World via the transatlantic slave trade, and has merged over the centuries with the religious concepts and practices of the French colonists.[6] Here, efforts by the colonial masters to evangelise the slaves resulted in the latter's acquisition of Catholic beliefs and practices, and ultimately in a broader development of the spirituality of various African ethnic groups in secluded social spaces. Contemporary Haitian vodou has adapted to this experience and claims to practise both religions in mutual synergy and complementarity, otherwise referred to as *religious syncretism*.[7] Comparable to other African-American religions, Haitian vodou can be described as a polytheistic,[8] syncretistic and nondogmatic religion, whose content, structure and rituals are subjected to generally accepted rules that can be varied by the believers and adapted to the needs of the respective groups. A central element of Haitian vodou is the community of believers, the so-called *sosjeté*. In Haiti, the concept of *sosjeté* is based on the family's place of living, the yard, which is referred to as *laku*. Furthermore, spiritual reference is based on the family's associated *hounfor*, or temple. The members of a *sosjeté* are connected via their collective tribute to the spirits of the family within this territory (Larose 1977: 95; Métraux 1958: 51). Laënnec Hurbon, a leading specialist on Haitian vodou, stresses the significance of religious specialists, *houngans* and *mambos*, who occupy key positions in the *sosjeté* and whose prestige affects the level of importance attached to it. Due to their knowledge (*konesans*) and influence (*pouvwa*) in local communities, these religious leaders are known as *Papa-lwa* or *Maman-lwa*, referring to their integrative function.[9] *Hounsis*, believers, who have already undergone the first phase of initiation and are now aspirants to the priesthood, assist at the ceremonies and are known as *timoun*, children of the house (Hurbon 2002: 92). Despite this apparently hierarchical structure, vodou cannot be compared to clerical units such as Catholicism or the Protestant Churches, since its structures are institutionalised to only a minor degree.[10] Vodou's loose, decentralised and informal composition must be noted as one of its specific characteristics, which can further be observed in the autonomous position of religious cult communities and their social unity, where religious knowledge is transferred in nondogmatic ways.

As described above, Haitian vodou developed in the course of migration and the transport of African religious ideas and practices to the New World. In the twentieth century, when *vodouissants*, vodou believers, again left their Haitian homes for a new life in foreign places, vodou continued its journey to the urban centres of North America. It became part of a second diaspora, this time the Haitian diaspora, and was once again adapted to the needs of the migrants and their new living conditions.

The characteristics of Haitian migration in the Caribbean and North American area have been largely discussed in various disciplines of the social sciences.[11] Particularly the Haitian way of life, which asserts itself as a circulation between a former home and a new dwelling place, has received considerable attention, and is today regarded as a typical characteristic of the migrant concept now referred to as 'transnationalism' (Basch et al. 1994; Fouron and Glick Schiller 1997; Glick Schiller et al. 1992). Haitian transmigrants who commute between Haiti and other places of residence, such as New York, Miami, Boston or Montréal, not only make economic and political reference to more than one place of living, but also develop religious practices that are shaped in a 'transnational social space' (Pries 1999) spanned between Haiti and the Haitian diaspora.

Montréal, a bilingual city in a multicultural nation, is an attractive place for Haitian immigrants to live. The fact that most of them speak French in addition to Haitian Creole gives them an advantage over non-francophone immigrants, for instance, when they look for work or accommodation. In general, Canadian multiculturalism provides suitable conditions for social and political integration (Dejean 1990). Several centuries of immigration from Europe, Asia, Africa, Latin America and the Caribbean has led to the development of a multiethnic environment in the city, where multiple religious fields meet, blend and interweave.[12] This diversity provides migrants with an opportunity to continue their native religious practices, thereby creating a familiar home in a foreign place, and to practise trans-ethnic world religions, such as Christianity, Buddhism or Islam, at the same time. Due to different and on occasion complementary motives for taking up or sustaining a particular religious practice, religious identities can be lived in parallel in order to facilitate access to individual, sometimes competing, social fields. Hence it has been observed that some migrants belong to a number of religious communities as a means of getting in touch with several social security providers (see Rohregger in this volume for a similar case).[13]

The fact that migrants use religion as a tool for integration into their multicultural host society – that is, for expressing proximity, but also to articulate feelings of distance to it – applies in equal measure to the Haitian community. Haitians in Montréal draw on religious practices to create a space in which they can maintain, design and establish their ethnic identity.

Furthermore, shared religious worship allows them to come into contact with other ethnic groups. Similar to the situation in Haiti, many members of the Haitian community in Montréal practise both religions – vodou and Catholicism – simultaneously (Drotbohm 2005). While Haitians form a significant percentage of practising Catholics in Québec parishes,[14] many of them continue to practise vodou in the private sphere. They adapt their performances to the conditions of urban life and continue to stay in touch with other localities in the Haitian diaspora through religious practice.

Translocal Haitian Vodou Societies

During my fieldwork in Montréal, I focused primarily on the activities of two vodou *sosjetés*: Sosjeté Tèt Ansamn and Sosjeté Daho.[15] It is important to note that these *sosjeté* networks do not exist independently, but evolved through the activities of the priests who continued or took up their services in Montréal, successively integrating more and more vodou practitioners into their groups. Neither of the networks is bound by territory or neighbourhood. Their members are scattered throughout the various quarters of the city, but maintain links with *sosjeté* members living in other areas of the Haitian diaspora, be it Toronto, Boston, New York or Miami. As in Haiti, the *sosjeté* in Montréal is a religious community with a hierarchical structure. It has a spiritual leader, the *houngan* or the *mambo*, and subordinate assistants, the *hounsis*. The concept of the *sosjeté* is one of membership, that is, of ritual initiation into the inner circle, although these groups in Haiti and the diaspora have no fixed boundaries in quantitative terms. One *mambo* estimated that membership of her *sosjeté* varied between forty and sixty people. The *sosjetés* are open and flexible in the sense that some of those already initiated have the option of participating for a certain amount of time and later, if preferred, of withdrawing their religious involvement. Others come and go as they wish. Some members intensify their involvement in times of need, that is, when they are already in close contact with the priest, receive consultations and participate in ritual activities. Yet others merely attend rituals in honour of certain spirits. The priests, again at the centre of these activities, know precisely who has to be contacted before a major ceremony and who is currently travelling and therefore unable to participate; they also know who is in the process of losing interest in *sosjeté* activities. Due to its translocal connectedness, spanning communication and social practice in several places and across country borders, and to its flexible, open-ended and constantly changing structure, the term *network* seems more appropriate than *group* or *community* (see introductory remarks in this volume).

In the following I will exemplify the particular characteristics of these networks with Florence's *sosjeté*. Florence left Haiti at the end of the 1980s, when it was clear that the termination of the dictatorial regime under Francois Duvalier and his son would not suffice to bring about the long-awaited economic and political change. It was around this time that Florence finally decided to follow her husband, who had left the country earlier on. Once in Canada, however, she discovered that her husband had developed a relationship with another woman, with whom he already had several children. Despite this sudden and unexpected social isolation, Florence managed to cope in the first few years with the help of her extended family.[16] She explained the evolution of her *sosjeté* as follows:

Vodou was always in my life. However, at the beginning I knew nobody who practised in Montréal. Regardless, I carried out my services [the tribute to the spirits
by means of a private home altar] regularly. I managed to get on with my life here.
I found a job and did not return to Haiti, despite problems with the immigration
office. After a year or two a good friend of mine was not doing well. He felt weak. You
know, it's a typical sign of someone having been sent an evil spirit. I told him that I
had already practised these things in Haiti and could do something for him. Later he
was cured; he was very glad and told all his friends, who then came to see me. Finally
I was able to establish my practice here in Montréal, the people need it desperately!

Florence alludes to the living conditions of first-generation migrants, who, in
her view, have to balance out a continuous transitory moment between different life-worlds. In the course of time, she discovered that most members of
her ethnic community had specific needs arising from a sense of vulnerability,
the result of an ongoing process of transit and integration. The constructive
character of needs (Benda-Beckmann 1994) becomes apparent when at the
very beginning of her practice in Montréal, Florence treated a particular group
of Haitians, namely, the first-generation immigrants who had upheld strong
links with their native country and had to face political change that would be
decisive for their eventual return. Their living conditions were different from
those the younger generations, who developed a closer attachment to Canada,
so that Florence saw herself faced with issues such as negotiating between here
and there, between transience and rootedness, and with the open-end character of the migrants' stay. Furthermore, many of her clients spoke of their difficulties in dealing with expectations and demands, not only within the migrant
community itself but especially on the part of families and friends still living in
Haiti. Those who 'made it' out of the country and managed to live their lives in
Canada had the impression they were surrounded by the jealousy and expectations of those who faced even greater difficulties. Suspicion of evil attacks
were thus a major issue in discussions with the priest or priestess, who had to
mediate the powers between evil forces, vodou spirits, clients, their friends and
enemies, and finally, themselves (I will come back to this point later).

On the whole, Florence was confident she could cope with these problems,
and saw herself as the moral backbone of those with whom she shared a connection to the home country as well as to life in the diaspora. In the years
that followed she held consultations, first of all with her friends and family
members, and later with strangers. During this period, Florence gained an
excellent reputation and considerable prestige within the group. From the
perspective of group members, Florence possesses key qualities for the distinguished position of a priest: she is discreet to strangers and loyal to her clients.
She does not attempt to profit financially from the sufferings of her clients and
has proved to be highly intuitive in resolving conflict in her own *sosjeté*. As
her services gradually became established over the years, the circle of clients

expanded. In the first few years, her practice was mostly consulted by Haitians from working-class backgrounds. Over time, wealthier clients began to appear – lawyers, doctors and politicians.[17] (When I enquired about the differences between the various groups, she smiled and said: 'The poor come during the day, the rich at night. The later it is, the richer they are!'). The great majority of network members, however, are migrants who see themselves as belonging to the poorer, more marginalised sections of society. More recently Florence has been consulted by people of different ethnic backgrounds. People with Caribbean or African background form the majority, but Asians and Latin Americans as well as Québécois also visit her, request consultations and occasionally participate in religious ceremonies.[18] The contacts that evolved were initially linked bilaterally to her person. Only the collective performance of ceremonies allowed these personal connections to develop into a more complex network, which also involved direct links between two or more members. Whereas initially the group was merely a loose bond, it became a more stable unit in the course of time, with the open-ended, fluid structure described above. Many of the people who are today members of Florence's *sosjeté* already knew each other in Haiti and had invited their friends and families to become part of the network once they had migrated to Canada. Others had heard of her offers and turned to her in moments of crisis, as will be described below.

The decision of whether to make someone an 'official member' of the vodou network (i.e. permit their participation in ceremonies and later perhaps their initiation by a priest) is based on the dialogue between the spirits and the priest. A trance during a ceremony is interpreted as explicit approval and acceptance by the spirit that intends to bind the person concerned to itself. Should this person continue to cultivate his or her connection to the spirits, participate regularly in ceremonies and finally integrate him- or herself into the social life of the *sosjeté*, nothing can stand in the way of initiation. This method of constructing the network's inner circle allows both Haitians and people of different ethnic backgrounds access to the *sosjeté*. Everything depends on the intensity of their engagement with other members and with the spirits.

Today, Florence represents a significant instance of trust within the group, since she acts as a centre of communication, counselling and exchange. In talks with members of the *sosjeté*, it transpired that networks had strong daily-based functions, and that numerous members turned to the priest with practical questions of organisation. Those looking for a job, an apartment, a used car, child care or a favourable private loan can simply make a request; Florence then activates her network in search of suitable contacts. However, the quality of this kind of service, which is common for many priests in Montréal, should not be reduced to the profane activities element of the religious network, but rather interpreted as supplementing other informal networks based on the family, the neighbourhood or the migrant community.

Besides this role as a networker in the group, mediating between demand and supply, Florence has close contact to other *mambos* and *houngans*, some of whom she herself had initiated. Moreover, similar to the *mambos* and *houngans* I met in Montréal, she practises her art in a translocal space, directing her services not only at potential clients in Québéc or the rest of Canada but also in the US and Haiti. The spiritual centres of both vodou societies – Sosjeté Tèt Ansamn and Sosjeté Daho – lie in Haiti, and therefore most believers (have to) maintain a close relationship with their native island.[19] An annual journey to Haiti is of utmost importance for members of the *sosjetés*. Florence travels to Haiti on a regular basis to carry out the principal rituals for the spirits with her family and members of the *sosjeté*. She also has a desire to refresh her spiritual knowledge, to visit the local cemetery and to find essential ingredients, such as certain oils, herbs and plants, which are then distributed on her return among *sosjeté* members living in Montréal.[20] She travels frequently to Boston and occasionally to Miami, where some financially important clients live. Others who live further away prefer to visit her at her home in Montréal and stay in a neighbourhood motel for a few days or weeks – depending on the duration of the consultation.[21]

My previous descriptions presented the priests and priestesses as network nodes, mediating between different localities, among actors from different ethnic backgrounds and between different social classes. According to the members of both *sosjetés*, their interest and motivation in becoming part of such a network focuses on two aspects of religious practice: firstly, the collective performance of ceremonies for the spirits and secondly, certain services, such as the spiritual consultations with *houngans* or *mambos*. In the following I will concentrate on these two areas of religious practice and elaborate on them in terms of their social construction of mutuality and responsibility.

Religious Ceremonies: Creating a New Place of Emotional Security

There are several practical problems attached to holding a celebration of vodou spirits, or *sermoni*, in the middle of Montréal.[22] First of all, the enormous cost for food, drink, decorations and Haitian drummers has to be covered. Space is another crucial point. A proper *sermoni* must be carried out under an open sky and with direct access to the earth. This is not easy in Montréal, since it is frequently too cold and neighbours might feel disturbed by the drums or the frenzy of the dancers who are possessed. On the other hand, the *sermoni* cannot be conducted in a small apartment. A soundproof basement, ideally equipped with a concrete floor and cooking facilities, would be a feasible solution. Animal sacrifices represent a further difficulty. A pig sacrificed for Ogou, one of the main spirits, would make too much noise by Montréal standards and risk calling the attention of animal rights activists. Hence they favour chickens or, in particularly grave cases, possibly a goat. A basement, however, lacks direct access to the earth, which is supposed to absorb the blood devoted to the spirits. Certain elements of nature, such as spring water, rocks and specific plants are a prerequisite. Many of the *vodouissants* regret the adaptation of their religious practice to urban conditions and the minimalism of the ceremonies. Despite or perhaps precisely because of these constraints, an occasion of this kind is greatly appreciated by the *sosjeté* members and enhances the reputation of the priests.

The annual cycle contains two significant occasions that are celebrated with spectacular ceremonial events in Montréal. The first is the feast of the dead, the *Gédé*, which is celebrated on the first day of November, and is also known as the Catholic All Saints Day. The second is the feast for Ti Jean, the spirit of fire, which is held in mid-June. Given the decentralised structure of vodou societies as described above, these ceremonies are performed separately by each *sosjeté*. The feast provides the opportunity for a certain circle of people to gather, and for newcomers to be integrated. All three ceremonies I visited, for instance, were open to noninitiated foreigners like myself. However, I had to be invited by a member of the *sosjeté*. On the whole, the participation of newcomers is accepted and perceived as an appreciation of their religious practice. Along with her friends and the *hounsis*, Florence prepares the feast over a period of days. Some *sosjeté* members living in other parts of the Haitian diaspora will join her on this occasion. The feast, which begins in the early evening and continues until the early morning of the next day, proceeds according to a common pattern I have described elsewhere (Drotbohm 2005: 139–47, 241–45). Here, I would like to remark on two main aspects of the *sermoni* in order for its significance in terms of social security in the religious network to be understood.

Firstly, the ritual plays a decisive role in the imaginative formation of an inner structure to the religious network, and the definition of insiders and outsiders. Membership of this group is defined in accordance with a ritualised dialogue between spirits and participants, and thus emphasises that the ceremony serves to mark both proximities and distances, thereby defining Selves and Others.[23] This admission confirms other research on African-American religions, which highlights the element of exclusivity and the attempt to create a boundary line for outsiders. As Karen McCarthy Brown has said, 'The religions of the African diaspora can be said to be preoccupied with drawing boundaries around the inside group, defining its structure and modus operandi, and starkly contrasting this "family" group with the outside "foreign" power structures, structures which all too often seek to dominate and control' (1995: 212).

Indeed, belonging to this network should not be understood as rigid and exclusive but as part of the permanent negotiation of identities. Constructing the belonging of the individual actor to an inside group, particularly in relation to the diasporic experience, could be significant in shaping collective experience and expressing situational affiliations in this multicultural context, where different and changeable belongings are at hand. Thus, remapping the network in the ritual context reminds its members that they are part of something bigger, which provides sociability and connectedness in life-worlds that often appear dislocated and adrift. The second aspect of religious practice in diasporic cultures that is prevalent in ritual is the inherent characterisation or acquisition of space – understood as the interrelation of the social and physical dimensions of human life.[24] This diasporic transformation of space refers to the changing sense of religious orientation and implies remapping the interrelatedness of personal identity, social space and religious imagination. Several decades of research on African-American religiosity have indicated that the cultic moment serves to display a collective past on the one hand, and to reconstruct a localisable cultural identity on the other, which was lost with the deportation of slaves to the New World (Larose 1977; Brown 2001). Hurbon, for example, refers to the vodou cult as the place par excellence, 'où l'Haïtien s'efforce de retrouver son identité disloquée par l'arrachement physique à la terre de l'Afrique' (2002: 97). In his view, the desire to return to cultural origins becomes most apparent here, since the cult serves to envision a lost Africa, to make ancestors reappear and to construct a bridge to the past.[25]

This role of the ceremony, namely to raise consciousness for a lost home and to serve as an imaginary passage between the present and the past, also applies to ritual performance in the Haitian diaspora in Canada. Interviews with participants about the meaning of ceremony and the subjective connotations attached showed that the imaginary mapping of lost homelands is still of strong significance. However, the individual memories and inherent powers of imagination revolved around Haiti, and not an abstract, spiritual Africa. Myrielle, who regularly attends the network ceremonies, uses the following words to describe the meaning of these events: 'When we dance, I remember my home, my country that I had to leave and that I miss so much. The songs and the rhythms also remind me of Haiti.' It is obvious here that ancestral Africa, which occupies a key position in vodou cult, undergoes a shift in meaning on Canadian ground. In the Haitian diaspora the image of a lost relocation of African images to Haiti is evident in the descriptions of the believers, who link memories of their childhood to those of their home country. Let's again listen to Myrielle: 'We are in our country during the whole ceremony and exchange memories of our families and our childhood. This really produces a strong bond between us.'

The ceremony helps to counterbalance the sense of loss and to share the pain of separation, particularly in the case of migrants who spent their formative years in Haiti. Furthermore, performing ceremonies allows believers to express mutual solidarity, a fundamental aspect of the *sosjeté*. Interestingly enough, even non-Haitian *sosjeté* members became aware of this. Without knowing Haiti, they too felt the evocation of memories of their lost homes. However, these members, who were also migrants, referred to the loss of their own homes, their own native countries. It can be assumed that by means of collective reference in the ritual moment, the network creates a place of its own, that is, a social space without connection to a physical or national territory within the religious spectrum. Hence the religious network creates a place of emotional security when people are faced with transience, separation and loss.

Consultations: Mediating Transnational Needs and Obligations

The second important element of religious practice in the *sosjeté* is the above-mentioned consultation of vodou priests or priestesses.[26] While some of the clients integrate visits to Florence in their everyday lives, others consult her in moments of deep mental crisis and physical suffering. A diffuse sense of imbalance, for example, is a frequent occasion to consult a priest. The person feels unwell, has recently suffered disappointments and now wants to gather information about her position in her social context. After some initially vague insinuations, those who seek advice usually begin their consultation by recounting notions of being cursed,[27] followed by expressions of fear and mistrust with regard to their immediate social environment. Consulting a *mambo* or *houngan* is frequently the last resource, when nothing else has worked.

In the course of the first consultation, which is followed by others depending on the severity of the case, Florence endeavours to localise clients in their personal community, and to reconstruct roots, boundedness and connectedness in an effort to identify their strengths and weaknesses. Her task is to interpret the clients' position in the context of their personal environment and in relation to family members and friends (most of whom live in different localities). Furthermore, she has to understand and illustrate their relation to the spirits in order to present ideas, or give hints and instructions on behaviour that might reinforce these personal and spiritual relations. A consultation can last between a couple of minutes and several hours, or continue, with interruption, for months or even years.[28]

During my research I had the opportunity to be present at some of Florence's consultations and to discuss the issues raised with the priestess and some of the clients prior to or after the consultation.[29] On the whole, the issues advanced differed in terms of geographical localisation. In some consultations the cause of conflict was rooted in interpersonal relationships within the Haitian community in Montréal. Clients spoke of general difficulties in day-to-day life, ranging from matters of the heart and partnerships, through conflict at the workplace or with the Canadian judiciary, to quarrels between the different generations of the family. In these cases it was up to the priestess to detect the background to the conflict and suggest solutions in the form of concrete instructions for magical treatment and suitable behaviour. In her consultations Florence reverts to her extensive knowledge of the essential problems and conflicts in the diaspora. In addition, she works with spiritual knowledge, *konesans*, which refers to her exact understanding of the vodou pantheon, the principal magical operations, divination and binding techniques, the dealing with herbs and the appropriate recitations.[30] Fundamental to her understanding of each client's individual situation is her capacity for empathy, which allows her to situate each individual case in its specific personal and familial context and also to consider the background of the specific migration history. As a religious specialist, she has the task of identifying the protagonists in each case and must ask the correct questions without unduly emphasising her personal assessment of the situation. One *houngan* described this skill in the following manner: 'You have to open up for the people. You have to see things. What does the person want? What are they looking for? Sometimes they just want a fast treatment that works, sometimes they just want to talk.' Karen McCarthy Brown, who interprets consultations as a therapeutic system specific to Haiti, and compares vodou with Western types of treatment, underlining the conciliatory dimensions of these, offers, 'Healing, forgiveness and connection were the desired ends' (1997: 132). She emphasises the reconciliatory role of the priest and the demanding job of strengthening one's own migrant community, which is strongly divided along racial and class lines. Besides these aspects inherent in the community, the great majority of problems discussed in consultations are rooted in the transnational field, which connects Florence's clients with their home country and the family members still living there. Given the particular meaning of this interconnectedness, I will identify some of the most prevalent fields of conflict Florence has had to deal with.

The biggest part of the problems presented during the consultations were imbalances and dependencies between those still living in Haiti and those living in the diaspora. Many clients reported at length about their feelings of guilt that they developed vis-à-vis the hardship their family members in Haiti have to endure, be it in terms of material poverty, frequent supply crisis, political troubles or the repeating news about kidnappings. Due to the fact that jealousies and envy, in the context of vodou, is imagined to be expressed by means of evil attacks, so-called *pwens*, many migrants link their current problems to having been attacked by evil spirits or to curses sent from Haiti.[31] According to the clients, these attacks are habitually the result of envy and mistrust on the part of family members or others who remained in Haiti and have enormous expectations of them. It is a common occurrence that those living in Canada are unable to meet the financial and material demands of their kin in

Haiti, not to mention their hopes. Issues such as financial aid in the form of monthly remittances, but also other kinds of material as well as organisational support – for instance, in organising visas – surface regularly when migrants get in touch with family members staying in the home country. The dialogical moment between formulating expectations, on the one hand, and sending support, on the other, requires constant balancing and negotiation. These difficulties are aggravated when the family member living in Canada is part of a binational partnership. The non-Haitian spouse will occasionally attempt to block the sending of remittances to Haiti, which can result in serious conflicts both among the couple themselves as well as between family members in Canada and those in Haiti. A further minefield of conflict are the frequent visits of Haitian kin to Montréal, who stay for a couple of weeks, a few months or even a year or more. Haitian migrants in Montréal are frequently expected to accommodate the children of their friends and relatives, who come to Canada to attend high school or take up university studies. Other clients talked about their fear of the frustration or even hatred of those they were unable to accommodate. The same applies to other services, such as letters of invitation, support in obtaining a visa, etc. The entire context of interpersonal and intrafamily negotiations becomes even more strained in the case of disease or death, due to emotional distress and the high costs that have to be covered. Some of Florence's clients spoke of how they had neglected their duties vis-à-vis their kin living in Haiti, and of their subsequent sense of guilt. They also talked of their ambivalence between a desire to flee their responsibility vis-à-vis their families in Haiti and the moral duty to express solidarity with the fate of the island.

I would like to advance two possible interpretations of these confessions. First of all, the possibility that clients attempt to shift their responsibility and acts of reciprocity to the spiritual realm should be considered. In other words, was it their intention to find out whether the neglect of family obligations was morally acceptable to the priest and could be compensated by a sacrifice or other ritual act. Secondly, consultations could mean a desire for reconciliation and the liberation from ambivalence and fear of personal failure. In most cases the priest tried to map out a constellation of individuals and to detect whether a curse had been sent from family members in Haiti. Apart from potential interventions and methods of healing, all the priest I interviewed on this aspect always advised the person to revive relations and accomplish their duties. Florence and the other *mambos* and *houngans* I interviewed in Montréal strongly supported the transfer of money between Canada and Haiti, encouraging migrant family members to send as many remittances as possible. Florence explained this as follows:

> Heike, imagine if they stopped sending money to Haiti. The whole country would starve to death. This is not just about our families. The whole Haitian nation

depends on us, since the state doesn't function. Tomorrow or the day after, when it's our children's turn, the entire system will collapse because they've never seen Haiti. Their moral duty is not as strong because they were born here. That's why we have to send as much money as possible now; otherwise there'll be no Haiti left tomorrow.

In this description, she links the notion of responsibility for one's own kind to providing for the Haitian nation.[32] This observation refers to the general phenomenon of public discourse in the migrant community, where individual, collective and national levels of vulnerability and mutual responsibility are frequently interwoven. In their positions as participant, observer and therapist for intimate relations in the migrant community, priests manage to keep a detached view of the social situation in the community, as well as economic and political developments in the home country, anticipating the struggle to ensure long-term stability for future life in Haiti. These descriptions demonstrate that the priest, at the moment of consultation, not only takes the individual case into account, but includes the particularities of translocal bonds of kin and friends. Her reference to various circles of solidarity shows that the religious specialist is in a position to analyse parallel perspectives and to view these often contradictory interests from different angles. Whereas the idea of security in the former paragraph referred to emotional and mental healing, the consultations described here tend to serve practical needs of translocal communication and mutual support, also in a material sense.

Conclusion

Religious networks have multiple meanings both within and for communities in the diaspora. They function as points of contact for immigrants who have recently arrived and are in need of orientation and support in a foreign country – be it in a financial, logistic, psychological or spiritual form. They appear as knots in the web of transnational lives, connecting the home country with other localities in the diaspora. Dialogue between the generations of the migrant community serves as structures of communication for the transmission and negotiation of cultural identities. In the case of Haitian vodou, religious networks operate in a translocal and transnational space. They transgress the national boundaries of Canada and Haiti and do not halt before class or racial barriers.

The exchange, responsibility and security that evolve in the context of these networks have been described in two dimensions, varying significantly in their spatial focus. Firstly, the network had a reconcilable effect on the situation in the diaspora, since in ritual acts, which are a mainstay of religious practice, the loss of home and the sense of separation were shared. Furthermore, the religious specialists, *houngans* and *mambos*, fulfilled the position of network-ers within their group by knowing how to redistribute material resources and information, and by counselling. In their function as nodal points in these groups, they act as central authorities in promoting dialogue in the transna-tional community. This refers to the life of the migrant community in Mon-tréal as well as to the struggles and contention with family members still in the home country. In this respect, obvious differences in the needs and expecta-tions of the respective groups towards priests and priestesses have been identi-fied. While Haitians living in Canada look for spiritual and emotional support and concentrate their expectations primarily on interpersonal conflict and assumptions of sorcery, family members in Haiti tend to look for material and financial support as well as for signs of solidarity.[33] In the case of vodou, reli-gious specialists assume a balancing and mediating role in order to transform concurrence into a complementary system. An important research finding was the fact that personal networks under pressure from processes of transna-tionalisation have been strengthened by religious specialists. Thus, *mambos* and *houngans* constitute vital intercessors on the receiving side of remittances, since they remind migrants of their solidarity duties. In summary, it should be noted that compensation for a sense of personal loss and social isolation, and the concurrence and complementarity between familial and religious networks are the essential characteristics of vodou networks bridging the gap between Haiti and its diaspora. The members of the network and particularly the priest as its most important nodal point exchange a variety of social securities. They bind lives that are on the move together, strengthen responsibility and con-nectedness, and remap sociabilities in a social context, where disintegration and separation represent the dark side of the translocal way of life.

Notes

1. Haitian vodou borrows numerous terms from Christianity, such as *prèt* (priest), *temp* (tem-ple) or *mès* (messe). However, there are very few structural similarities between Christian institutions and those of vodou, and most of the terms used in this text should be under-stood as indigenous concepts from the realm of the polytheistic, nondogmatic universe of Haitian belief. The position and role of priests, *mambos* (female) and *houngans* (male), is that of mediumistic religious specialists who promote dialogue between human beings and vodou spirits (*lwas*).
2. The following descriptions are based on anthropological fieldwork, which was carried out in Haiti and Montréal in 2000, 2002 and 2003 (between two and seven months each time) and generously supported by a doctoral scholarship from the Land Hesse (Germany) and the Centre d'Études Ethniques (CEETUM) at the University of Montréal (Canada). My project

discussed the images of and discourses on vodou spirits, which constitute a vital system of reference in the Haitian migrant community in Montréal. For the content and methodology of the research, see Drotbohm (2005).

3. The conversation with Florence took place in July 2002. This and all other personal statements quoted in the course of this text were collected during my stay in Montréal in 2002 and 2003.

4. For detailed descriptions of some 'cases' treated during these consultations, see Drotbohm (2005: 147–83).

5. This does not mean that immigrants in Canada in general and Haitians in particular are not faced with economic marginalisation and poverty. Diasporic networks can help to mitigate the worst aspects of poverty, and transnational communities represent a process of empowerment for numerous underprivileged groups. See, for instance, Kennedy and Roudometof (2001).

6. For the evolution of Haitian vodou and the interaction between vodou and Catholicism, see, for instance, Deren (1992 [1953]), Desmangles (1990, 1992), Hurbon (1995), and Mintz and Trouillot (1995).

7. For detailed elaborations on Haitian vodou and the anthropological concept of 'syncretism', see Bastide (1970) and Desmangles (1990, 1992). In general, the concept of syncretism is problematic, because it might suggest the existence of 'pure' religions in contrast to mixed ones and neglect the fact that any kind of religion undergoes constant changes and modifications. I have gone more into detail on the concept of syncretism and anti-syncretism with regard to the Haitian community in Montréal in Drotbohm (2007). See also endnote 13.

8. Fernández Olmos and Paravisini-Gebert see Haitian vodou as a monotheistic religion, since its practitioners recognise a supreme god, or *gran mèt*. However, they also reflect on the core position of the *lwas*, spiritual entities interpreted as gods, spirits, etc. (Fernández Olmos and Paravisini-Gebert 2003: 105).

9. Hurbon (2002: 91); see also Métraux (1958: 54–57) and Fernández Olmos and Paravisini-Gebert (2003: 107).

10. Vodou was declared the official state religion of Haiti in 2002 by the then president, Jean-Bertrand Aristide. This may affect its institutionalisation in the long run.

11. From the mid-1950s onwards, a great many Haitians fled their country, the poorest in the western hemisphere, as a result of political persecution, structural violence and *la mizè*, increasing poverty. The first wave of migrants who arrived in Montréal consisted mainly of intellectuals and political activists who had fled the Duvalier dictatorship (1957–1986). The next surge in the 1970s left a strong imprint of Haitian immigration in Québéc. Today, approximately 1.5 million people of Haitian origin live outside Haitian territory (Glick Schiller and Fouron 2001: 12). Besides the Haitian community in Montréal with about 40,000 to 70,000 people of Haitian origin (Dejean 1990; Labelle et al. 1983), there are bigger communities in the US (450,000 altogether; 150,000 in both New York City and Miami, 30,000 in Boston) (Stepick 1998: 5) and between 10,000 and 15,000 in Paris (Delachet-Guillon 1996).

12. Gagnon and Germain (2001). African-American religions, such as the Brazilian candomblé, Cuban santería or Haitian vodou, were not considered in this survey. The lack of a centralised structure and the parallel belonging to several religious groups would have complicated their statistical coverage.

13. Warner and Wittner (1998). This point will not be treated extensively here, but I was frequently informed that people are initiated into several religious networks in the course of their lives. One young woman, for instance, told me she had been baptised at least five times and thus received permission to participate in Catholic, Protestant, Muslim and Buddhist celebrations.

14. With regard to the migrants' desire for native spaces, it should be added that not only Haitian vodou, but also Catholicism as it is practised in areas dominated by Haitians is undergoing

a process of adaptation and transformation, whereby Haitian elements are integrated into Catholic rituals and liturgy (Drotbohm 2007).

15. Both *sosjeté* names express core concepts of Haitian culture. The Creole expression *Tèt Ansamn* can be translated as 'heads together' and refers to a vital group dynamic in moments of collective work or political activities. *Daho* is an abbreviation of 'Dahomey' and refers to the old kingdom of Benin, where vodou is assumed to have originated. Since my research focused on other aspects of vodou, I explored these two *sosjetés* only, and as such, my descriptions cannot be considered representative. In the course of my fieldwork I became aware of at least three further *sosjetés*, whose activities were either less regular or had primarily addressed the execution of religious practice. According to indirect information, however, the essential characteristics described in this text also apply to these *sosjetés*.

16. The significance of family bonds in terms of social security, particularly in the first few years after arrival, has been explored extensively in the context of migration research. See, for instance, Foner (1997), Boyd (1989), Palloni et al. (2001) and Fog Olwig (2001).

17. Commitment to the practice of vodou has a strong class-based dimension. Even in Haiti the more prosperous classes prefer to assign themselves to Catholicism, while vodou is considered to be the religion of the rural population and the poor. However, the boundaries are fluent as a result of the syncretistic character of vodou. Hence an upper-class orientation in the direction of vodou could develop covertly. During my fieldwork, contact between vodou societies and the elite of the Haitian community in Montréal was confirmed by several academics, artists and writers. Yet others declared that members of the upper classes would consult a vodou priest in moments of crisis, but avoid becoming part of a *sosjeté*. For the class dimension of vodou, see Rey (1999).

18. The insignificant number of non-Haitian network members makes it difficult to estimate their role within the group. Nevertheless, those I spoke to could be designated as having a working-class background.

19. Specific elements of religious practice cannot be performed outside of Haiti. Initiations, for example, are only possible to a certain degree in Montréal. Wedding ceremonies with a particular spirit and the initiation of a *hounsi* may be carried out, but not the initiation to a *mambo* or a *houngan*, which constitutes the final step.

20. Today, various vodou paraphernalia can be acquired in the *botanicàs* of Montréal, but for most people who practise vodou, they merely represent a compromise, since their origins are unknown. Moreover, materials bought in Haiti have the reputation of being 'simply stronger'.

21. Another possibility of transcending local boundaries to reach new groups of clients is the Internet, where numerous *mambos* and *houngans* offer their services. For the appearance of African-American religions on the Internet, see, for instance, Kremser (2000).

22. For detailed descriptions of vodou ceremonies in Haiti, see Métraux (1958: 159–88) and Deren (1992: 209–70). For studies on vodou in the diaspora (New York City), see Brown (2001: 275–352) and Schmidt (2002: 258–60).

23. See Arweck (2002) for the group-defining dimension of rituals.

24. For the respatialisation in the ritual moment, see, for instance, Vertovec (2000: 19).

25. Hurbon (2002: 97). For the place-reproducing component of African-American religions, see Bastide (1970). Taking the example of candomblé in Brazil, he demonstrates that African soil is recreated in the religious context as a kind of image in the *mémoire collective*.

26. The following descriptions are a generalising synthesis of a range of discussions with Florence and several *mambos* and *houngans*.

27. The idea of intruding evil spirits and curses sent by enemies looms large in the imagination of *vodouissants*.

28. For Florence's diagnosis and treatment techniques, see Drotbohm (2005: 176–80).

29. For methodological aspects, see Drotbohm (2005: 147–52).

30. For the concept of *konesans*, see Brown (1997) and Métraux (1958: 53–54).
31. Karen Richman has published in detail on vodou curses circulating between Haiti and the Haitian diaspora (2005).
32. Although the number of remittances sent to Haiti varies from year to year, they are undeniably a key factor for economic survival in Haiti (see Basch et al. 1994: 161; Glick Schiller and Fouron 2001: 60–74).
33. My research includes the perspective of the diaspora population and not that of members of the networks still living in Haiti. Hence my interpretations regarding the network from the Haitian side can only remain partial.

References

Arweck, E., ed. 2002. *Theorizing Faith: The Insider, Outsider Problem in the Study of Ritual*. Birmingham: University of Birmingham Press.

Basch, L., N. Glick Schiller and C. Szanton Blanc. 1994. *Nations Unbound: Transnational Projects, Postcolonial Predicaments and Deterritorialized Nation-States*. Amsterdam: OPA (Overseas Publishers Association).

Bastide, R. 1970. 'Mémoire Collective et Sociologie du Bricolage'. *L'Année Sociologique (Paris)* 3. Série, 21: 65–108.

Baumann, G. 1999. *The Multicultural Riddle: Rethinking National, Ethnic and Religious Identities*. New York: Routledge.

Benda-Beckmann, K. von. 1994. 'Social Security in Developing Countries; A Mixed Blessing', in *Social (In)Security and Poverty as Global Issues*, ed. M. T. W. Meereboer. The Hague: Ministry of Foreign Affairs, Development Information Department, 10–26.

Boyd, M. 1989. 'Family and Personal Networks in International Migration: Recent Developments and New Agendas'. *International Migration Review*, New York, The Center for Migration Studies, 23(3): 638–69.

Brown, K. McCarthy. 1995. 'Serving the Spirits: The Ritual Economy of Haitian Vodou', in *Sacred Arts of Haitian Vodou*, ed. D. Cosentino. Los Angeles: University of California Press, 205–23.

———. 1997. 'Systematic Remembering, Systematic Forgetting: Ogou in Haiti', in *Africa's Ogun: Old World and New*, ed. S. T. Barnes. Bloomington: Indiana University Press, 65–89.

———. 2001. 'Telling a Life through Haitian Vodou: An Essay Concerning Race, Gender, Memory, and Historical Consciousness', in *Religion and Cultural Studies*, ed. S. Mizruchi. Princeton, NJ: Princeton University Press, 22–37.

Dejean, P. 1990 [1978]. *D'Haiti au Québec*. Montréal: Cidihca.

Delachet-Guillon, C. 1996. *La Communauté Haïtienne en Île-de-France*. Paris: L'Harmattan.

Deren, M. 1992 [1953]. *Der Tanz des Himmels mit der Erde. Die Götter des haitianischen Vodou*. Vienna: Promedia.

Desmangles, L. G. 1990. 'The Maroon Republics and Religious Diversity in Colonial Haiti'. *Anthropos* 85: 475–82.

———. 1992. *The Faces of the Gods: Vodou and Roman Catholicism in Haiti*. Chapel Hill: University of North Carolina Press.

Drotbohm, H. 2005. *Geister in der Diaspora: Haitianische Diskurse über Geschlechter, Jugend und Macht in Montréal, Kanada*. Marburg: Curupira.

———. 2007. 'Comment habiller la Vierge? Syncrétisme et anti-syncrétisme haïtien à Montréal Canada'. *Diversité Urbaine* 7(1): 31–50.

Fernández Olmos, M. and L. Paravisni-Gebert. 2003. *Creole Religions of the Caribbean: An Introduction from Vodou and Santería to Obeah and Espiritismo*. New York, London: New York University Press.

Fog Olwig, K. 2001. 'New York as a Locality in a Global Family Network', in *Islands in the City: West Indian Migration to New York*, ed. N. Foner. Berkeley: University of California Press, 142–60.

Foner, N. 1997. 'The Immigrant Family: Cultural Legacies and Cultural Changes'. *International Migration Review*, Special Issue: Immigrant Adaptation and Native-Born Responses in the Making of Americans, 31(4): 961–74.

Fouron, G. E. and N. Glick Schiller. 1997. 'Haitian Identities at the Juncture between Diaspora and Homeland', in *Caribbean Circuits: New Directions in the Study of Caribbean Migration*, ed. P. Pessar. New York: Center for Migration Studies, 127–59.

Gagnon, J. E. and A. Germain. 2001. *Espace urbain et religion: Esquisse d'une géographie des lieux de culte minoritaire de la région de Montréal*. Paper of the INRS-Urbanisation, Culture et Société. Université de Montréal.

Glick Schiller, N., L. Basch and C. Blanc-Szanton, eds. 1992. *Towards a Transnational Perspective on Migration: Race, Class, Ethnicity, and Nationalism Reconsidered*. New York: The New York Academy of Sciences.

Glick Schiller, N. and G. E. Fouron. 2001. *Georges Woke Up Laughing: Long-Distance Nationalism and the Search for Home*. Durham, NC: Duke University Press.

Hurbon, L. 1995. *Voodoo: Search for the Spirit*. Paris: Gallimard.

_____. 2002. *Dieu dans le vodou haïtien*. Paris: Maisonneuve & Larose.

Kennedy, P. and V. Roudometof. 2001. 'Transnationalism in a Global Age', in *New Immigrants and Transnational Cultures*, ed. P. Kennedy and V. Roudometof. London, New York: Routledge, 1–26.

Kremser, M., ed. 2000. *ADDR, Afrikanische Digitale Diaspora Religionen*. Reihe: Afrika und ihre Diaspora, Bd. 2. Münster: Lit-Verlag.

Labelle, M., S. Larose and V. Piché. 1983. 'Émigration et immigration: Les Haitiens au Québec'. *Sociologie et Sociétés* 15(2): 73–88.

Larose, S. 1977. 'The Meaning of Africa in Haitian Vodu', in *Symbols and Sentiments: Cross-cultural Studies in Symbolism*, ed. I. Lewis. London: Academic Press, 85–116.

Levitt, P. 1998. 'Local-level Global Religion: The Case of U.S.-Dominican Migration'. *Journal for the Scientific Study of Religion* 37(1): 74–89.

_____. 2001. 'Between God, Ethnicity, and Country: An Approach to the Study of Transnational Religion'. Paper presented at the Workshop on 'Transnational Migration: Comparative Perspectives', 30 June–1 July, Princeton University.

Métraux, A. 1958. *Le Vaudou Haïtien*. Preface by Michel Leiris. Paris: Gallimard.

Mintz, S. and M.-R. Trouillot. 1995. 'The Social History of Haitian Vodou', in *Sacred Arts of Haitian Vodou*, ed. D. Cosentino. Los Angeles: University of California Press, 123–47.

Orsi, R. A., ed. 1999. *Gods of the City: Religion and the American Urban Landscape*. Bloomington, Indianapolis: Indiana University Press.

Palloni, A., D. S. Massey, M. Ceballos, K. Espinosa and M. Spittel. 2001. 'Social Capital and International Migration: A Test Using Information on Family Networks'. *American Journal of Sociology* 106: 1262–98.

Pessar, P., ed. 1997. *Caribbean Circuits: New Directions in the Study of Caribbean Migration*. New York: Centre for Migration Studies.

Pries, L., ed. 1999. *Migration and Transnational Social Spaces*. Aldershot: Ashgate.

Rey, T. 1999. *Our Lady of Class Struggle: The Cult of the Virgin Mary in Haiti*. Asmara: Africa World Press.

Richman, K. E. 2005. *Migration and Vodou*. Gainesville: University Press of Florida.

Schmidt, B. E. 2002. *Karibische Diaspora in New York. Vom 'Wilden Denken' zur 'Polyphonen Kultur'.* Berlin: Reimer.

Stepick, A. 1998. *Pride against Prejudice: Haitians in the United States.* Boston, London: Allyn & Bacon.

Veer, P. van der. 2001. 'Transnational Religion'. Paper presented at the Conference on 'Transnational Migration: Comparative Perspectives'. Princeton University, 30 June–1 July.

Vertovec, S. 2000. 'Religion and Diaspora'. Paper presented at the Conference on 'New Landscapes of Religion in the West', School of Geography and the Environment, University of Oxford, 27–29 September.

Warner, S. R. and J. G. Wittner. 1998. 'Immigration and Religious Communities in the United States', in *Gatherings in Diaspora: Religious Communities and the New Immigration,* ed. S. R. Warner and J. G. Wittner. Philadelphia: Temple University Press, 3–36.

Contributors

Mirjam de Bruijn is a senior researcher at the African Studies Centre in Leiden, the Netherlands, where she is head of the research group 'Connections and Transformations'. In June 2007 she was named professor of African Studies (Contemporary History and Anthropology of West and Central Africa) at Leiden University. She has conducted research in Cameroon, Mali and Chad (in the period from 1986 to the present) and completed (interdisciplinary) projects on climate change, migration, conflict and poverty. Currently, she coordinates a research programme on local conflict dynamics in collaboration with CODESRIA. She was awarded a five-year research grant starting in 2008 for a project on marginality, communication and mobility in Africa. Recent publications include *Strength beyond Structure: Social and Historical Trajectories of Agency in Africa*, edited with Rijk van Dijk and Jan-Bart Gewald (Brill, 2007).

Catrine Christiansen is a research fellow at the Institute of Anthropology, University of Copenhagen. She has focused on links between faith, sociality and health-seeking behaviour in relation to conversion from mainline to charismatic Christianity. As a researcher at Nordic Africa Institute (2002–2005) she developed research on church-based social development projects for young people affected by HIV/AIDS in Uganda. Her principal research interests include religion, social development, youth, health and social organisation. She is the author of several articles and co-edited the book *Navigating Youth, Generating Adulthood: Social Becoming in an African Context* (Nordafrika Institutet, 2006).

Rijk van Dijk is an anthropologist at the African Studies Centre in Leiden. He has done extensive research on the rise of Pentecostal movements in urban areas of Malawi and Ghana and is the author of *Young Malawian Puritans* (ISOR Press, 1992). He co-edited *Modernity on a Shoestring* with Richard Fardon and

Wim van Binsbergen (EIDOS, 1999), *The Quest for Fruition through Ngoma* with Ria Reis and Marja Spierenberg (James Currey, 2000) and *Situating Globality: African Agency in the Appropriation of Global Culture* with Wim van Binsbergen (Brill, 2004). His current research focuses on the transnational dimensions of Ghanaian Pentecostalism, particularly in relation to the migration of Ghanaians to the Netherlands and Botswana. A recently published article, 'Localisation, Ghanaian Pentecostalism and the Stranger's Beauty in Bostwana' in *Africa*, deals with insights gained from this research.

Heike Drotbohm is an assistant professor at the Institute for Social and Cultural Anthropology, University of Freiburg. She has worked on Creole cultures in the Caribbean and in West Africa and has published on the transformation of religious imaginations in migratory circumstances. She has carried out anthropological fieldwork in Haiti as well as in Canada and has concentrated on the role of vodou spirits in relation to the everyday experiences of Haitian transmigrants. Her recent fieldwork in the Cape Verdean Islands focuses on transnationalism and creolisation in relation to social primary relations such as family and friendship. Recent publications include 'Of Spirits and Virgins: Situating Belonging in Haitian Religious Spaces in Montreal, Canada' in *Suomen Antropologi: Journal of the Finnish Anthropological Society* and *Geister in der Diaspora. Haitianische Diskurse über Geschlechter, Jugend und Macht in Montreal, Kanada* (Curupira, 2005).

Gertrud Hüwelmeier is a senior lecturer and research fellow at the Humboldt University of Berlin, Department of European Ethnology. She received her PhD in anthropology at the University of Tübingen and completed her habilitation in 2003 on gender and religion, specifically on processes of transformation among Catholic sisters. During a subsequent research project on 'transnational religion – women's congregations as actors in the process of globalisation', she carried out fieldwork in Europe, the US and India. Currently, she is the director of a research project on transnational networks, religion and new migration, focusing on Vietnamese and Ghanaian migrants.

Kristin Kupfer is a PhD candidate at the Institute of East Asian Politics, Ruhr University of Bochum. She is a trained political scientist and sinologist. Her research interests encompass religion and social change in contemporary China, with a special focus on new religious movements. In 2008 she was based in Beijing, China, as a freelance journalist and researcher.

Carolin Leutloff-Grandits is a research fellow at the University of Graz and lecturer at the University of Vienna. She received her PhD in social anthropology from the Martin Luther University of Halle-Wittenberg in 2005. From

2005–2006 she worked as a lead researcher in the EU-funded international project, Kinship and Social Security (KASS). She has carried out fieldwork in Serbia and Croatia on the topics of ethnic conflict, property relations, identity formation, kinship and social security, and is the author of the book *Claiming Ownership in Post-war Croatia: The Dynamics of Property Relations and Ethnic Conflict in the Knin Region* (LIT, 2006).

Anja Peleikis is a senior research fellow at the Institute of Social Anthropology at the Martin Luther University of Halle-Wittenberg, where she co-leads the project 'After the Survivors: Performing the Holocaust and the Jewish Past in the New Yad Vashem Museum and the Jewish Museum, Berlin'. She gained her PhD degree from the University of Bielefeld and led research projects at the Centre for Modern Oriental Studies, Berlin, and the Max Planck Institute for Social Anthropology, Halle/Saale. Her research interests include transnational migration, tourism, memory practices, the anthropology of museums, as well as social security and legal pluralism. She has carried out fieldwork on these topics in West Africa, Lebanon and Lithuania. She is author of the book *Lebanese in Motion: Gender and the Making of a Translocal Village* (Transcript, 2003).

Rosie Read is a senior lecturer at the Institute of Health and Community Studies, Bournemouth University. She gained her PhD in social anthropology from Manchester University in 2002. Her research interests encompass anthropological and feminist theories of gender, emotional labour, care, volunteering, welfare and the state, and she has conducted ethnographic research in the Czech Republic on these themes. She is the author of several articles and has edited with Timothy Hall *Changes in the Heart of Europe: Recent Ethnographies of Czechs, Slovaks, Roma, and Sorbs* (Ibidem-Verlag, 2006). She has also co-edited and published a joint article with Tatjana Thelen on the theme of social security and care after socialism in a special issue of *Focaal: European Journal of Social Anthropology* (2007).

Barbara Rohregger is a political scientist and social anthropologist. She has been conducting research on social, economic, legal and political aspects of social security in developing countries for ten years, focusing mainly on sub-Saharan Africa. The dynamics of formal and informal social security mechanisms in the context of migration and urbanisation in Malawi was the subject of her PhD at the Erasmus University Law School, Rotterdam. Based on her experience as a researcher, she is currently working in development cooperation, dealing with the establishment of context-driven systems of social protection.

Tatjana Thelen gained her PhD at the Free University of Berlin and is the author of the book *Privatisierung und soziale Ungleichheit in der osteur-opäischen Landwirtschaft. Zwei Fallstudien in Ungarn und Rumänien (Privati-sation and Social Inequality in Eastern European Agriculture: Two Case Studies from Hungary and Romania)* (Campus, 2003). Currently, she teaches social anthropology at the University of Zurich and leads the research project 'Local State and Social Security in Rural Hungary, Romania and Serbia', funded by the Volkswagen Foundation, based at the Max Planck Institute for Social Anthro-pology in Halle/Saale. She has also been a lead researcher in the EU-funded international project, Kinship and Social Security (KASS). Her findings have been published in several articles, and she co-edited with Rosie Read 'Social Security and Care after Socialism', which appeared in a special issue of *Focaal: European Journal of Social Anthropology* (2007).

Index